AT THE MOUNTAINS OF MADNESS

AT THE MOUNTAINS OF MADNESS

A GRAPHIC NOVEL

ADAPTED FROM THE ORIGINAL NOVEL BY
H.P. LOVECRAFT
TEXT ADAPTED AND ILLUSTRATED BY
I.N.J. CULBARD

STERLING
New York

STERLING
New York

An Imprint of Sterling Publishing
387 Park Avenue South
New York, NY 10016

First published 2010
by SelfMadeHero
A division of Metro Media Ltd
5 Upper Wimpole Street
London W1H 6BP
www.selfmadehero.com

Illustrator and Adaptor: I.N.J. Culbard
Cover Designer: I.N.J. Culbard
Layout Designer: Andy Huckle
Textual Consultant: Nick de Somogyi
Publishing Director: Emma Hayley
Marketing Director: Doug Wallace
With thanks to: Dan Lockwood

Dedication
For Katy, Joseph and Benjamin
- I.N.J. Culbard

ISBN 978-1-4027-8042-4

Distributed in Canada by Sterling Publishing
c/o Canadian Manda Group, 165 Dufferin Street
Toronto, Ontario, Canada M6K 3H6

For information about custom editions, special sales, and premium
and corporate purchases, please contact Sterling Special Sales
at 800-805-5489 or specialsales@sterlingpublishing.com.

Manufactured in the China

2 4 6 8 10 9 7 5 3 1

www.sterlingpublishing.com

FOREWORD

Written in 1931, *At the Mountains of Madness* is a key work in H.P. Love-craft's canon. Originally rejected by *Weird Tales*, the novel has since become a firm favorite with readers of the macabre. A haunting combination of science and fantasy in its own right, the novel also explains and connects various elements of Lovecraft's "Cthulhu mythos." Indeed, these pages—with their references to Miskatonic University, the dreaded *Necronomicon*, and a host of monstrous beings—contain much that will be familiar to devoted Lovecraft fans. For those who have yet to venture into the unknown, *At the Mountains of Madness* is both accessible and exciting, and stands as one of Lovecraft's most successful tales.

Antarctica—then, as now, one of the least explored areas of the world—marks something of a departure for Lovecraft in terms of setting. As soon as his characters arrived on that mysterious continent, Lovecraft's imagination ran unchecked—he was able to fill the landscape with impossible, malevolent cities, safe in the knowledge that he was unlikely to be contradicted by scientific fact (for a while, at least). This freedom allowed for a sense of scale which is unmatched in Lovecraft's other works. The vast polar wasteland is swiftly established as an enthralling, terrifying location, producing a creeping atmosphere of horror before we have even been introduced to its inhabitants.

Infirm for much of his life, Lovecraft's intolerance (bordering on horror) of cold temperatures is reflected in the pervading sense of doom which runs through his tale. However, this abhorrence is somewhat countered by Lovecraft's fascination with polar exploration. As a result, *At the Mountains of Madness* is a compelling mixture of the repellent and the intriguing; the friction between these two states makes this one of Lovecraft's most powerful stories. Ian Culbard's sterling adaptation captures this antagonism perfectly, conjuring up the *Boy's Own* thrill of exploration before hitting us with a series of horrifying discoveries, each with greater implications for man's place in the universe.

"*At the Mountains of Madness* represents the most serious work I have attempted," Lovecraft wrote, "and its rejection was a very discouraging influence." Although he never found popular success during his lifetime, that dispiriting rejection has proved to be unfounded. This adaptation confirms the book's standing among the very best of genre fiction.

—Dan Lockwood
editor, *The Lovecraft Anthology: Vol I* (2011)

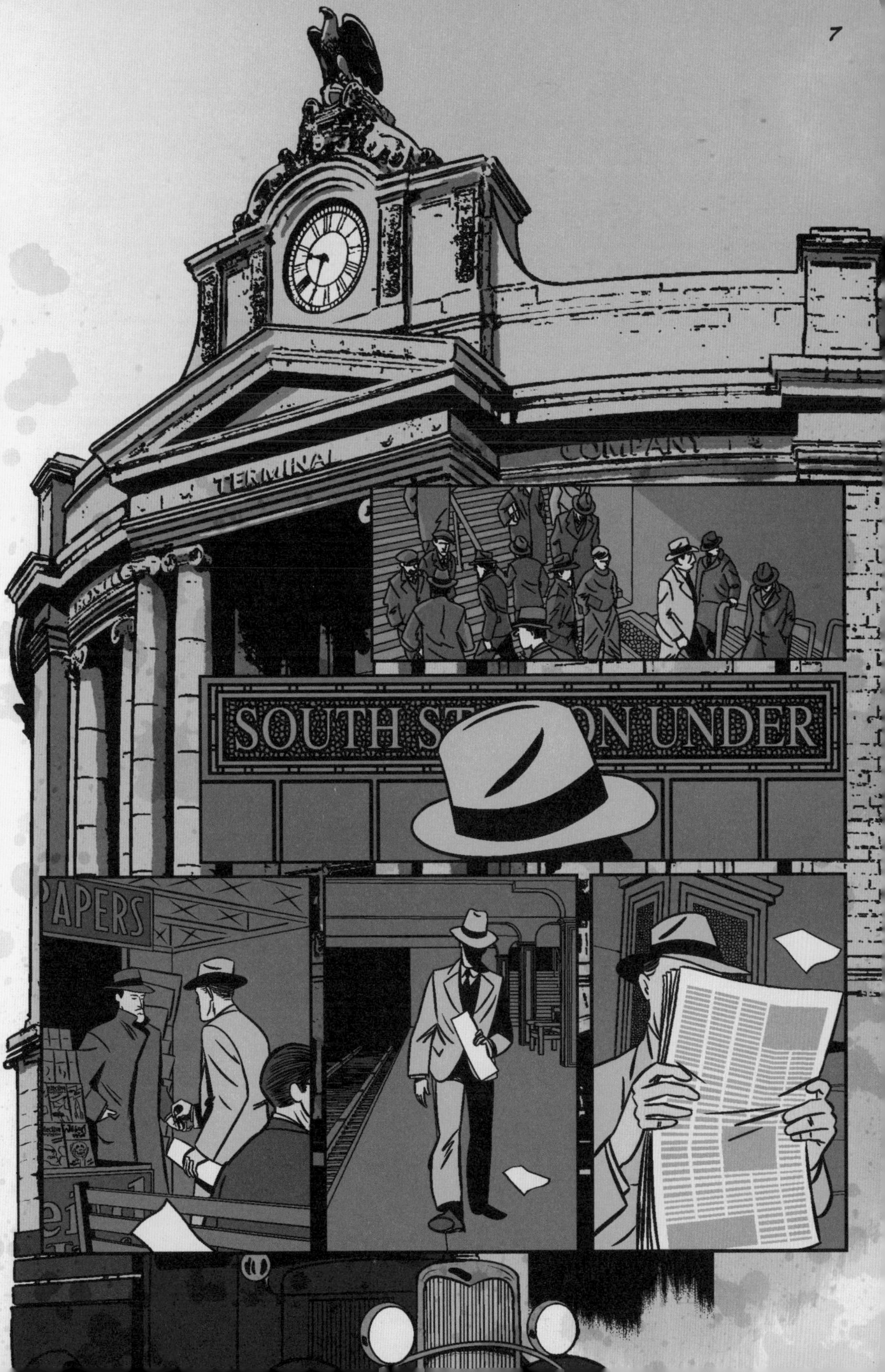
TERMINAL
COMPANY
SOUTH ST ON UNDER
PAPERS

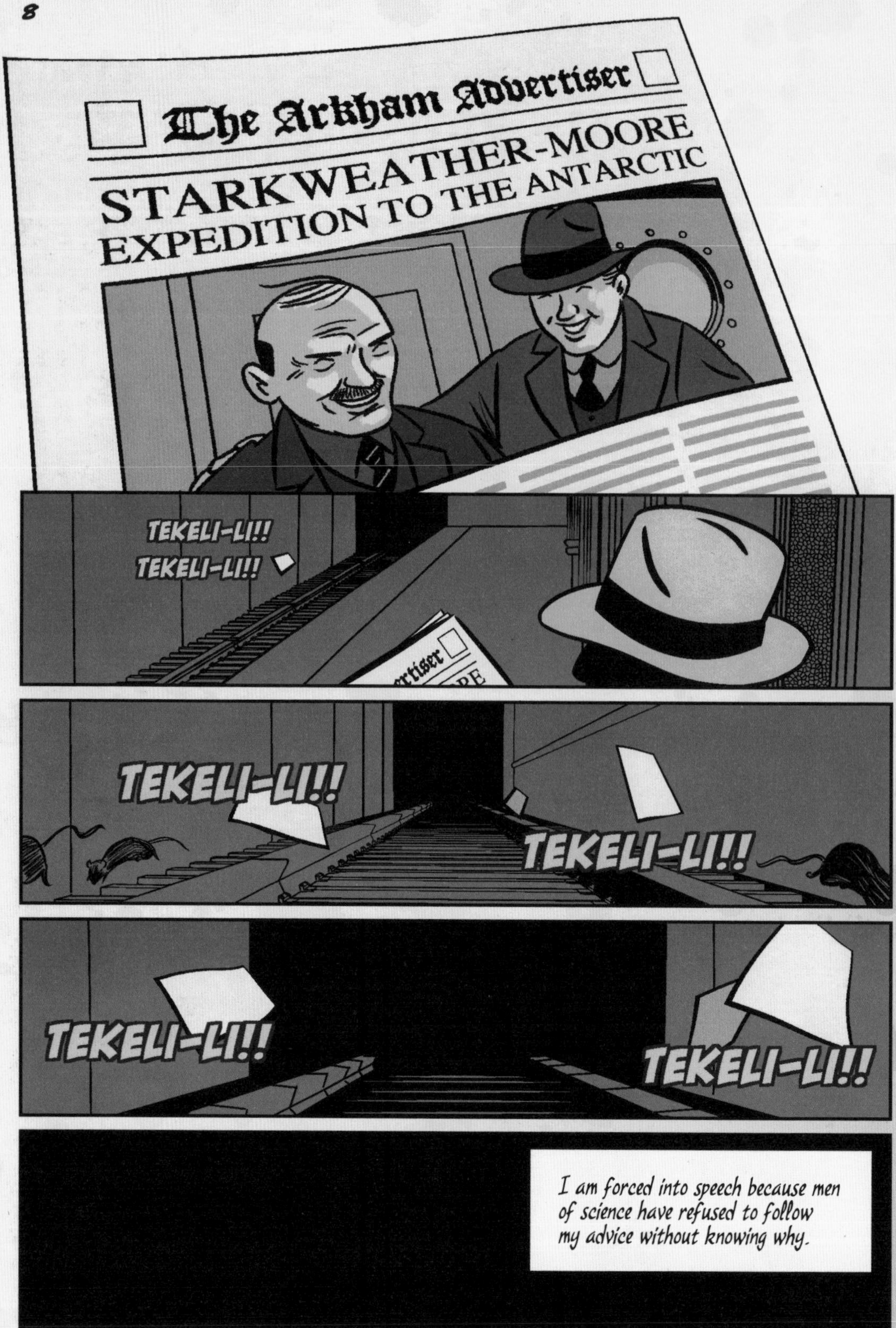

The Arkham Advertiser
STARKWEATHER-MOORE EXPEDITION TO THE ANTARCTIC
TEKELI-LI!!
TEKELI-LI!!
TEKELI-LI!!
TEKELI-LI!!
TEKELI-LI!!
TEKELI-LI!!
I am forced into speech because men of science have refused to follow my advice without knowing why.

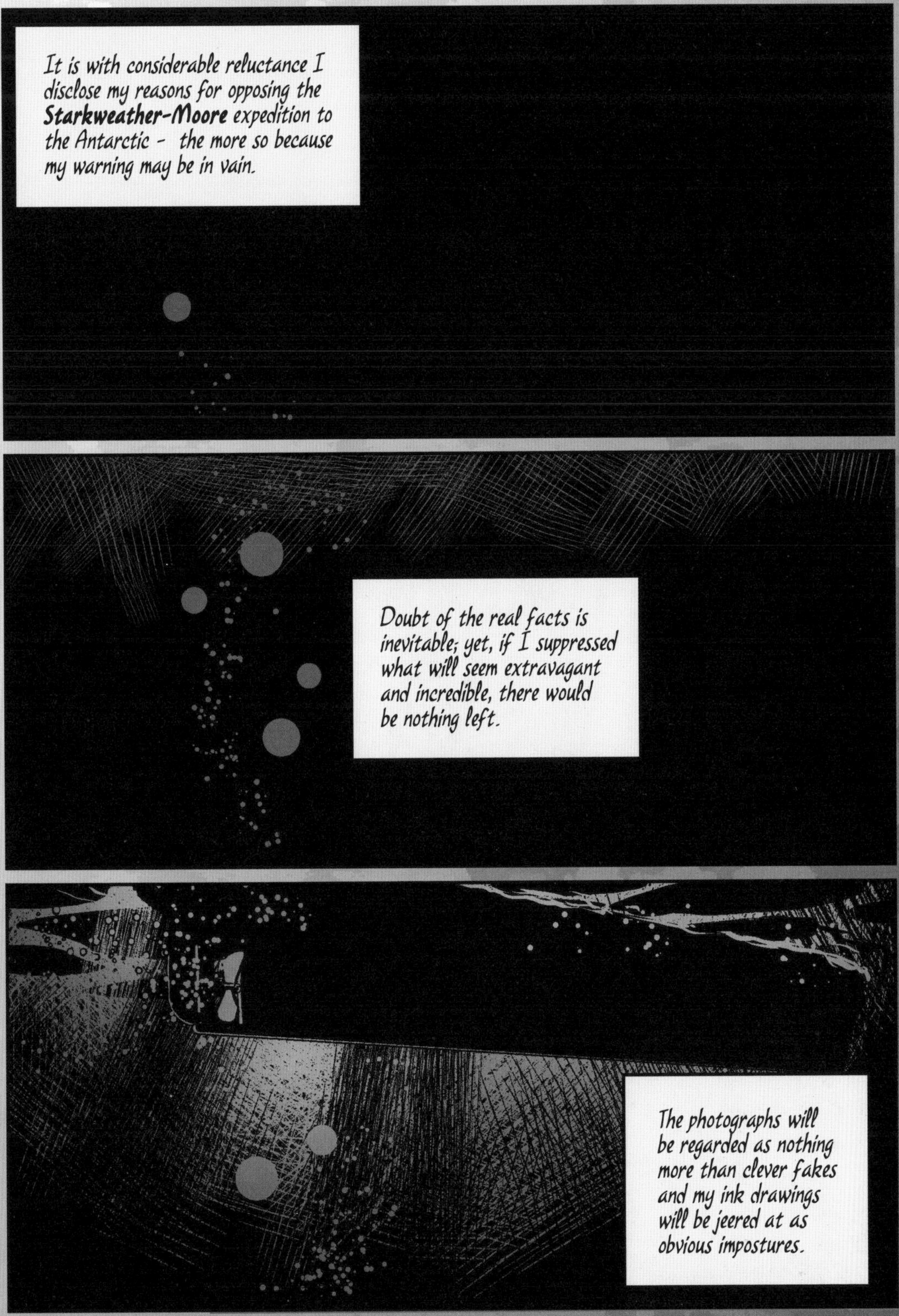
It is with considerable reluctance I disclose my reasons for opposing the **Starkweather-Moore** expedition to the Antarctic - the more so because my warning may be in vain.
Doubt of the real facts is inevitable; yet, if I suppressed what will seem extravagant and incredible, there would be nothing left.
The photographs will be regarded as nothing more than clever fakes and my ink drawings will be jeered at as obvious impostures.

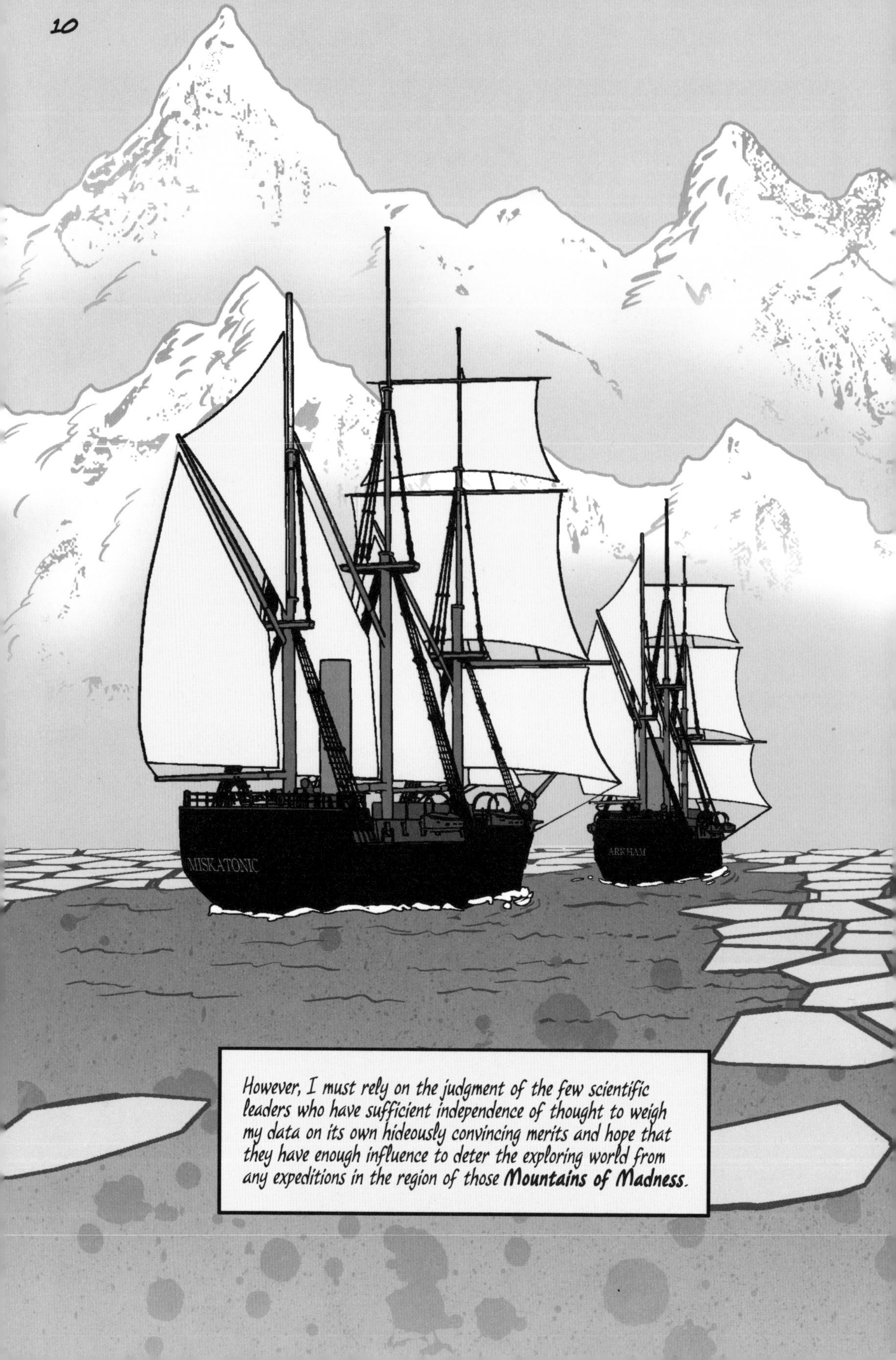
MISKATONIC
ARKHAM
However, I must rely on the judgment of the few scientific leaders who have sufficient independence of thought to weigh my data on its own hideously convincing merits and hope that they have enough influence to deter the exploring world from any expeditions in the region of those **Mountains of Madness**.

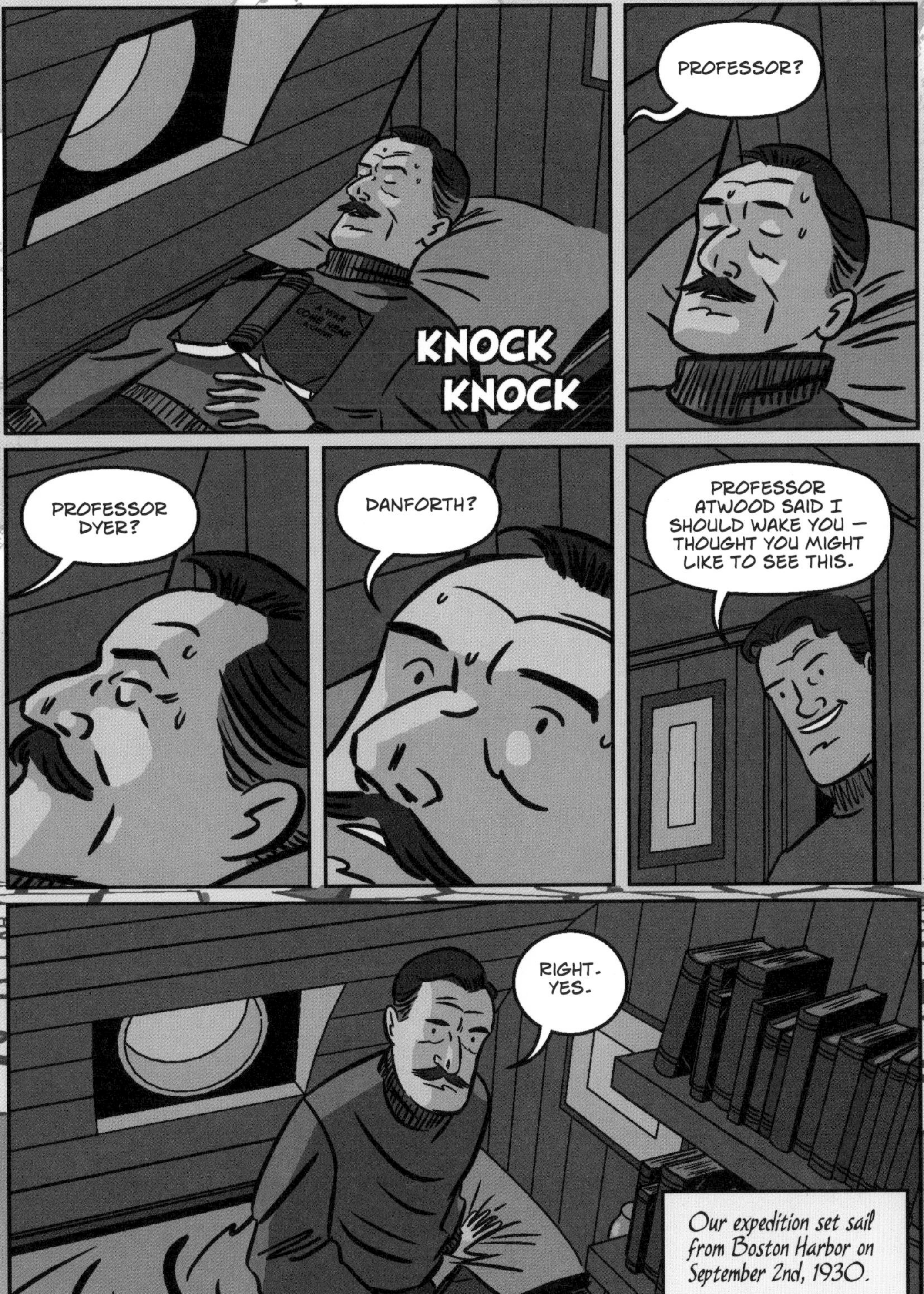
A WAR COME NEAR
KNOCK KNOCK
PROFESSOR?
PROFESSOR DYER?
DANFORTH?
PROFESSOR ATWOOD SAID I SHOULD WAKE YOU — THOUGHT YOU MIGHT LIKE TO SEE THIS.
RIGHT. YES.
Our expedition set sail from Boston Harbor on September 2nd, 1930.

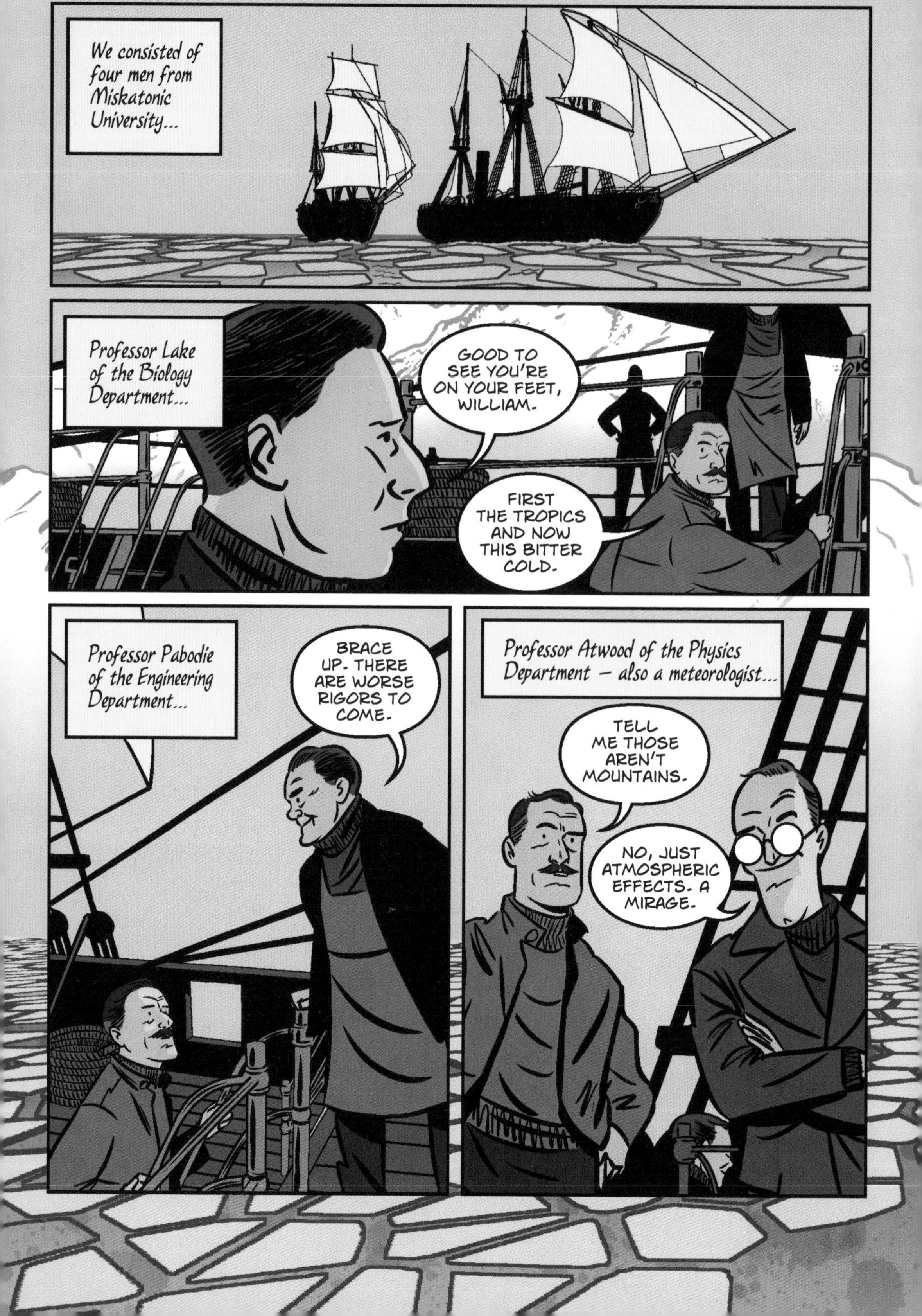
We consisted of four men from Miskatonic University...
Professor Lake of the Biology Department...
GOOD TO SEE YOU'RE ON YOUR FEET, WILLIAM.
FIRST THE TROPICS AND NOW THIS BITTER COLD.
Professor Pabodie of the Engineering Department...
BRACE UP. THERE ARE WORSE RIGORS TO COME.
Professor Atwood of the Physics Department – also a meteorologist...
TELL ME THOSE AREN'T MOUNTAINS.
NO, JUST ATMOSPHERIC EFFECTS. A MIRAGE.

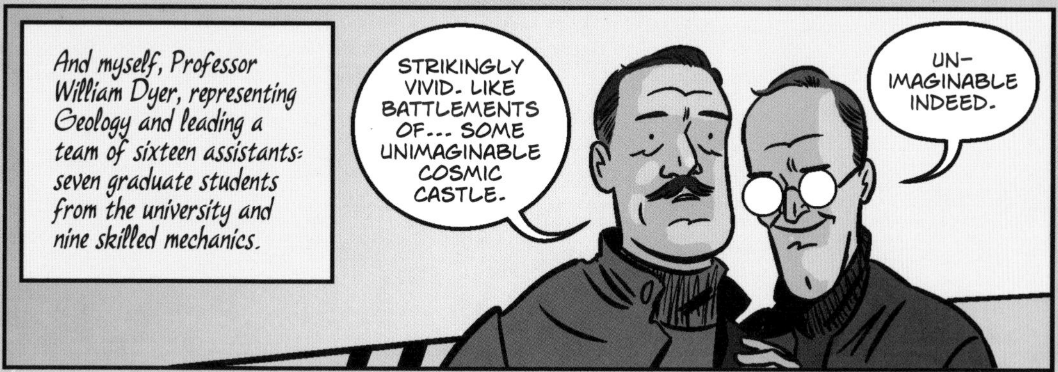
And myself, Professor William Dyer, representing Geology and leading a team of sixteen assistants: seven graduate students from the university and nine skilled mechanics.
STRIKINGLY VIVID. LIKE BATTLEMENTS OF... SOME UNIMAGINABLE COSMIC CASTLE.
UN-IMAGINABLE INDEED.

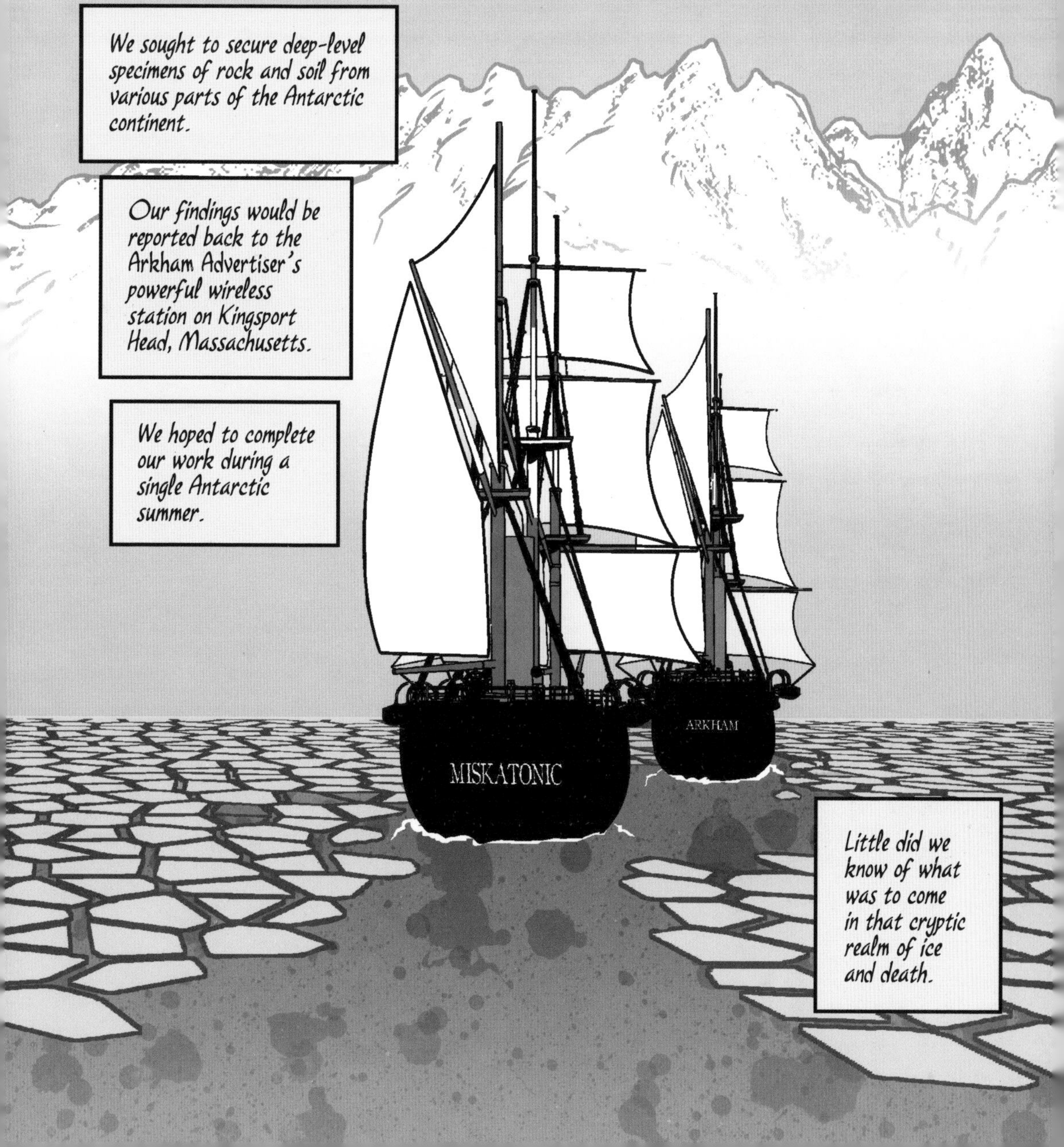
We sought to secure deep-level specimens of rock and soil from various parts of the Antarctic continent.
Our findings would be reported back to the Arkham Advertiser's powerful wireless station on Kingsport Head, Massachusetts.
We hoped to complete our work during a single Antarctic summer.
MISKATONIC
ARKHAM
Little did we know of what was to come in that cryptic realm of ice and death.

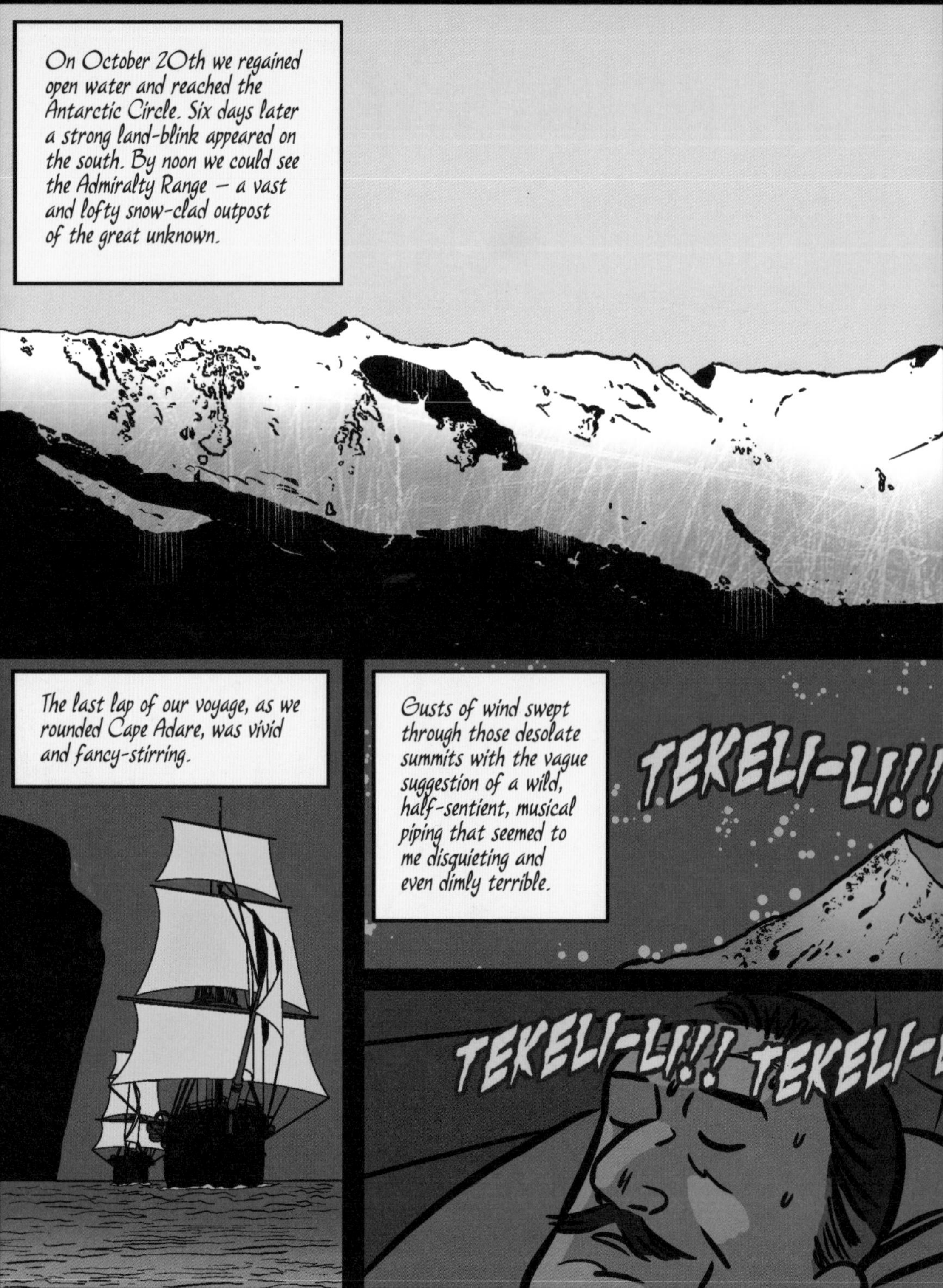
On October 20th we regained open water and reached the Antarctic Circle. Six days later a strong land-blink appeared on the south. By noon we could see the Admiralty Range — a vast and lofty snow-clad outpost of the great unknown.
The last lap of our voyage, as we rounded Cape Adare, was vivid and fancy-stirring.
Gusts of wind swept through those desolate summits with the vague suggestion of a wild, half-sentient, musical piping that seemed to me disquieting and even dimly terrible.
TEKELI-LI!!
TEKELI-LI!!

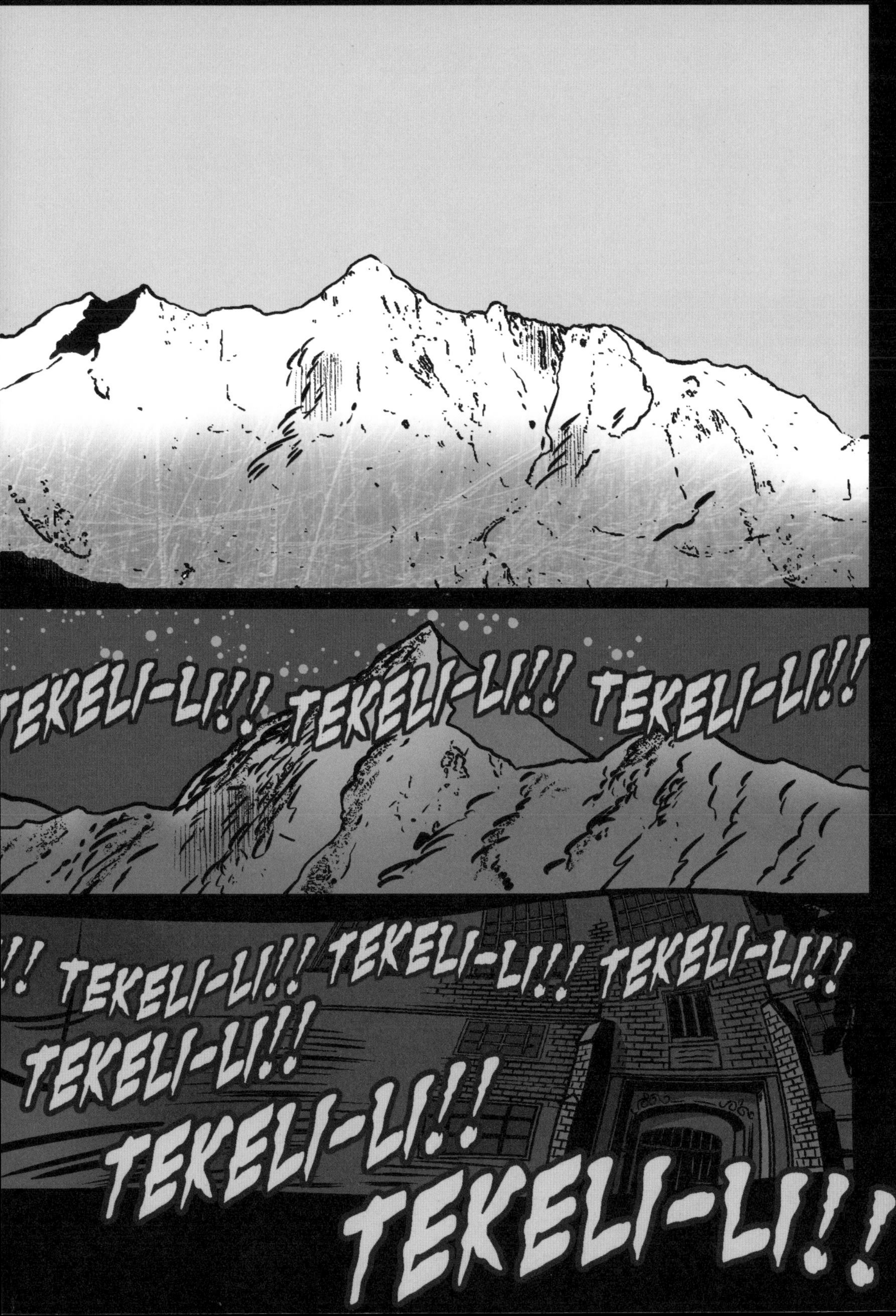
TEKELI-LI!! TEKELI-LI!! TEKELI-LI!!
!! TEKELI-LI!! TEKELI-LI!! TEKELI-LI!!
TEKELI-LI!!
TEKELI-LI!!
TEKELI-LI!!

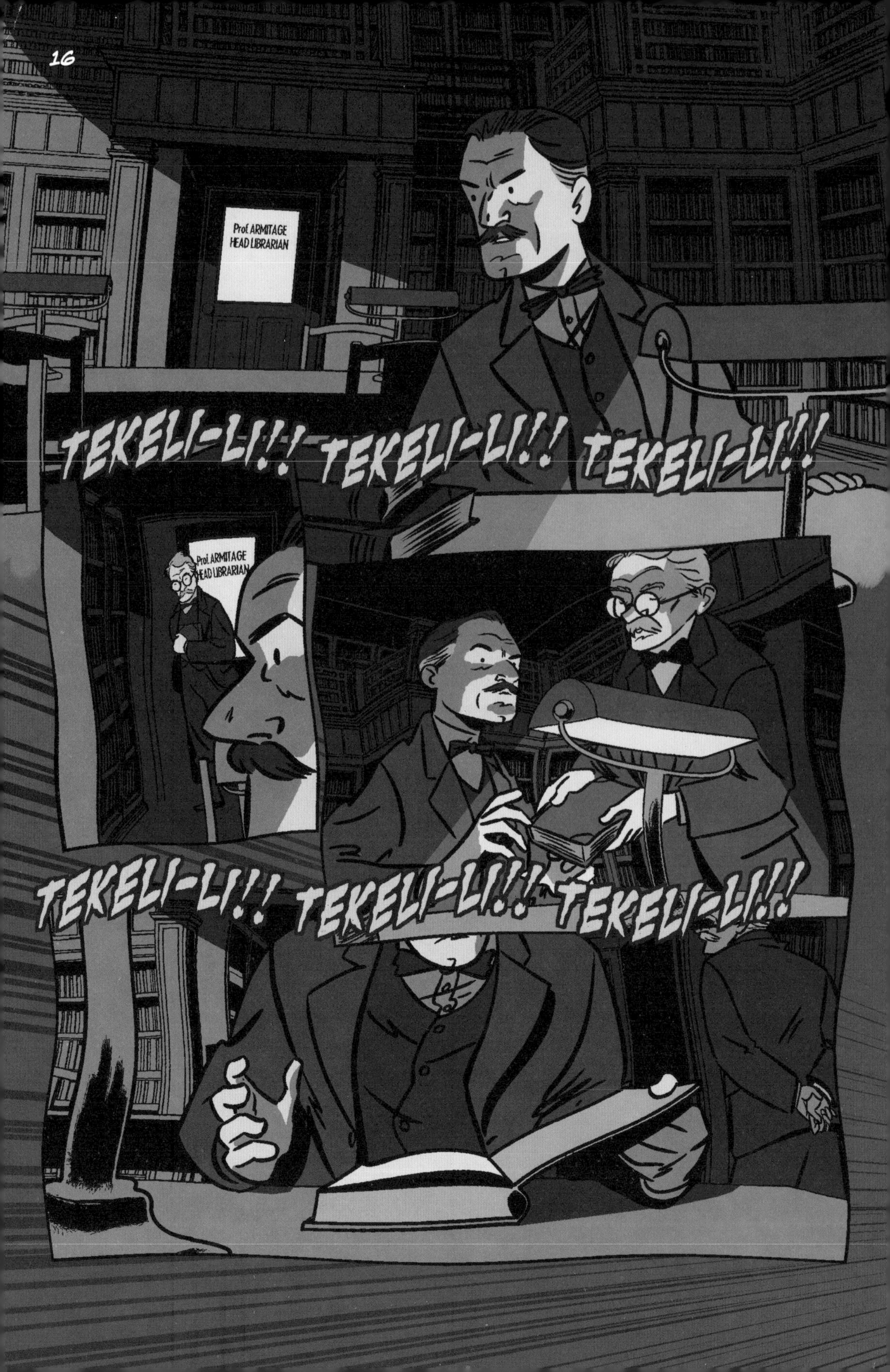

Prof. ARMITAGE
HEAD LIBRARIAN
TEKELI-LI!! TEKELI-LI!! TEKELI-LI!!
Prof. ARMITAGE
HEAD LIBRARIAN
TEKELI-LI!! TEKELI-LI!! TEKELI-LI!!

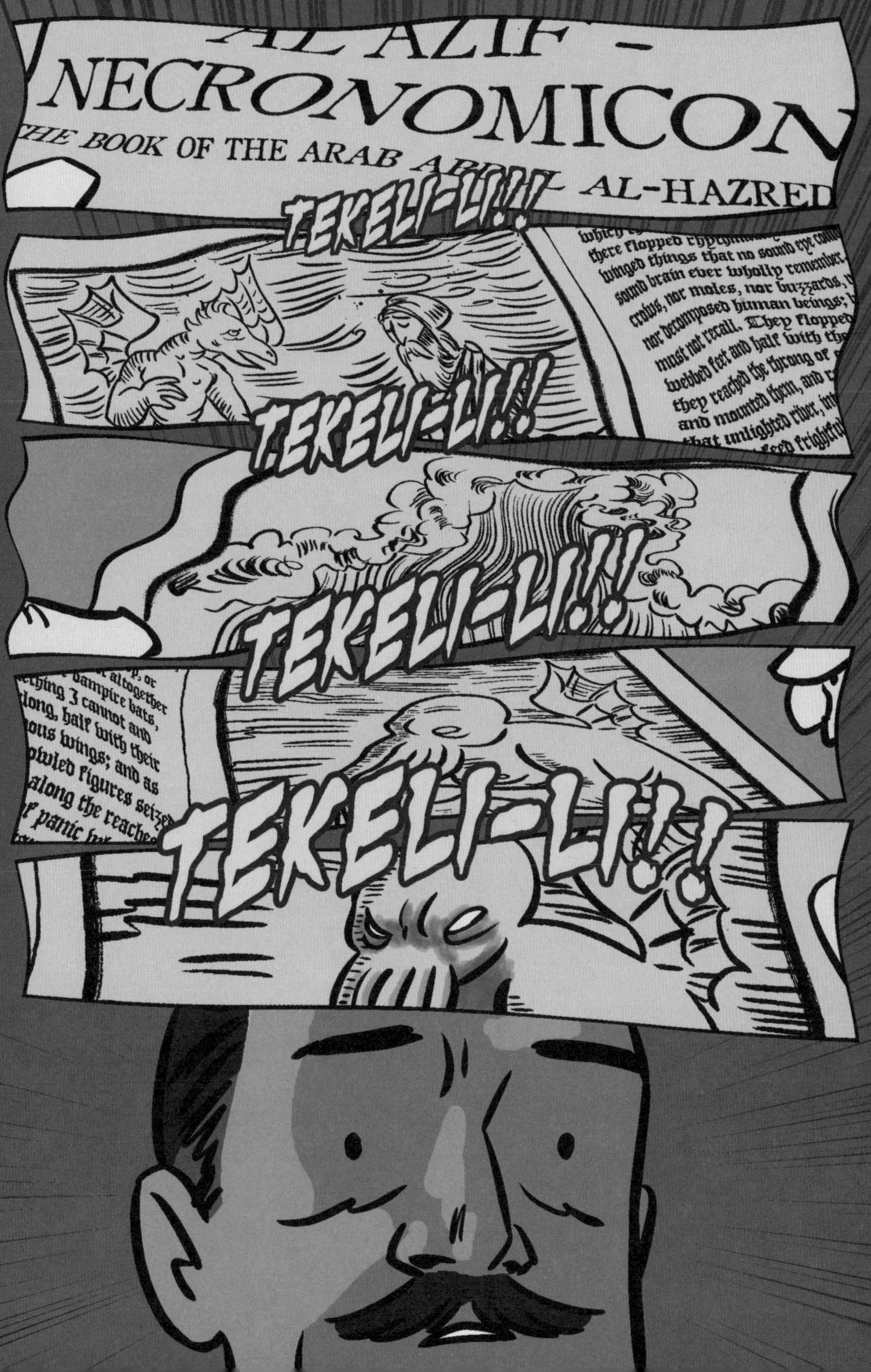
AL AZIF -
NECRONOMICON
THE BOOK OF THE ARAB
AL-HAZRED
TEKELI-LI!!
there flopped rhythmically
winged things that no sound eye could
sound brain ever wholly remember.
crows, nor moles, nor buzzards,
nor decomposed human beings;
must not recall. They flopped
webbed feet and half with the
they reached the throng of
and mounted them, and
that unlighted river,
TEKELI-LI!!
TEKELI-LI!!
vampire bats,
thing I cannot and
along, half with their
ous wings; and as
owled figures seized
along the reaches
panic
TEKELI-LI!!

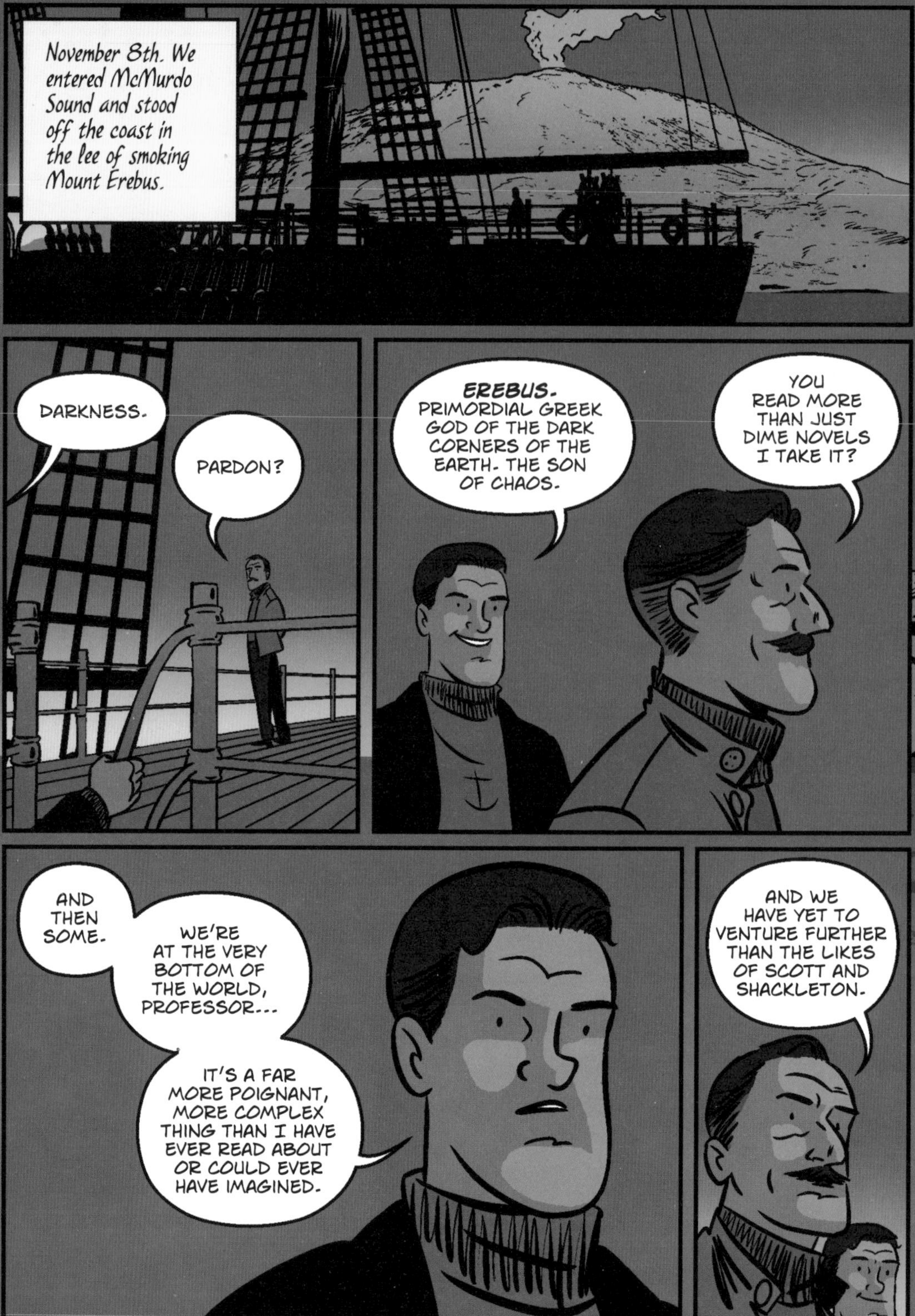
November 8th. We entered McMurdo Sound and stood off the coast in the lee of smoking Mount Erebus.
DARKNESS.
PARDON?
EREBUS. PRIMORDIAL GREEK GOD OF THE DARK CORNERS OF THE EARTH. THE SON OF CHAOS.
YOU READ MORE THAN JUST DIME NOVELS I TAKE IT?
AND THEN SOME.
WE'RE AT THE VERY BOTTOM OF THE WORLD, PROFESSOR...
IT'S A FAR MORE POIGNANT, MORE COMPLEX THING THAN I HAVE EVER READ ABOUT OR COULD EVER HAVE IMAGINED.
AND WE HAVE YET TO VENTURE FURTHER THAN THE LIKES OF SCOTT AND SHACKLETON.

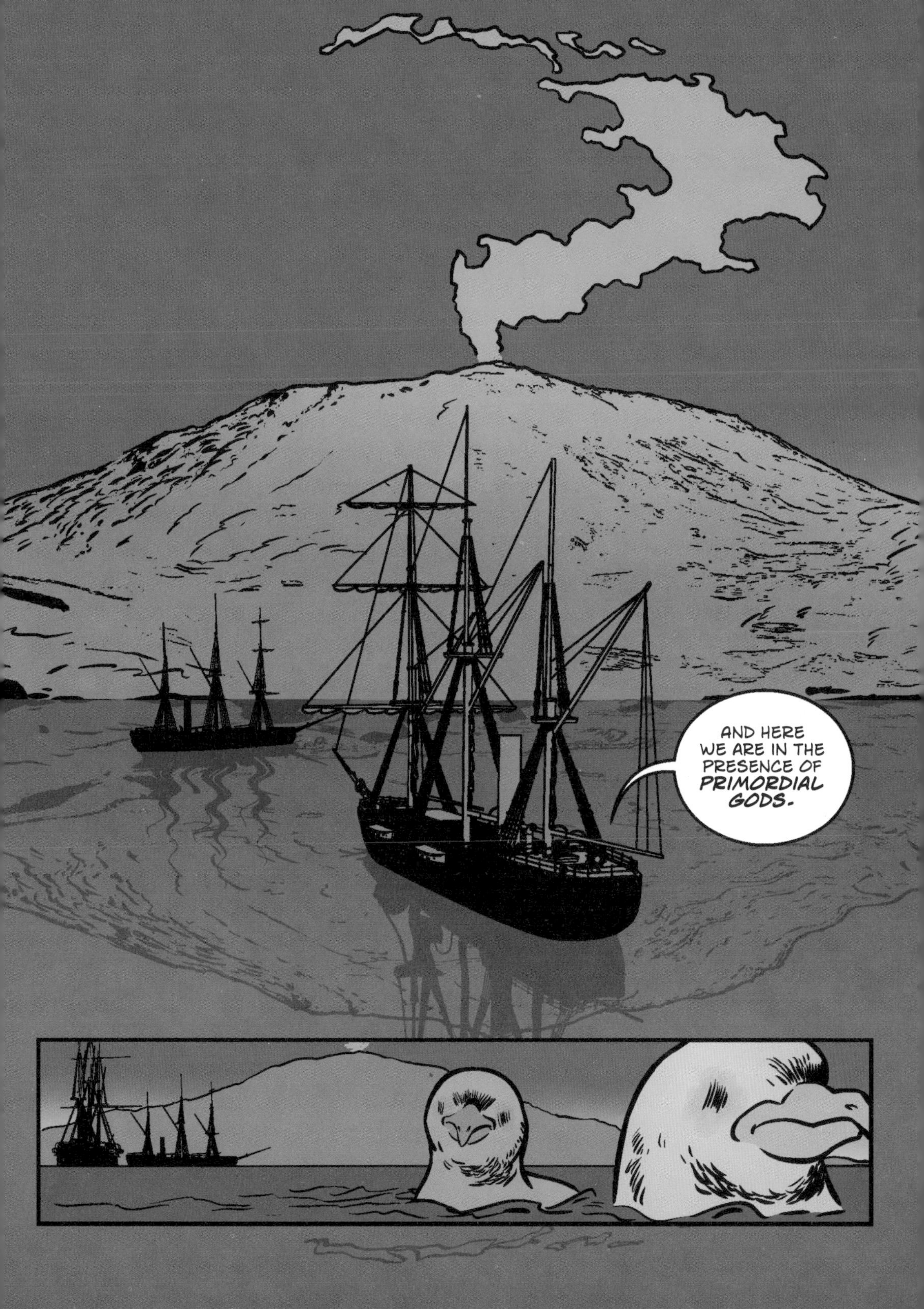
AND HERE WE ARE IN THE PRESENCE OF PRIMORDIAL GODS.

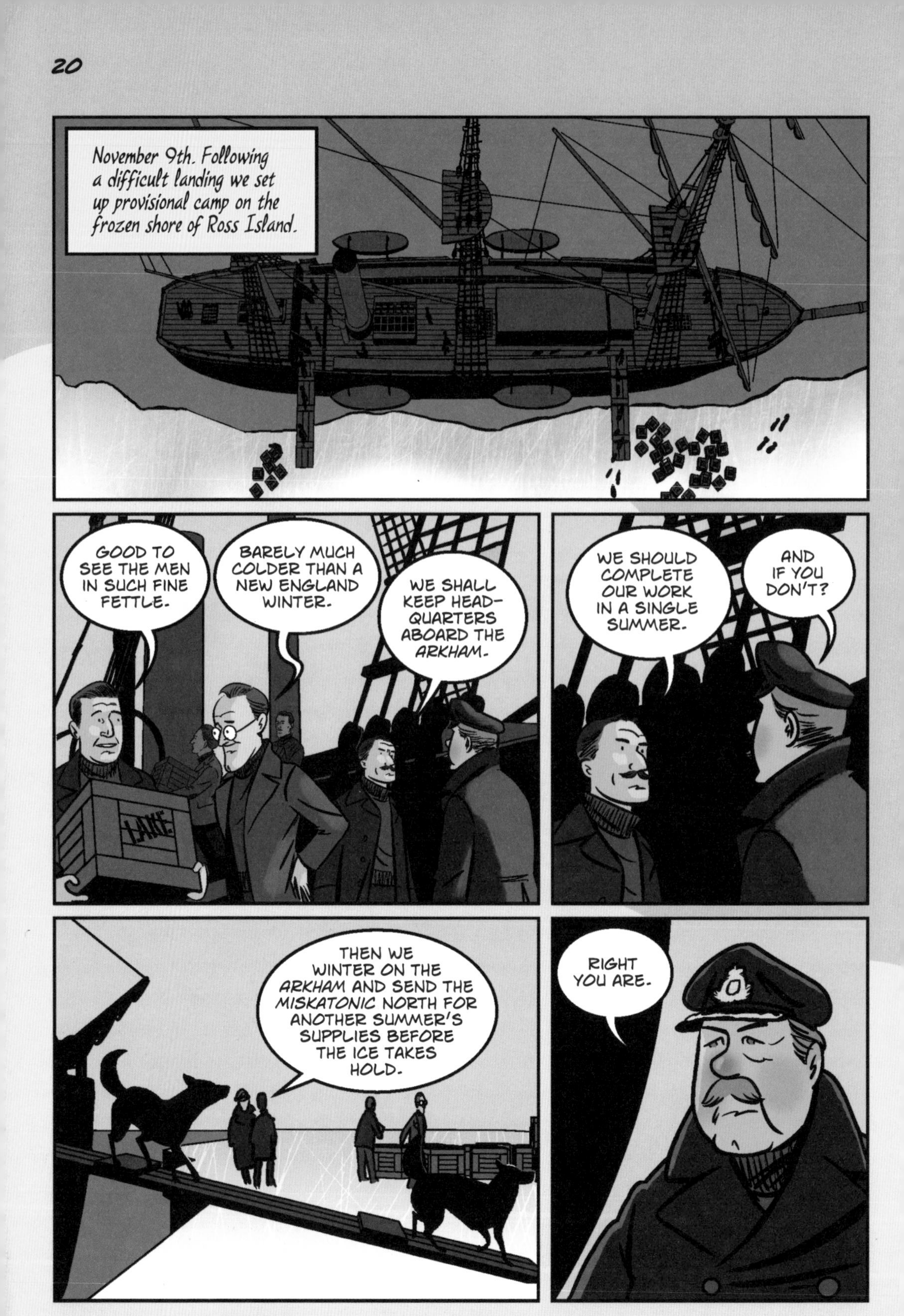
November 9th. Following a difficult landing we set up provisional camp on the frozen shore of Ross Island.
GOOD TO SEE THE MEN IN SUCH FINE FETTLE.
BARELY MUCH COLDER THAN A NEW ENGLAND WINTER.
WE SHALL KEEP HEAD-QUARTERS ABOARD THE ARKHAM.
LAKE
WE SHOULD COMPLETE OUR WORK IN A SINGLE SUMMER.
AND IF YOU DON'T?
THEN WE WINTER ON THE ARKHAM AND SEND THE MISKATONIC NORTH FOR ANOTHER SUMMER'S SUPPLIES BEFORE THE ICE TAKES HOLD.
RIGHT YOU ARE.

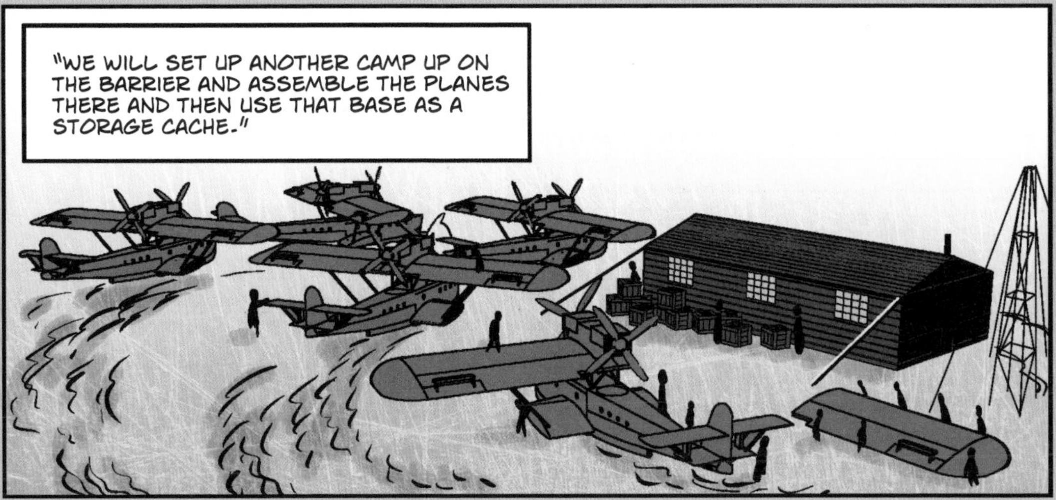
"WE WILL SET UP ANOTHER CAMP UP ON THE BARRIER AND ASSEMBLE THE PLANES THERE AND THEN USE THAT BASE AS A STORAGE CACHE."

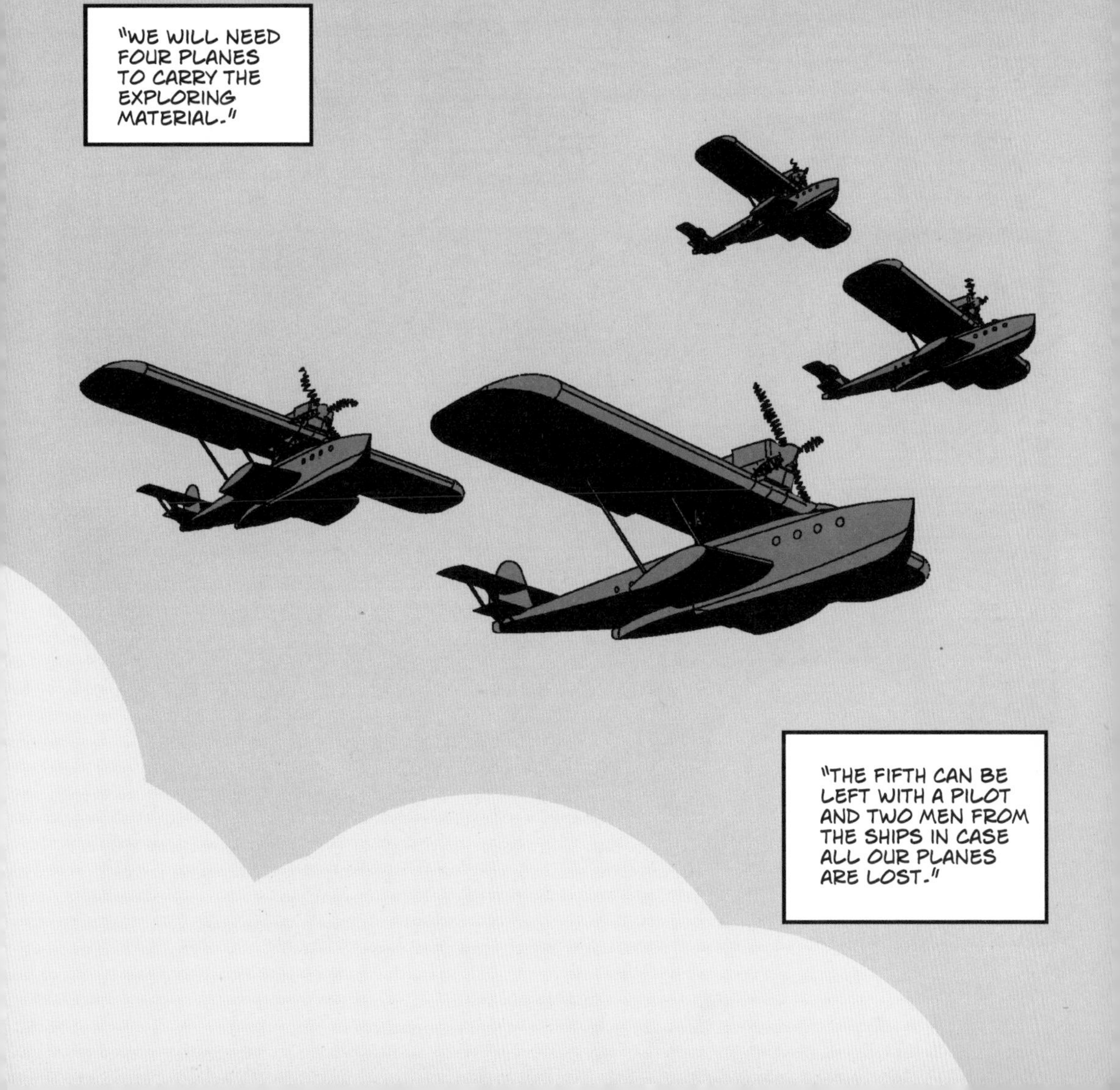
"WE WILL NEED FOUR PLANES TO CARRY THE EXPLORING MATERIAL."
"THE FIFTH CAN BE LEFT WITH A PILOT AND TWO MEN FROM THE SHIPS IN CASE ALL OUR PLANES ARE LOST."

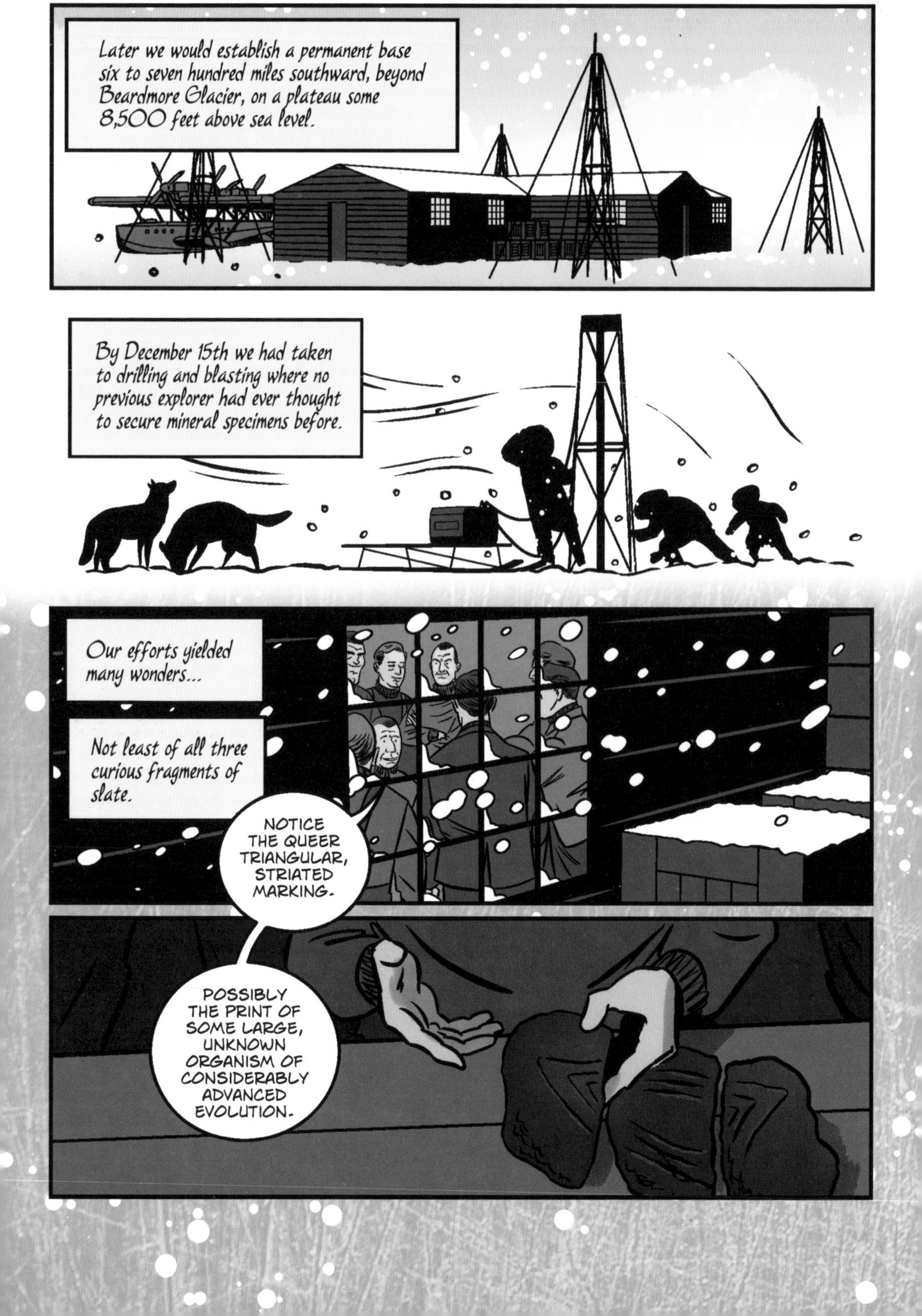
Later we would establish a permanent base six to seven hundred miles southward, beyond Beardmore Glacier, on a plateau some 8,500 feet above sea level.
By December 15th we had taken to drilling and blasting where no previous explorer had ever thought to secure mineral specimens before.
Our efforts yielded many wonders...
Not least of all three curious fragments of slate.
NOTICE THE QUEER TRIANGULAR, STRIATED MARKING.
POSSIBLY THE PRINT OF SOME LARGE, UNKNOWN ORGANISM OF CONSIDERABLY ADVANCED EVOLUTION.

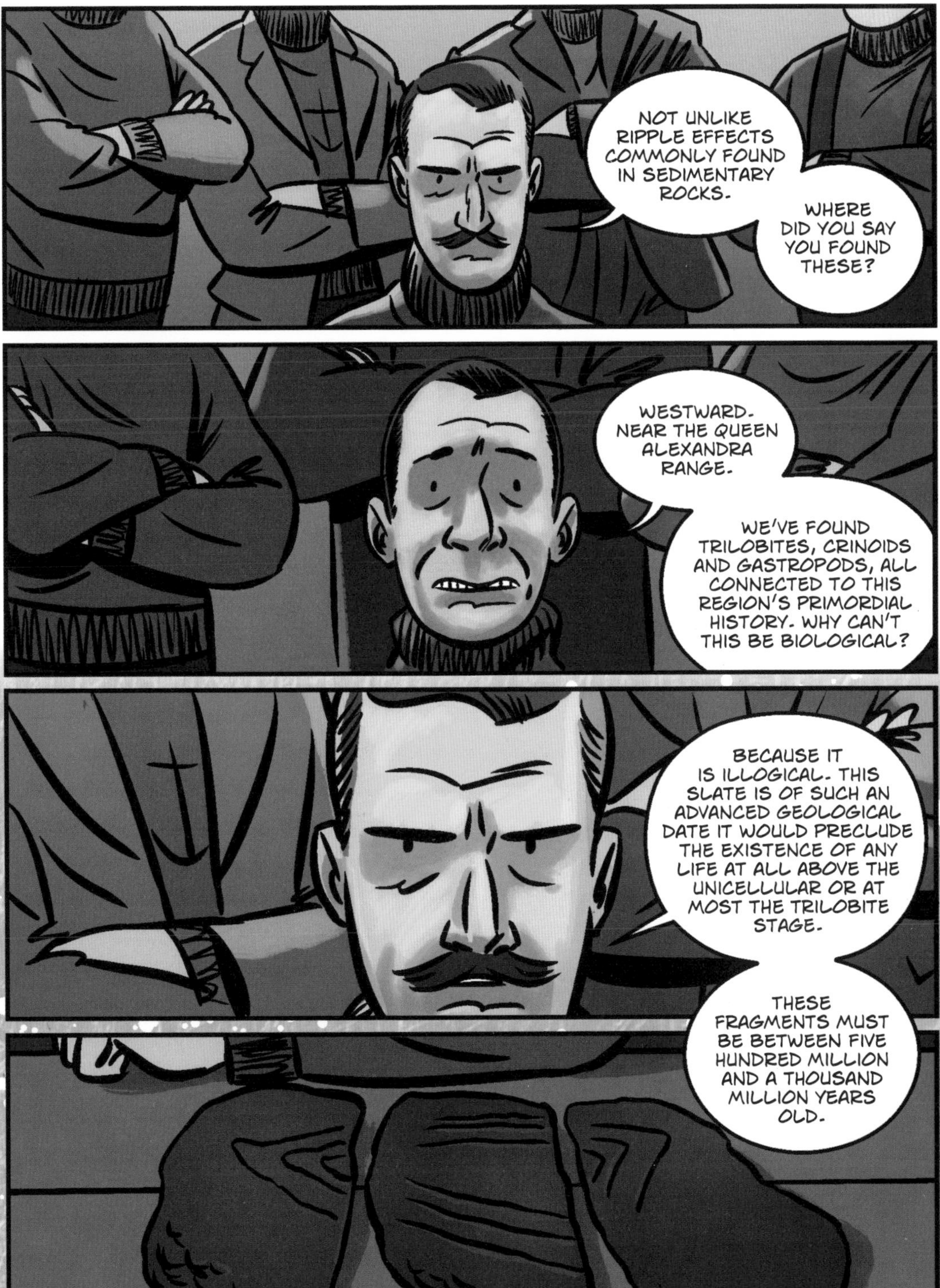
NOT UNLIKE RIPPLE EFFECTS COMMONLY FOUND IN SEDIMENTARY ROCKS.
WHERE DID YOU SAY YOU FOUND THESE?
WESTWARD. NEAR THE QUEEN ALEXANDRA RANGE.
WE'VE FOUND TRILOBITES, CRINOIDS AND GASTROPODS, ALL CONNECTED TO THIS REGION'S PRIMORDIAL HISTORY. WHY CAN'T THIS BE BIOLOGICAL?
BECAUSE IT IS ILLOGICAL. THIS SLATE IS OF SUCH AN ADVANCED GEOLOGICAL DATE IT WOULD PRECLUDE THE EXISTENCE OF ANY LIFE AT ALL ABOVE THE UNICELLULAR OR AT MOST THE TRILOBITE STAGE.
THESE FRAGMENTS MUST BE BETWEEN FIVE HUNDRED MILLION AND A THOUSAND MILLION YEARS OLD.

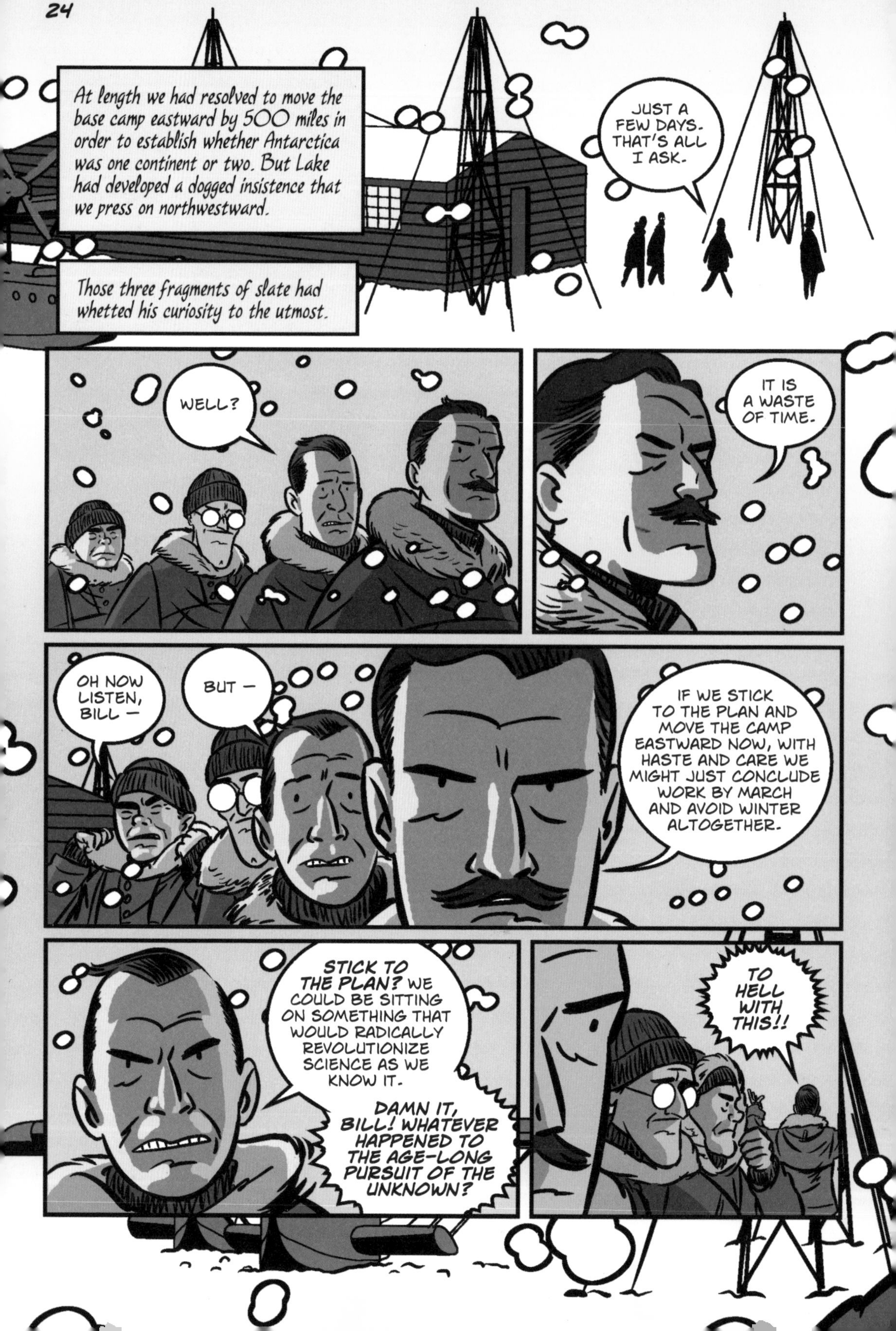
At length we had resolved to move the base camp eastward by 500 miles in order to establish whether Antarctica was one continent or two. But Lake had developed a dogged insistence that we press on northwestward.
JUST A FEW DAYS. THAT'S ALL I ASK.
Those three fragments of slate had whetted his curiosity to the utmost.
WELL?
IT IS A WASTE OF TIME.
OH NOW LISTEN, BILL —
BUT —
IF WE STICK TO THE PLAN AND MOVE THE CAMP EASTWARD NOW, WITH HASTE AND CARE WE MIGHT JUST CONCLUDE WORK BY MARCH AND AVOID WINTER ALTOGETHER.
STICK TO THE PLAN? WE COULD BE SITTING ON SOMETHING THAT WOULD RADICALLY REVOLUTIONIZE SCIENCE AS WE KNOW IT.
DAMN IT, BILL! WHATEVER HAPPENED TO THE AGE-LONG PURSUIT OF THE UNKNOWN?
TO HELL WITH THIS!!

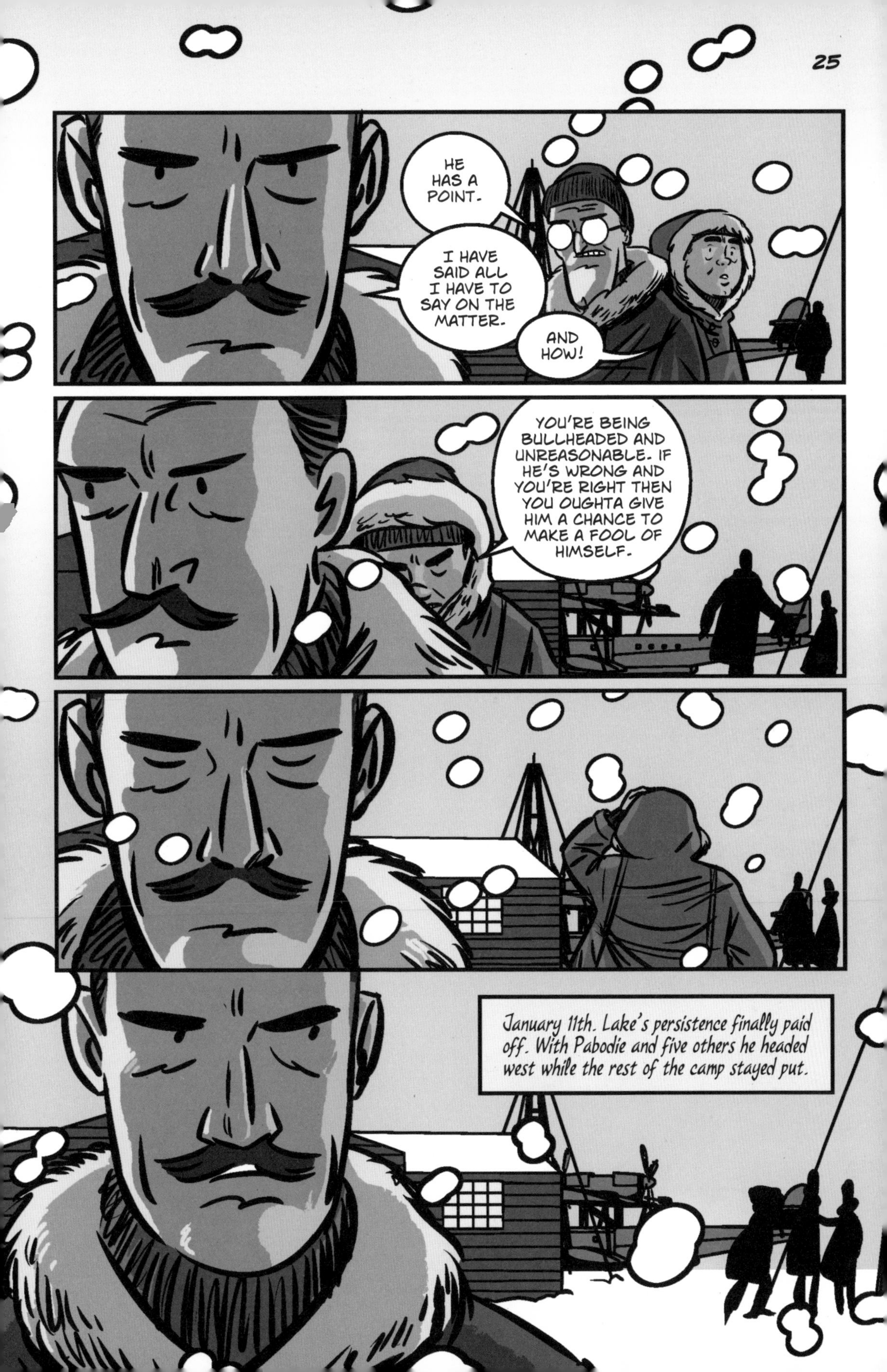
HE HAS A POINT.
I HAVE SAID ALL I HAVE TO SAY ON THE MATTER.
AND HOW!
YOU'RE BEING BULLHEADED AND UNREASONABLE. IF HE'S WRONG AND YOU'RE RIGHT THEN YOU OUGHTA GIVE HIM A CHANCE TO MAKE A FOOL OF HIMSELF.
January 11th. Lake's persistence finally paid off. With Pabodie and five others he headed west while the rest of the camp stayed put.

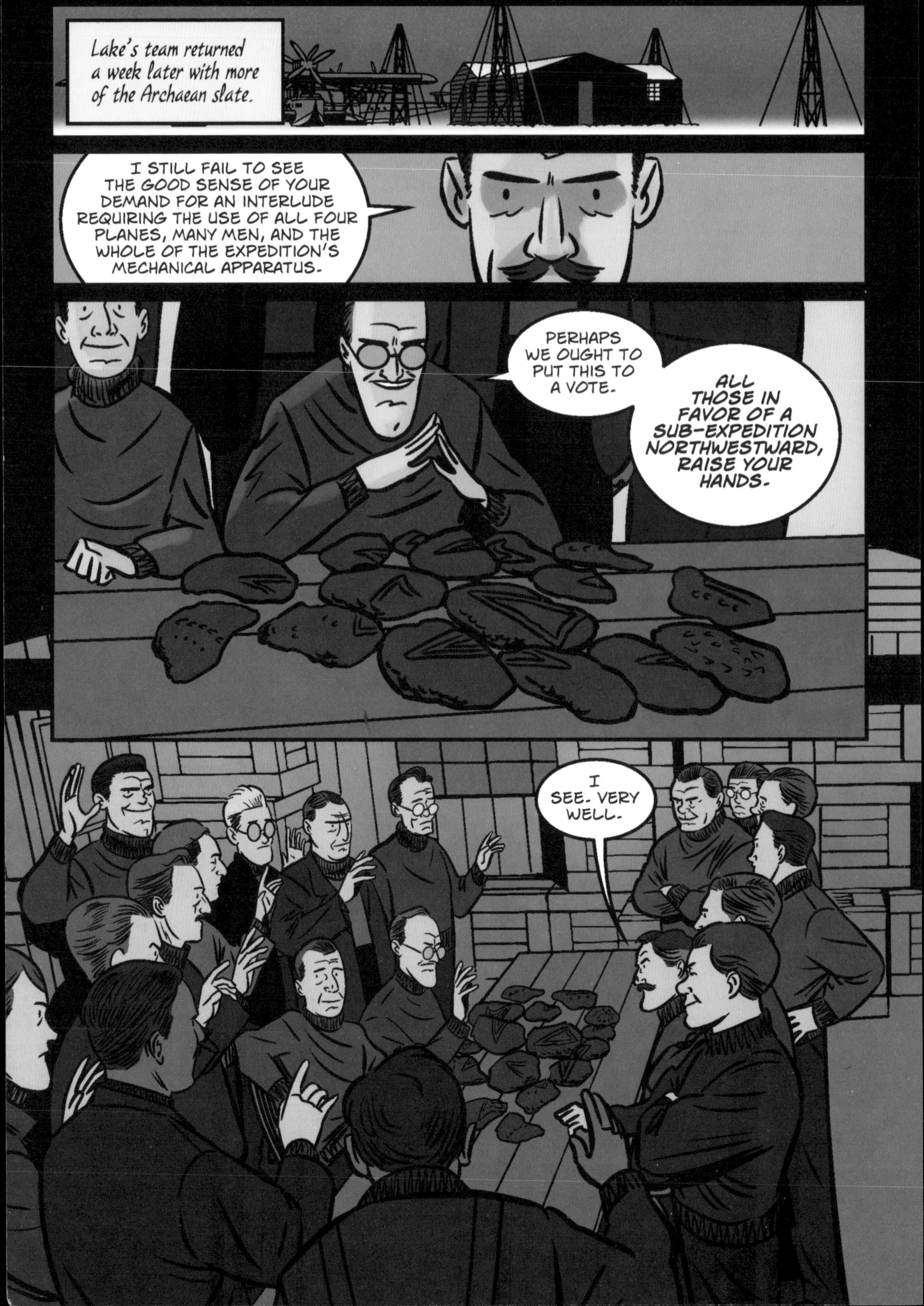
Lake's team returned a week later with more of the Archaean slate.
I STILL FAIL TO SEE THE GOOD SENSE OF YOUR DEMAND FOR AN INTERLUDE REQUIRING THE USE OF ALL FOUR PLANES, MANY MEN, AND THE WHOLE OF THE EXPEDITION'S MECHANICAL APPARATUS.
PERHAPS WE OUGHT TO PUT THIS TO A VOTE.
ALL THOSE IN FAVOR OF A SUB-EXPEDITION NORTHWESTWARD, RAISE YOUR HANDS.
I SEE. VERY WELL.

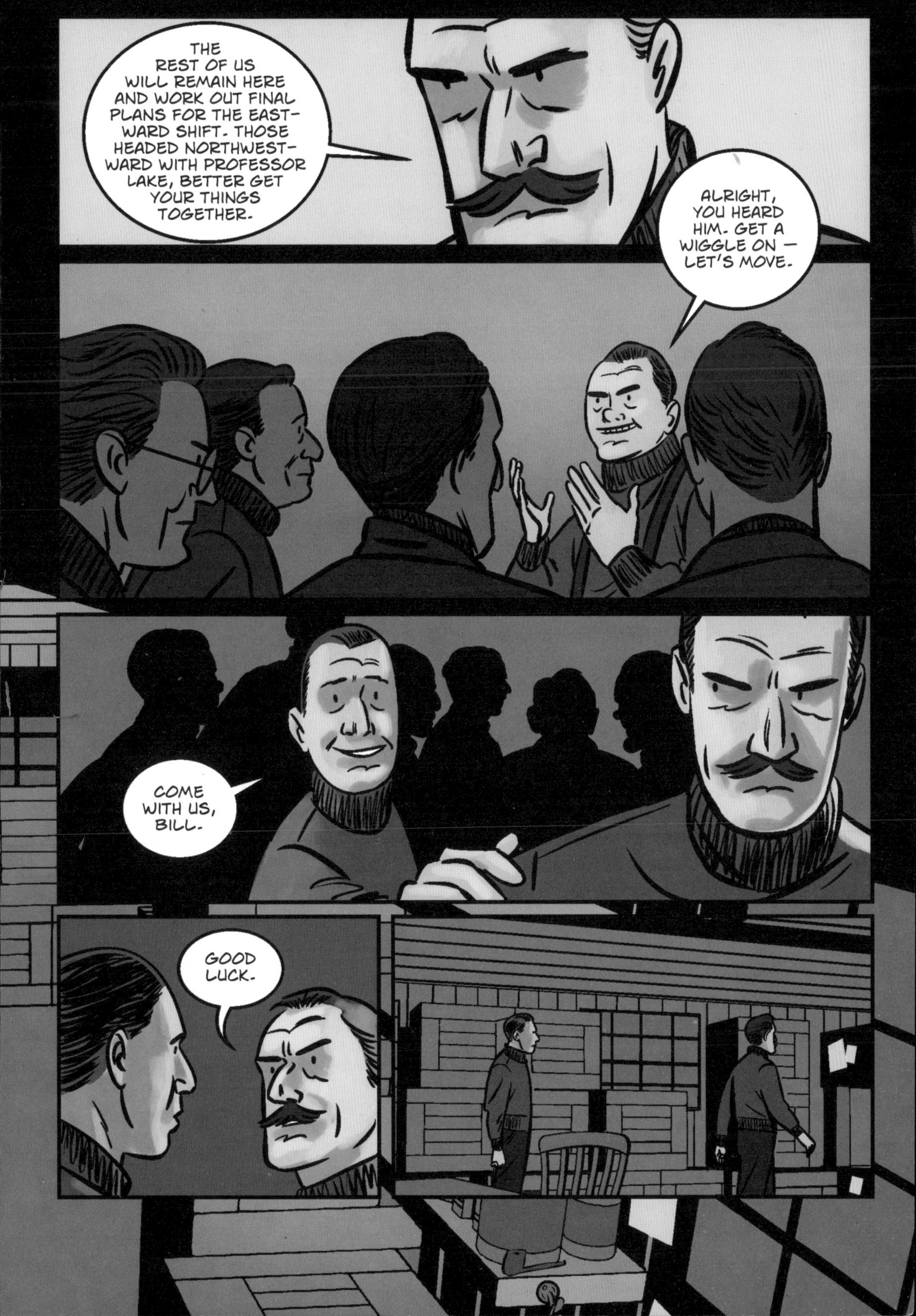
THE REST OF US WILL REMAIN HERE AND WORK OUT FINAL PLANS FOR THE EAST-WARD SHIFT. THOSE HEADED NORTHWEST-WARD WITH PROFESSOR LAKE, BETTER GET YOUR THINGS TOGETHER.
ALRIGHT, YOU HEARD HIM. GET A WIGGLE ON — LET'S MOVE.
COME WITH US, BILL.
GOOD LUCK.

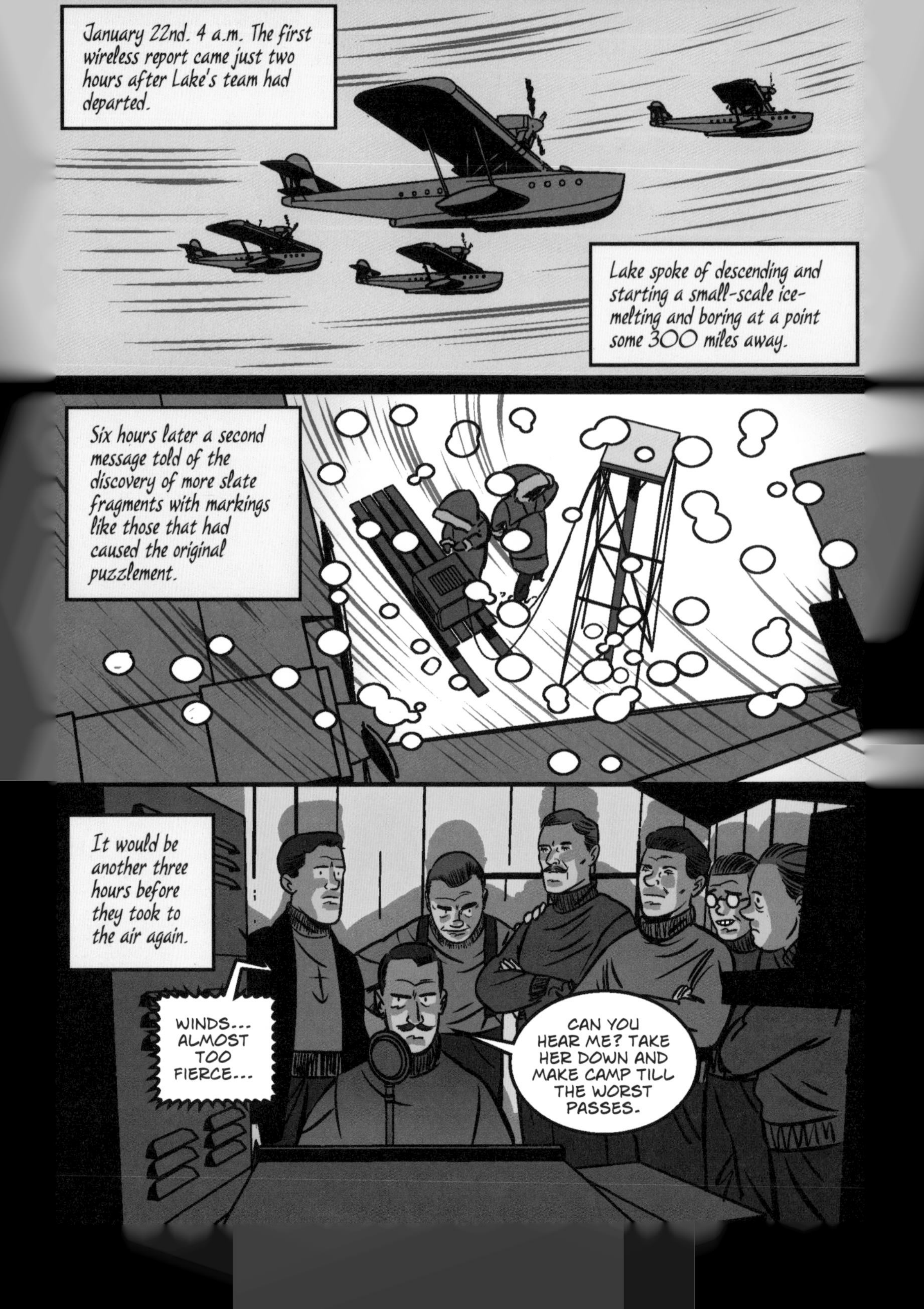
January 22nd. 4 a.m. The first wireless report came just two hours after Lake's team had departed.
Lake spoke of descending and starting a small-scale ice-melting and boring at a point some 300 miles away.
Six hours later a second message told of the discovery of more slate fragments with markings like those that had caused the original puzzlement.
It would be another three hours before they took to the air again.
WINDS... ALMOST TOO FIERCE...
CAN YOU HEAR ME? TAKE HER DOWN AND MAKE CAMP TILL THE WORST PASSES.

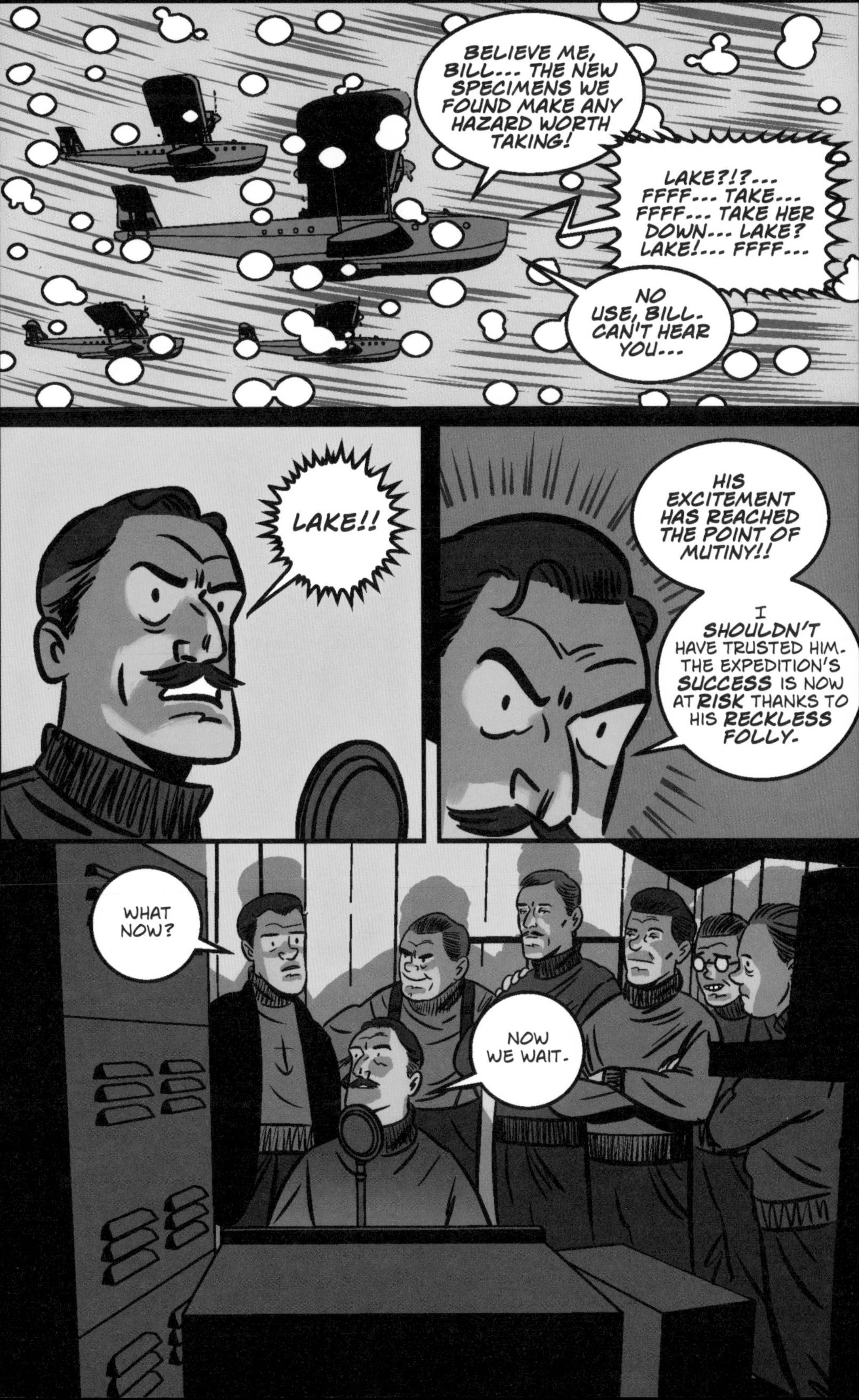
BELIEVE ME, BILL... THE NEW SPECIMENS WE FOUND MAKE ANY HAZARD WORTH TAKING!
LAKE?!?... FFFF... TAKE... FFFF... TAKE HER DOWN... LAKE? LAKE!... FFFF...
NO USE, BILL. CAN'T HEAR YOU...
LAKE!!
HIS EXCITEMENT HAS REACHED THE POINT OF MUTINY!!
I SHOULDN'T HAVE TRUSTED HIM. THE EXPEDITION'S SUCCESS IS NOW AT RISK THANKS TO HIS RECKLESS FOLLY.
WHAT NOW?
NOW WE WAIT.

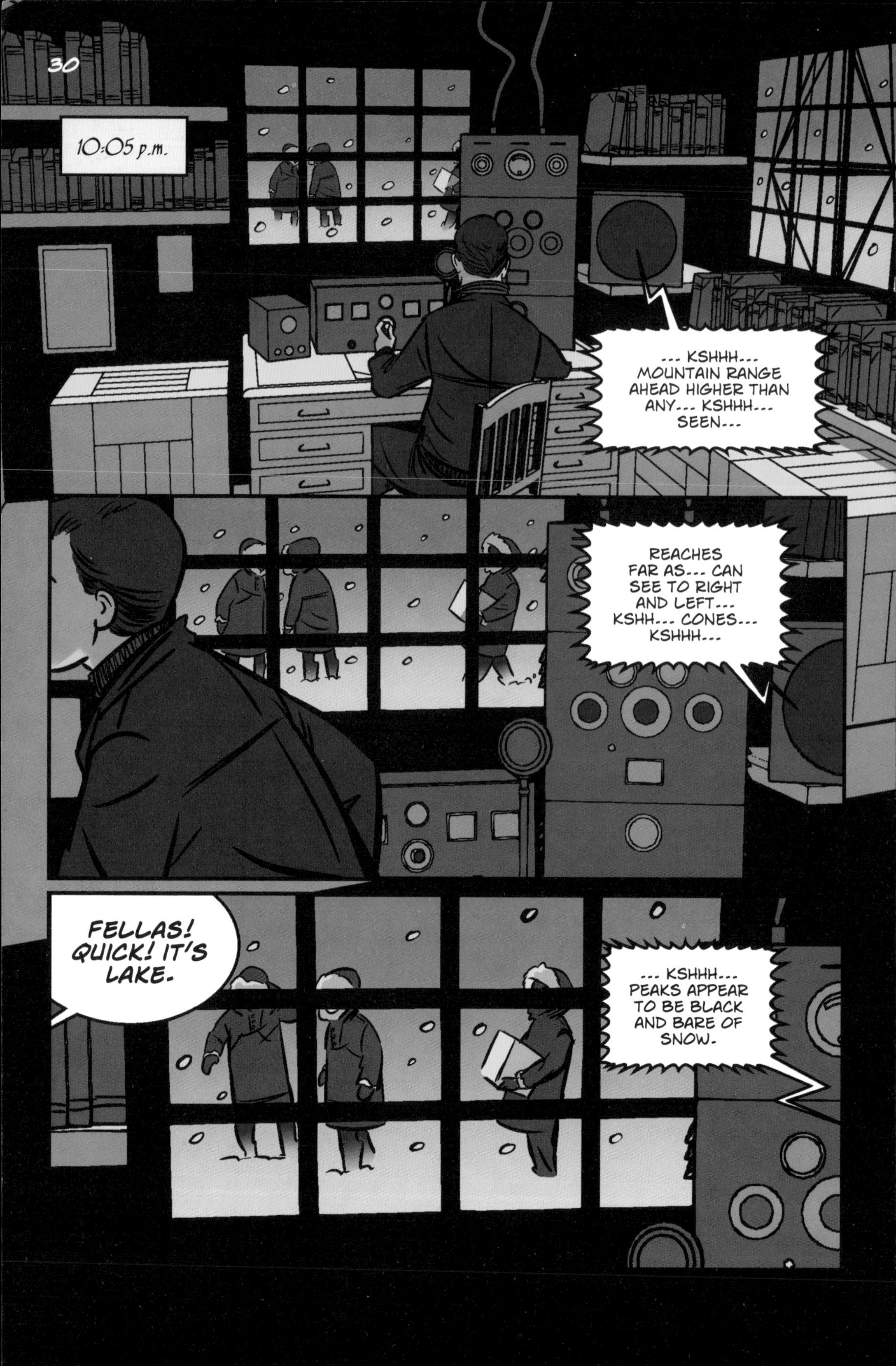
10:05 p.m.
--- KSHHH--- MOUNTAIN RANGE AHEAD HIGHER THAN ANY--- KSHHH--- SEEN---
REACHES FAR AS--- CAN SEE TO RIGHT AND LEFT--- KSHH--- CONES--- KSHHH---
FELLAS! QUICK! IT'S LAKE.
--- KSHHH--- PEAKS APPEAR TO BE BLACK AND BARE OF SNOW.

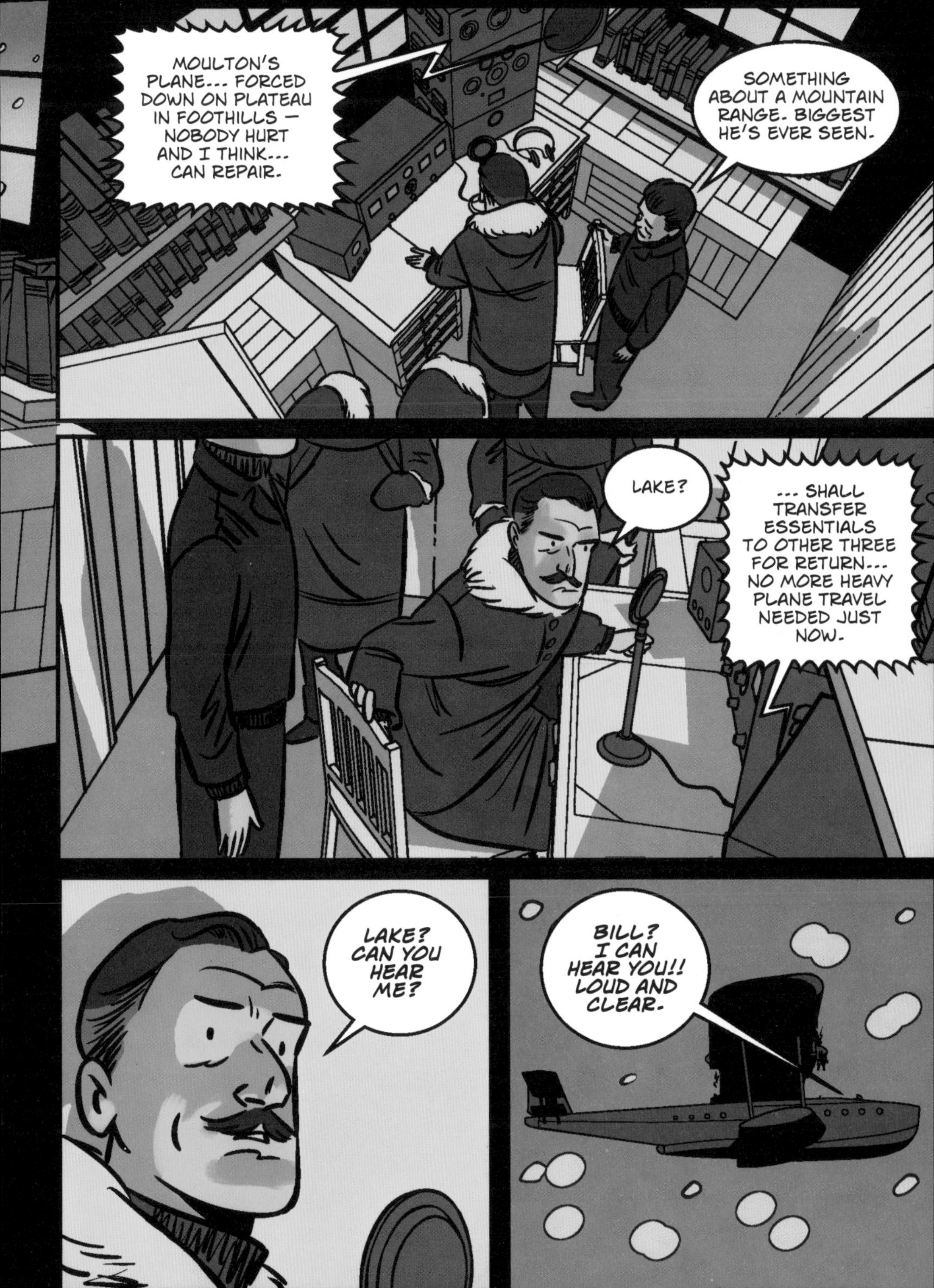
MOULTON'S PLANE... FORCED DOWN ON PLATEAU IN FOOTHILLS — NOBODY HURT AND I THINK... CAN REPAIR.
SOMETHING ABOUT A MOUNTAIN RANGE. BIGGEST HE'S EVER SEEN.
LAKE?
... SHALL TRANSFER ESSENTIALS TO OTHER THREE FOR RETURN... NO MORE HEAVY PLANE TRAVEL NEEDED JUST NOW.
LAKE? CAN YOU HEAR ME?
BILL? I CAN HEAR YOU!! LOUD AND CLEAR.

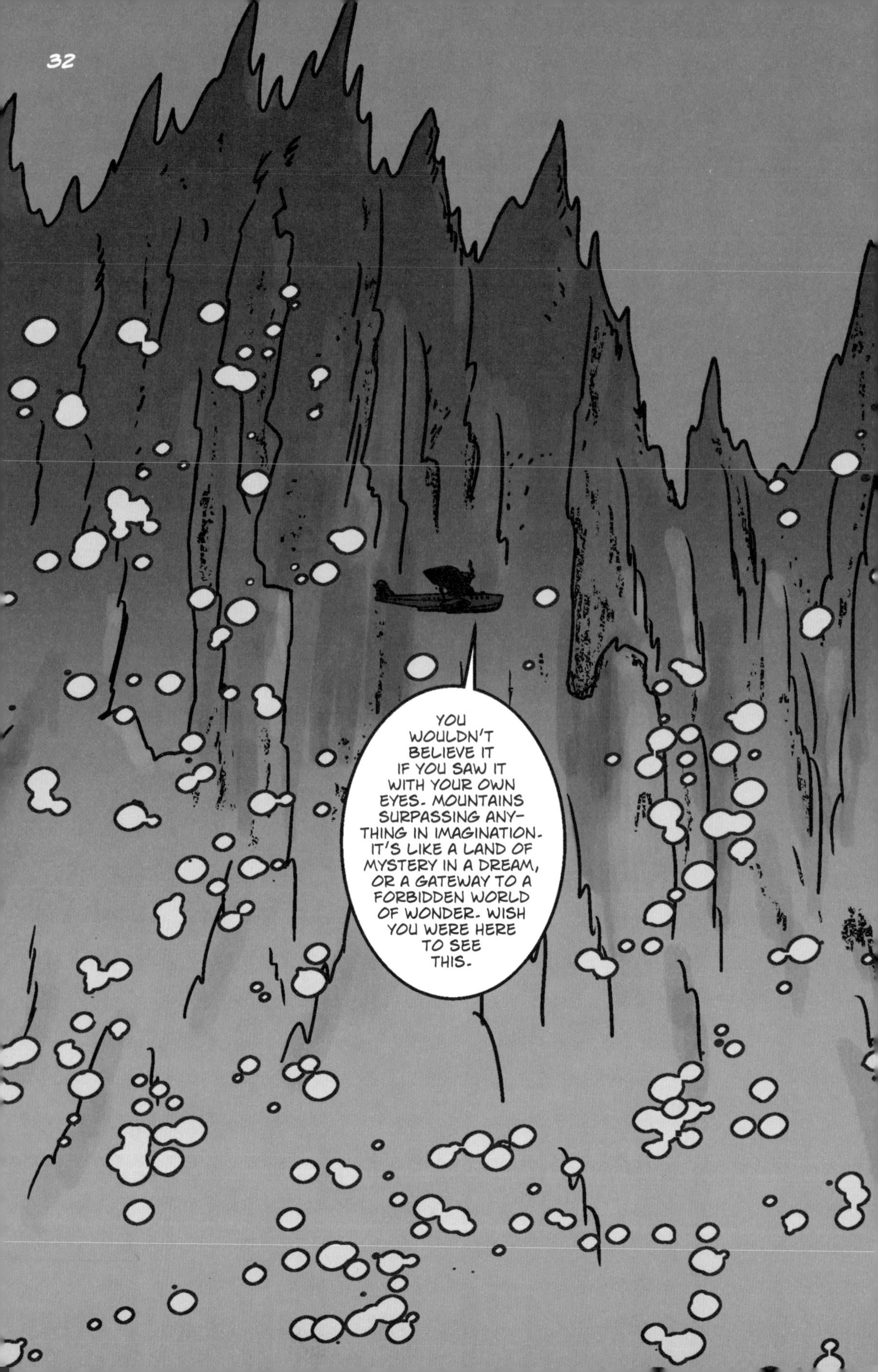
YOU WOULDN'T BELIEVE IT IF YOU SAW IT WITH YOUR OWN EYES. MOUNTAINS SURPASSING ANYTHING IN IMAGINATION. IT'S LIKE A LAND OF MYSTERY IN A DREAM, OR A GATEWAY TO A FORBIDDEN WORLD OF WONDER. WISH YOU WERE HERE TO SEE THIS.

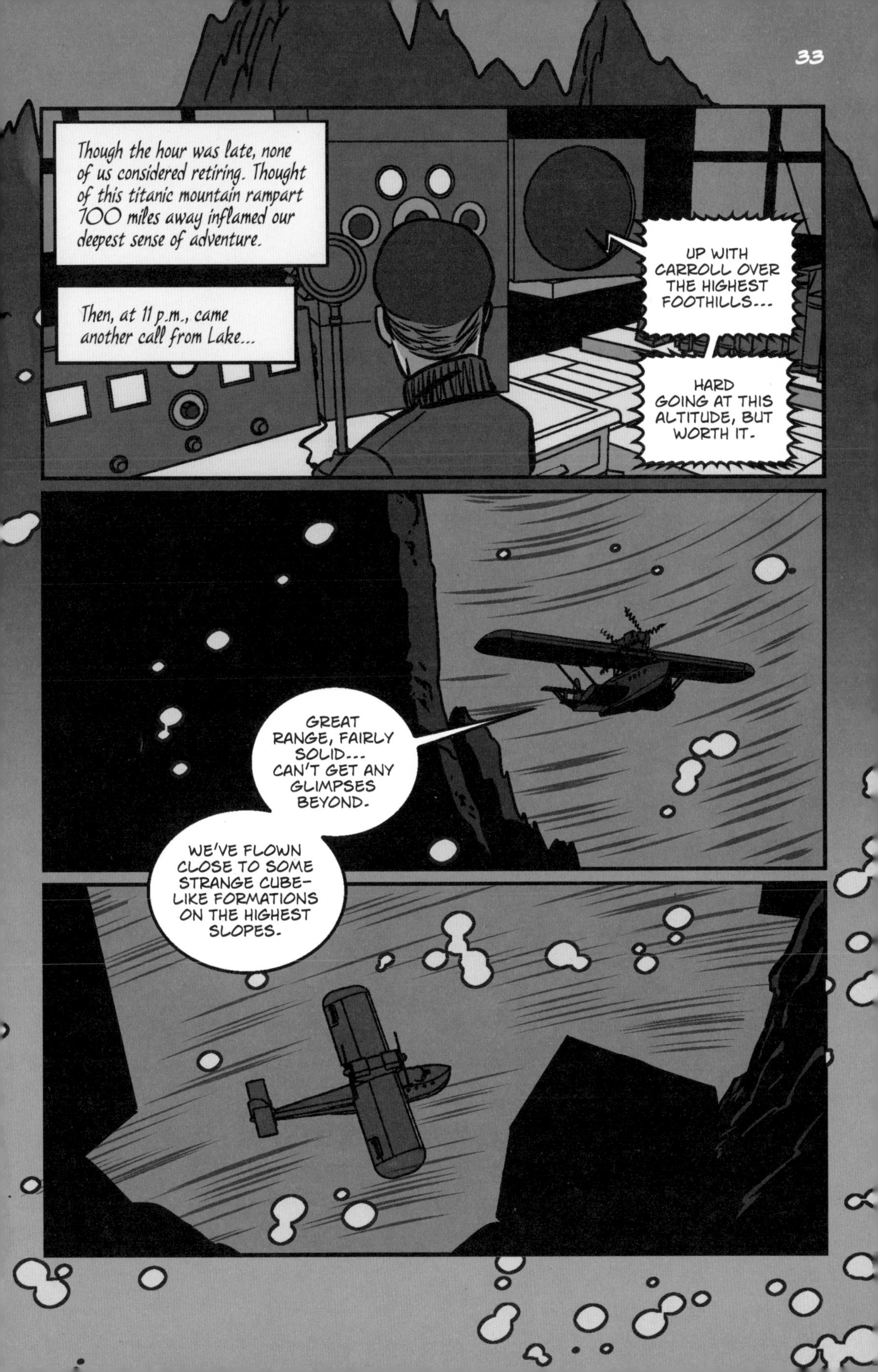
Though the hour was late, none of us considered retiring. Thought of this titanic mountain rampart 700 miles away inflamed our deepest sense of adventure.
Then, at 11 p.m., came another call from Lake...
UP WITH CARROLL OVER THE HIGHEST FOOTHILLS...
HARD GOING AT THIS ALTITUDE, BUT WORTH IT.
GREAT RANGE, FAIRLY SOLID... CAN'T GET ANY GLIMPSES BEYOND.
WE'VE FLOWN CLOSE TO SOME STRANGE CUBE-LIKE FORMATIONS ON THE HIGHEST SLOPES.

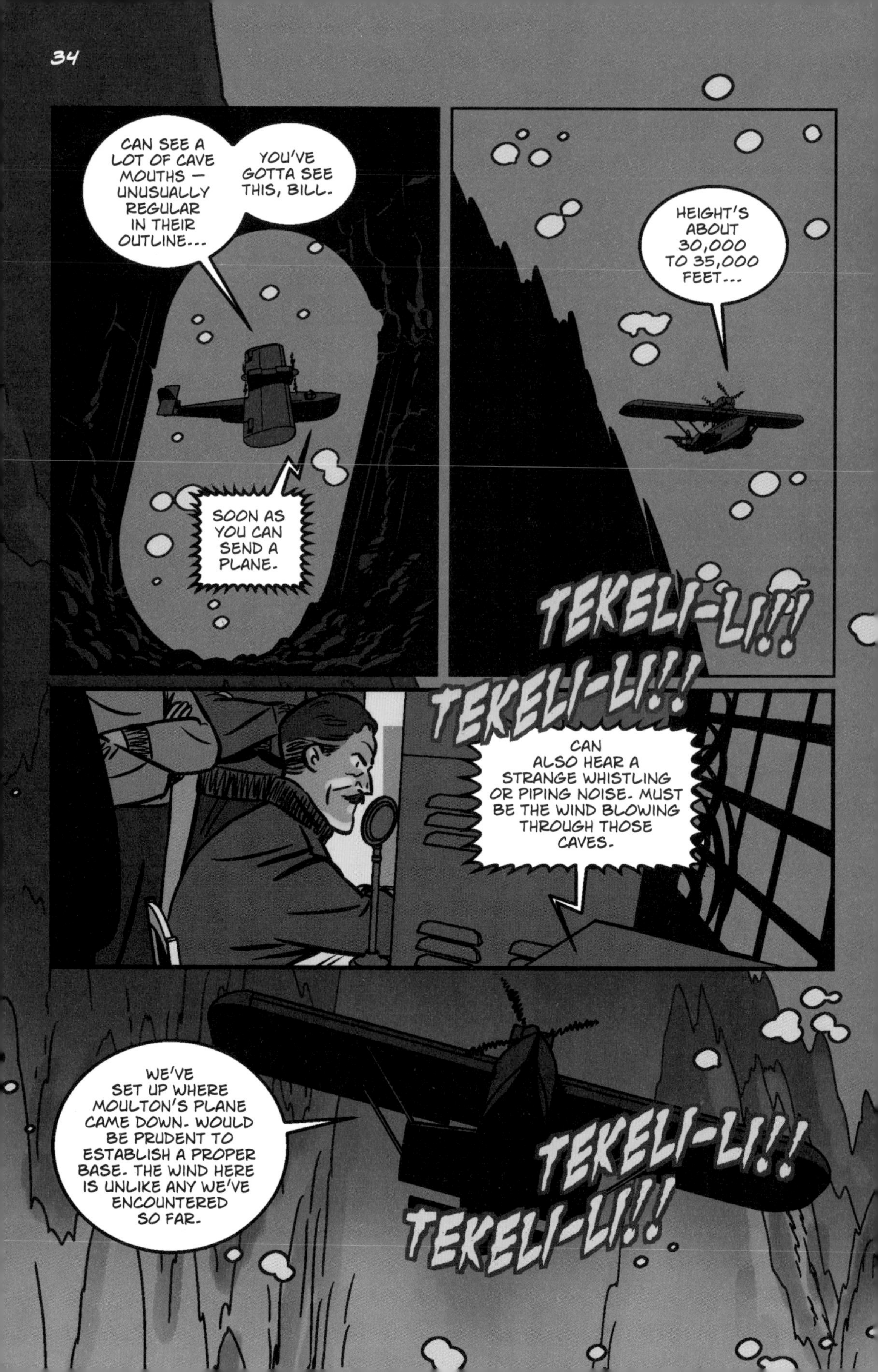
CAN SEE A LOT OF CAVE MOUTHS — UNUSUALLY REGULAR IN THEIR OUTLINE...
YOU'VE GOTTA SEE THIS, BILL.
SOON AS YOU CAN SEND A PLANE.
HEIGHT'S ABOUT 30,000 TO 35,000 FEET...
TEKELI-LI!!
TEKELI-LI!!
CAN ALSO HEAR A STRANGE WHISTLING OR PIPING NOISE. MUST BE THE WIND BLOWING THROUGH THOSE CAVES.
WE'VE SET UP WHERE MOULTON'S PLANE CAME DOWN. WOULD BE PRUDENT TO ESTABLISH A PROPER BASE. THE WIND HERE IS UNLIKE ANY WE'VE ENCOUNTERED SO FAR.
TEKELI-LI!!
TEKELI-LI!!

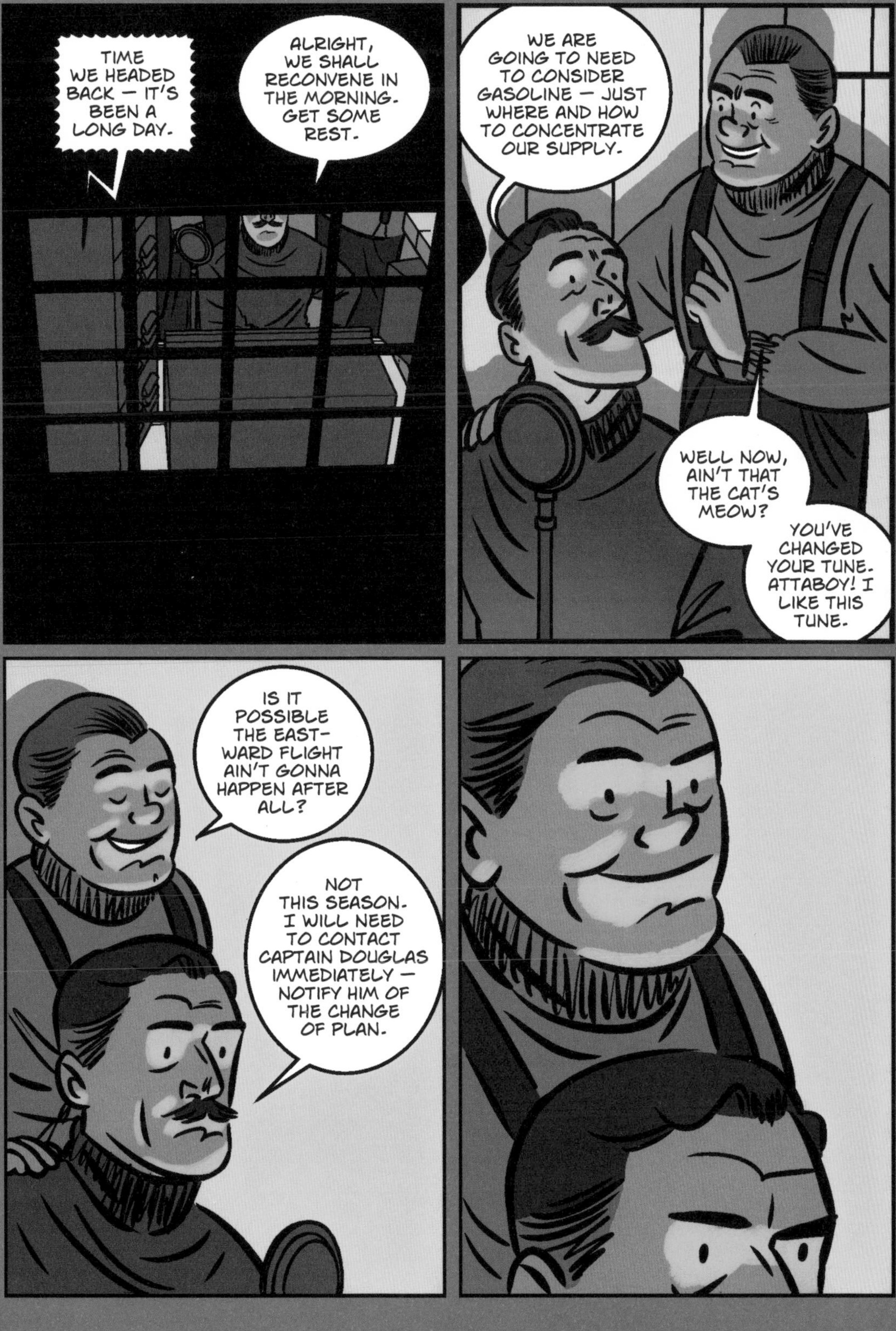
TIME WE HEADED BACK — IT'S BEEN A LONG DAY.
ALRIGHT, WE SHALL RECONVENE IN THE MORNING. GET SOME REST.
WE ARE GOING TO NEED TO CONSIDER GASOLINE — JUST WHERE AND HOW TO CONCENTRATE OUR SUPPLY.
WELL NOW, AIN'T THAT THE CAT'S MEOW?
YOU'VE CHANGED YOUR TUNE. ATTABOY! I LIKE THIS TUNE.
IS IT POSSIBLE THE EAST-WARD FLIGHT AIN'T GONNA HAPPEN AFTER ALL?
NOT THIS SEASON. I WILL NEED TO CONTACT CAPTAIN DOUGLAS IMMEDIATELY — NOTIFY HIM OF THE CHANGE OF PLAN.

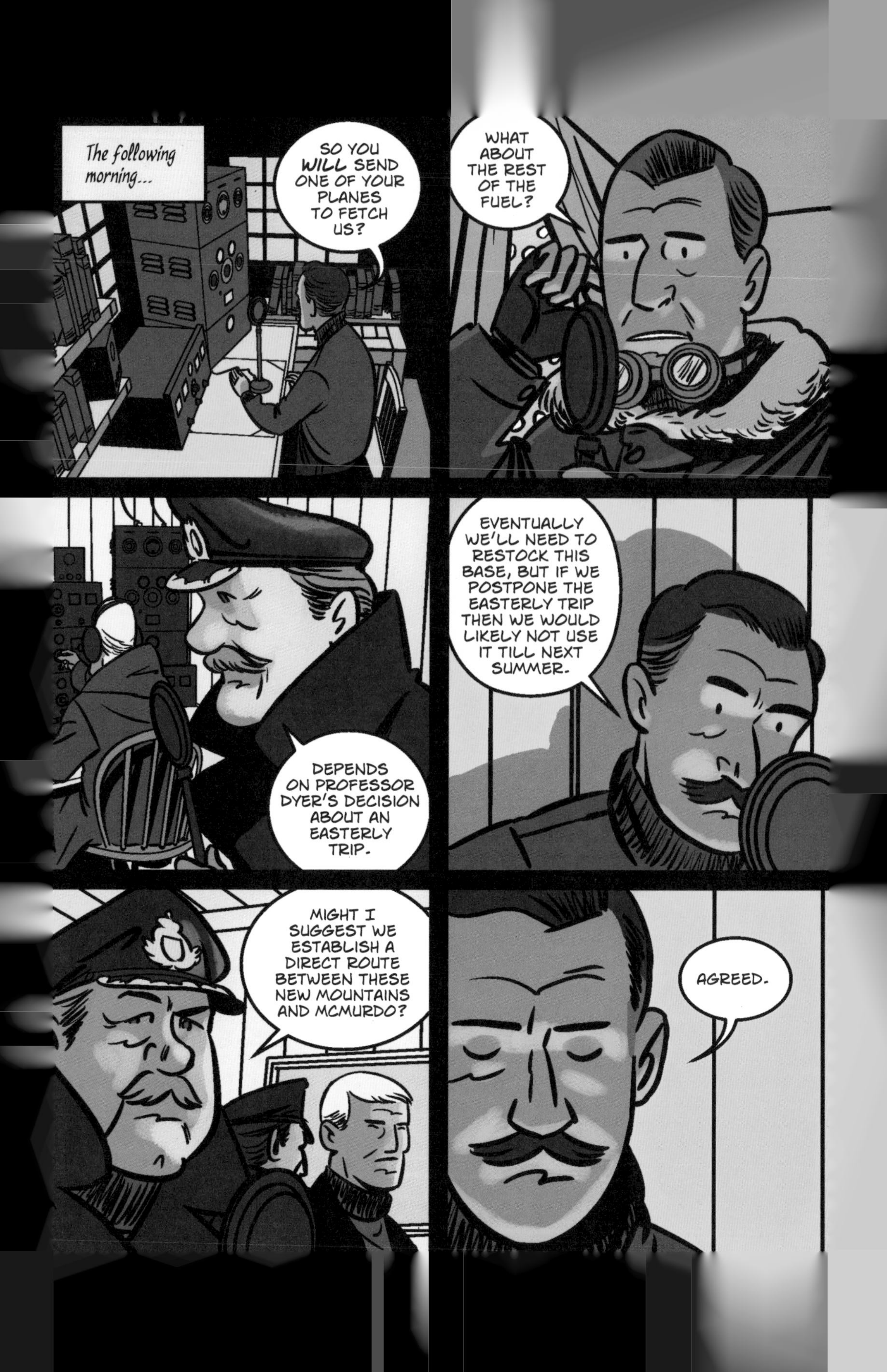
The following morning...
SO YOU WILL SEND ONE OF YOUR PLANES TO FETCH US?
WHAT ABOUT THE REST OF THE FUEL?
DEPENDS ON PROFESSOR DYER'S DECISION ABOUT AN EASTERLY TRIP.
EVENTUALLY WE'LL NEED TO RESTOCK THIS BASE, BUT IF WE POSTPONE THE EASTERLY TRIP THEN WE WOULD LIKELY NOT USE IT TILL NEXT SUMMER.
MIGHT I SUGGEST WE ESTABLISH A DIRECT ROUTE BETWEEN THESE NEW MOUNTAINS AND MCMURDO?
AGREED.

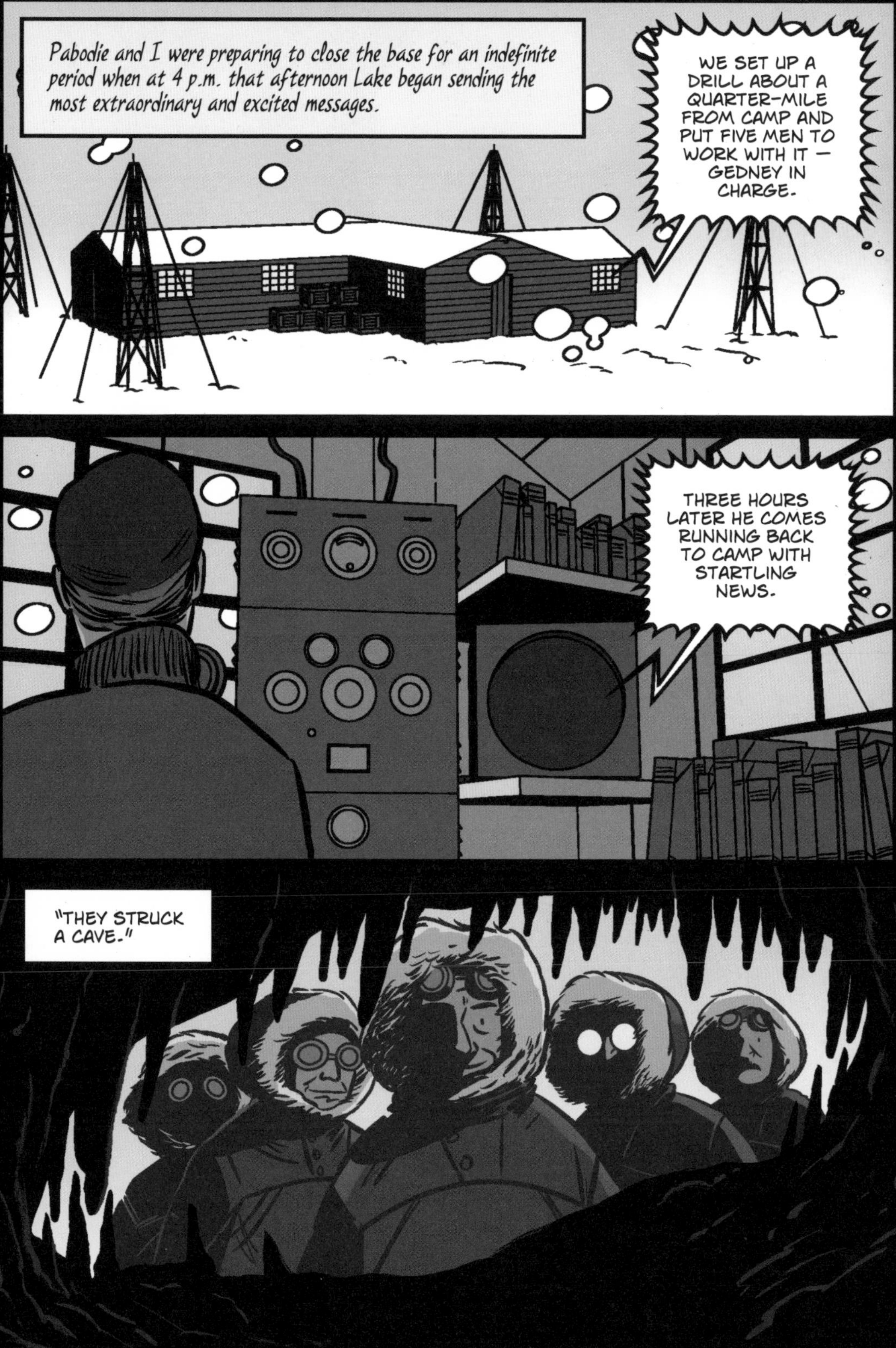
Pabodie and I were preparing to close the base for an indefinite period when at 4 p.m. that afternoon Lake began sending the most extraordinary and excited messages.
WE SET UP A DRILL ABOUT A QUARTER-MILE FROM CAMP AND PUT FIVE MEN TO WORK WITH IT — GEDNEY IN CHARGE.
THREE HOURS LATER HE COMES RUNNING BACK TO CAMP WITH STARTLING NEWS.
"THEY STRUCK A CAVE."

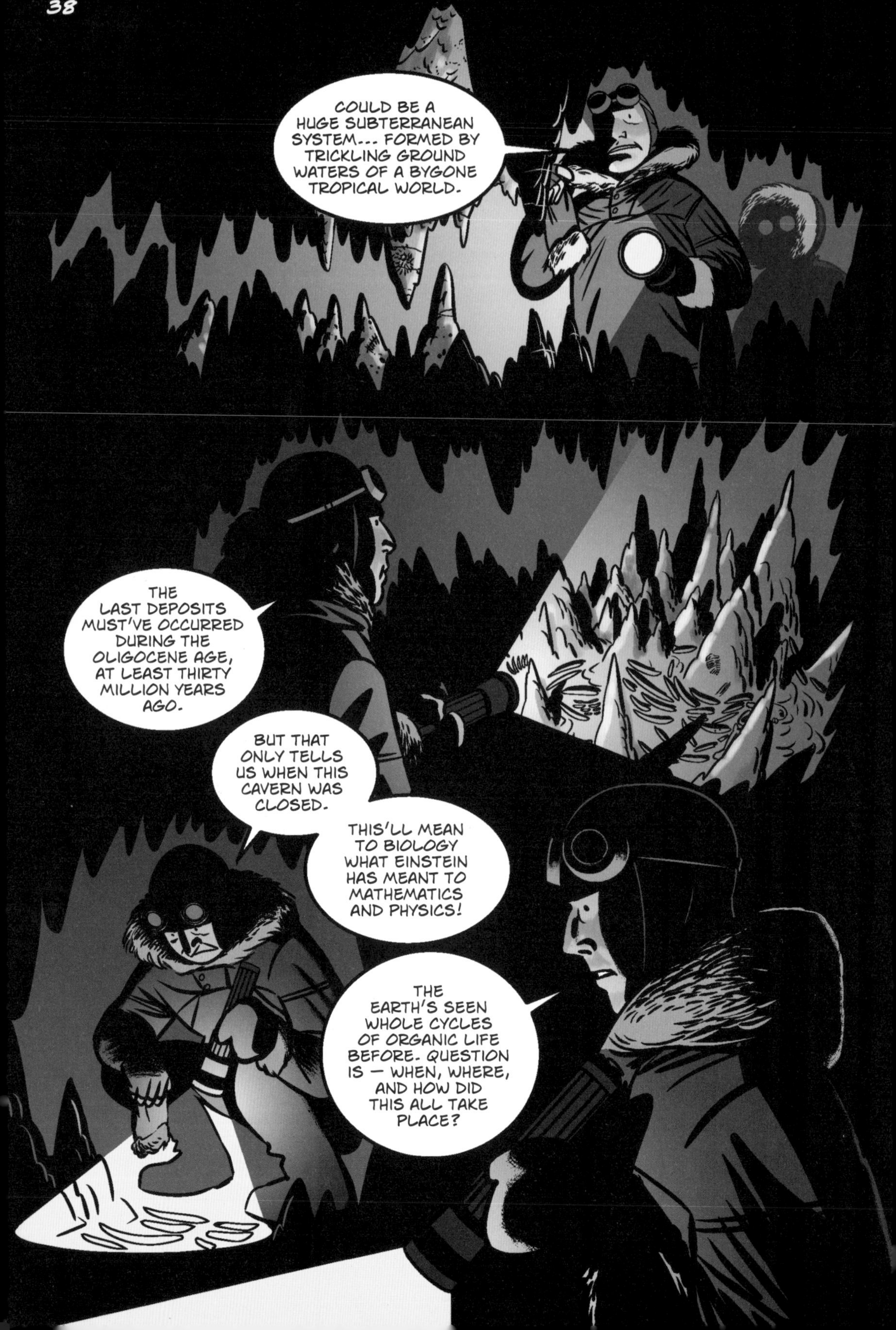
COULD BE A HUGE SUBTERRANEAN SYSTEM... FORMED BY TRICKLING GROUND WATERS OF A BYGONE TROPICAL WORLD.
THE LAST DEPOSITS MUST'VE OCCURRED DURING THE OLIGOCENE AGE, AT LEAST THIRTY MILLION YEARS AGO.
BUT THAT ONLY TELLS US WHEN THIS CAVERN WAS CLOSED.
THIS'LL MEAN TO BIOLOGY WHAT EINSTEIN HAS MEANT TO MATHEMATICS AND PHYSICS!
THE EARTH'S SEEN WHOLE CYCLES OF ORGANIC LIFE BEFORE. QUESTION IS — WHEN, WHERE, AND HOW DID THIS ALL TAKE PLACE?

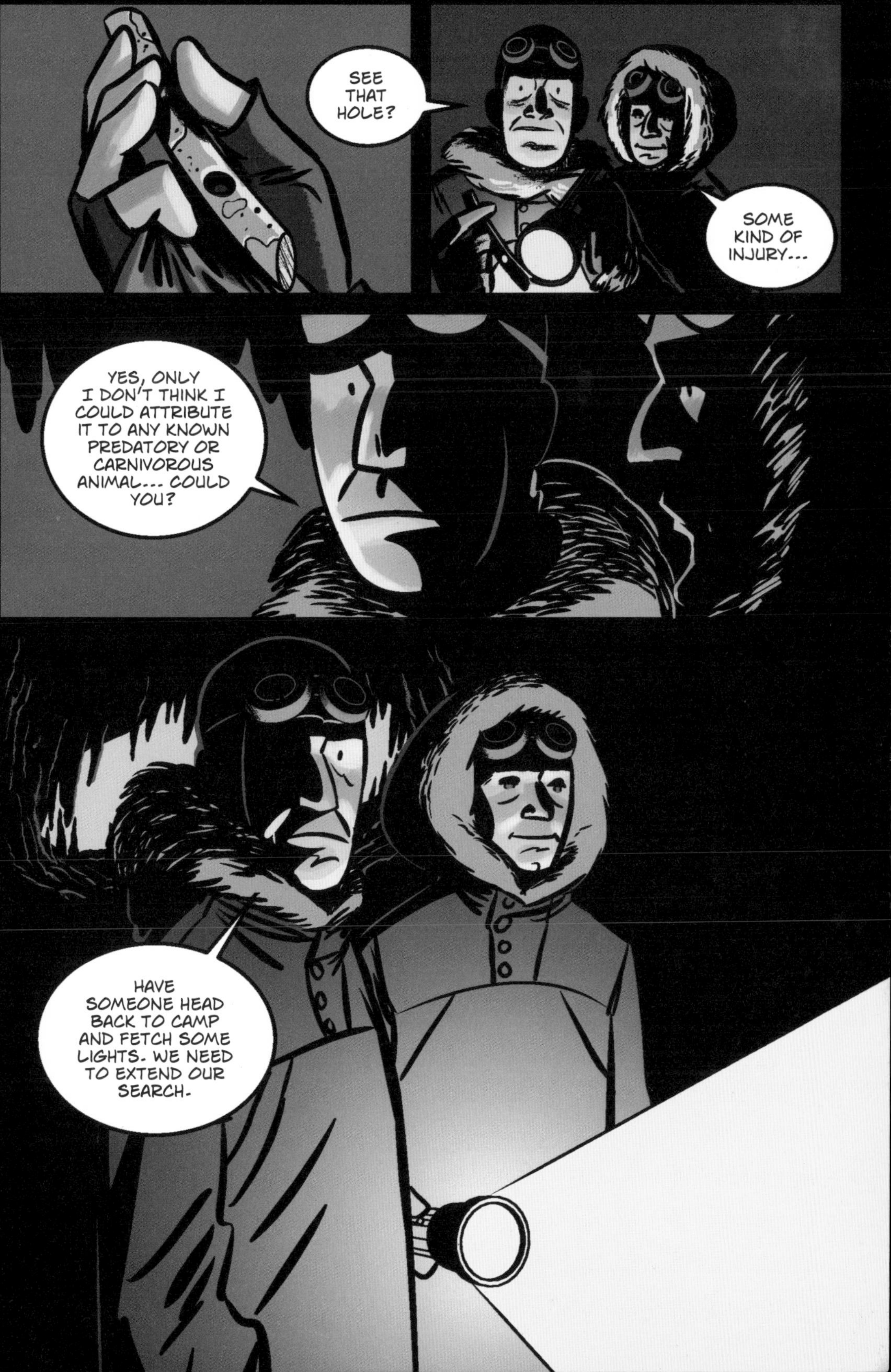
SEE THAT HOLE?
SOME KIND OF INJURY...
YES, ONLY I DON'T THINK I COULD ATTRIBUTE IT TO ANY KNOWN PREDATORY OR CARNIVOROUS ANIMAL... COULD YOU?
HAVE SOMEONE HEAD BACK TO CAMP AND FETCH SOME LIGHTS. WE NEED TO EXTEND OUR SEARCH.

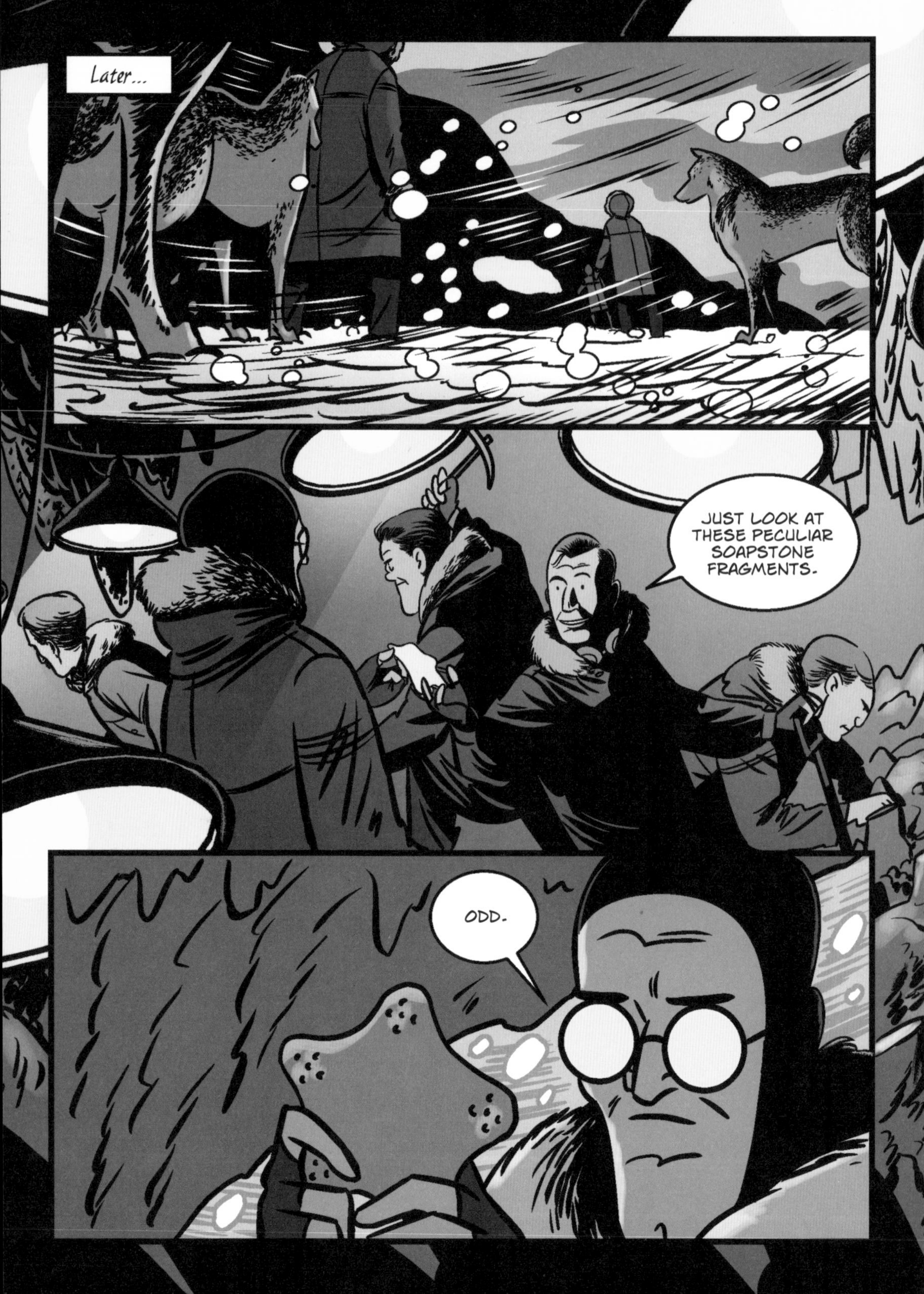
Later...
JUST LOOK AT THESE PECULIAR SOAPSTONE FRAGMENTS.
ODD.

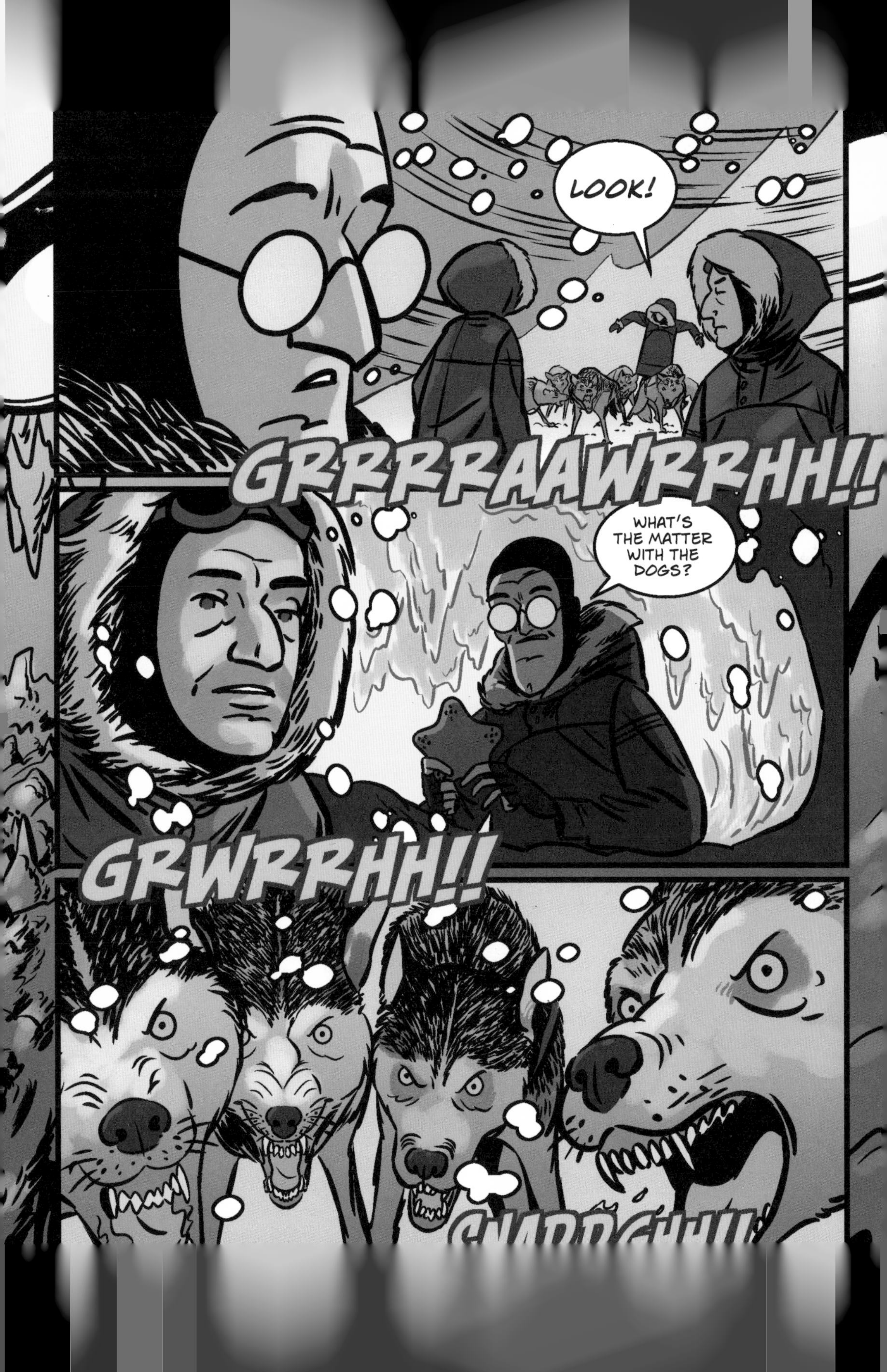
LOOK!
GRRRRAAWRRHH!!
WHAT'S THE MATTER WITH THE DOGS?
GRWRRHH!!

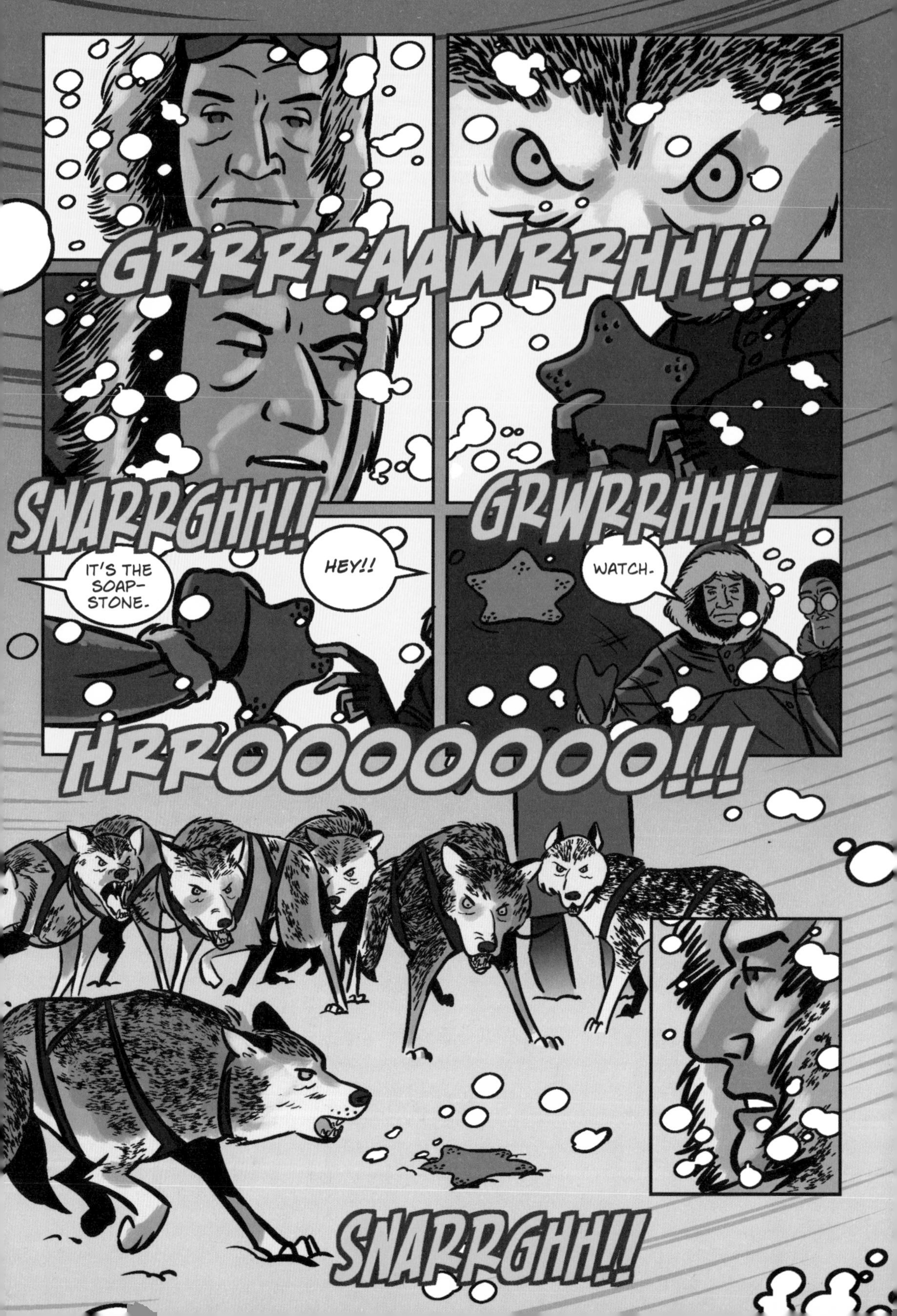
GRRRRAAWRRHH!!
SNARRGHH!!
GRWRRHH!!
IT'S THE SOAP-STONE.
HEY!!
WATCH.
HRROOOOOOOO!!!
SNARRGHH!!

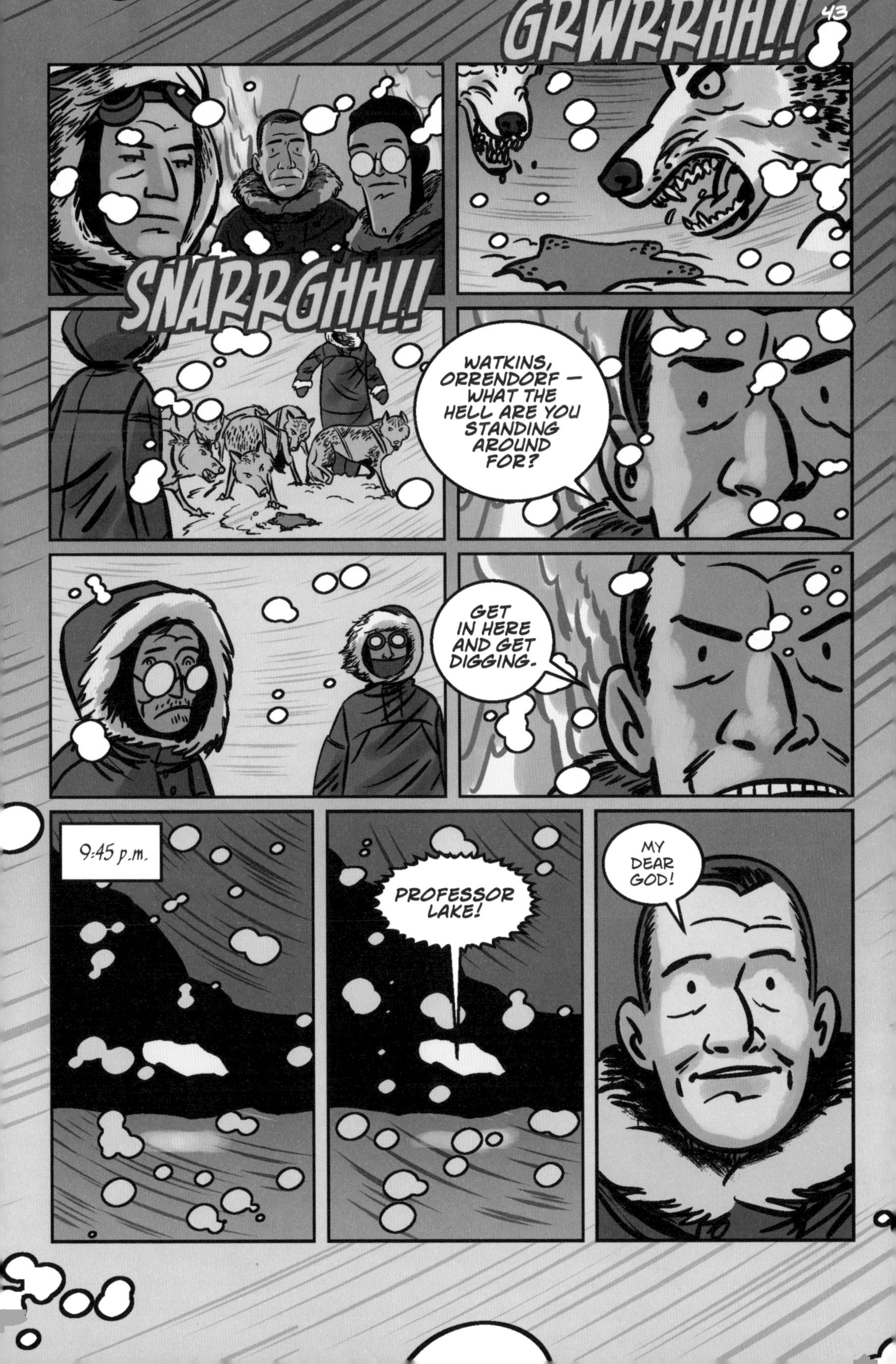
GRWRRHH!!
SNARRGHH!!
WATKINS, ORRENDORF — WHAT THE HELL ARE YOU STANDING AROUND FOR?
GET IN HERE AND GET DIGGING.
9:45 p.m.
PROFESSOR LAKE!
MY DEAR GOD!

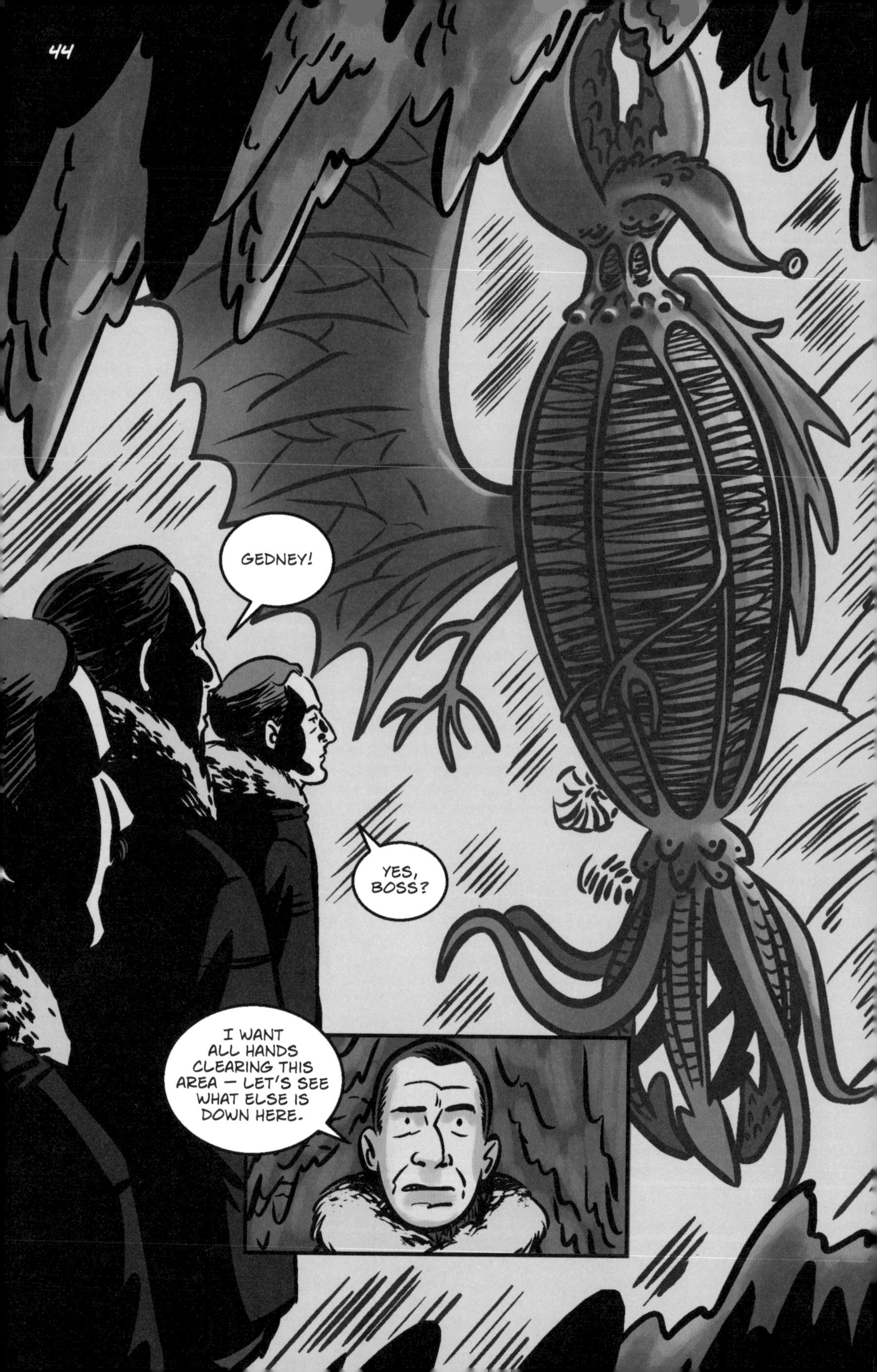
GEDNEY!
YES, BOSS?
I WANT ALL HANDS CLEARING THIS AREA — LET'S SEE WHAT ELSE IS DOWN HERE.

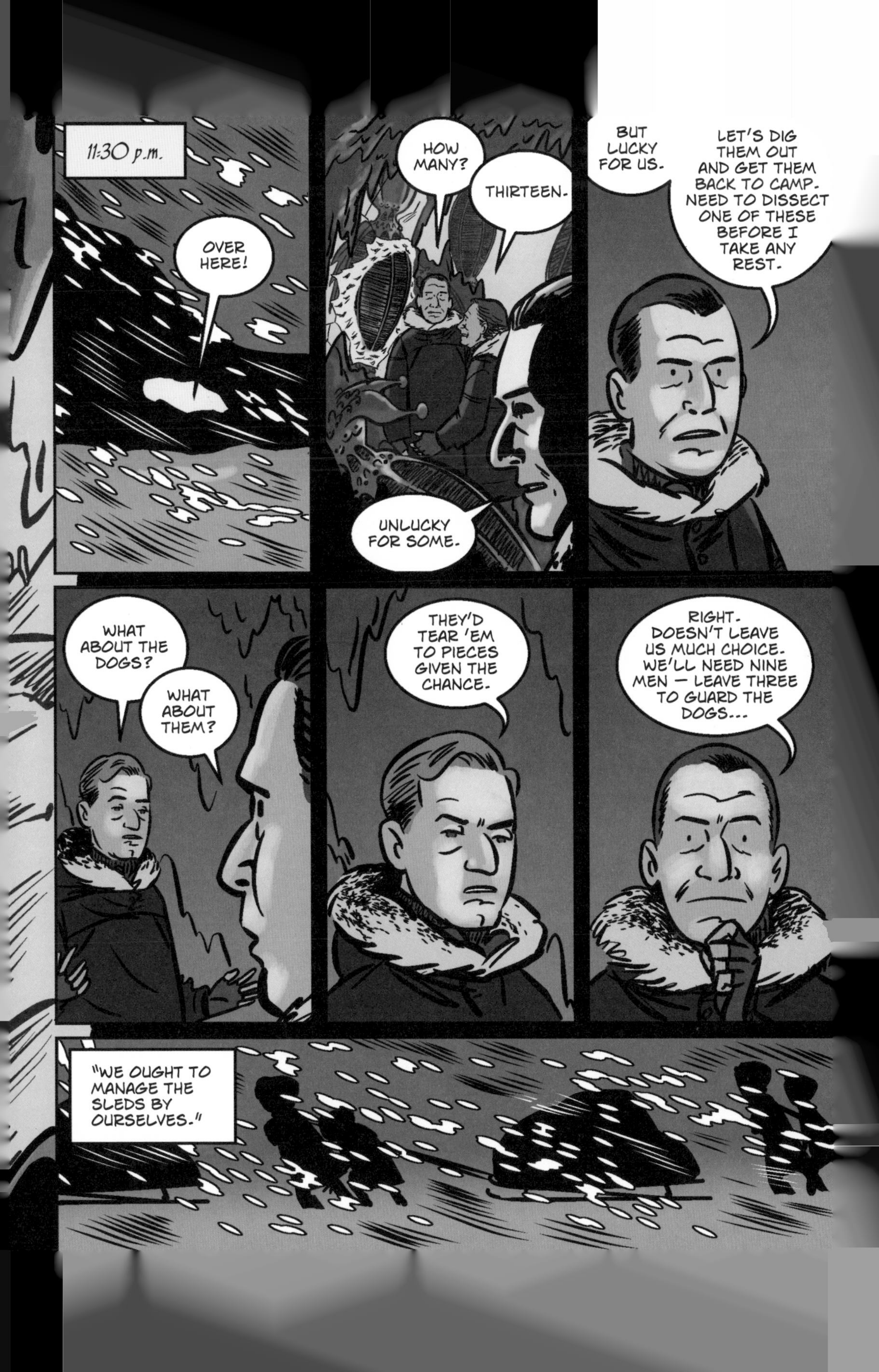
11:30 p.m.
OVER HERE!
HOW MANY?
THIRTEEN.
UNLUCKY FOR SOME.
BUT LUCKY FOR US.
LET'S DIG THEM OUT AND GET THEM BACK TO CAMP. NEED TO DISSECT ONE OF THESE BEFORE I TAKE ANY REST.
WHAT ABOUT THE DOGS?
WHAT ABOUT THEM?
THEY'D TEAR 'EM TO PIECES GIVEN THE CHANCE.
RIGHT. DOESN'T LEAVE US MUCH CHOICE. WE'LL NEED NINE MEN — LEAVE THREE TO GUARD THE DOGS...
"WE OUGHT TO MANAGE THE SLEDS BY OURSELVES."

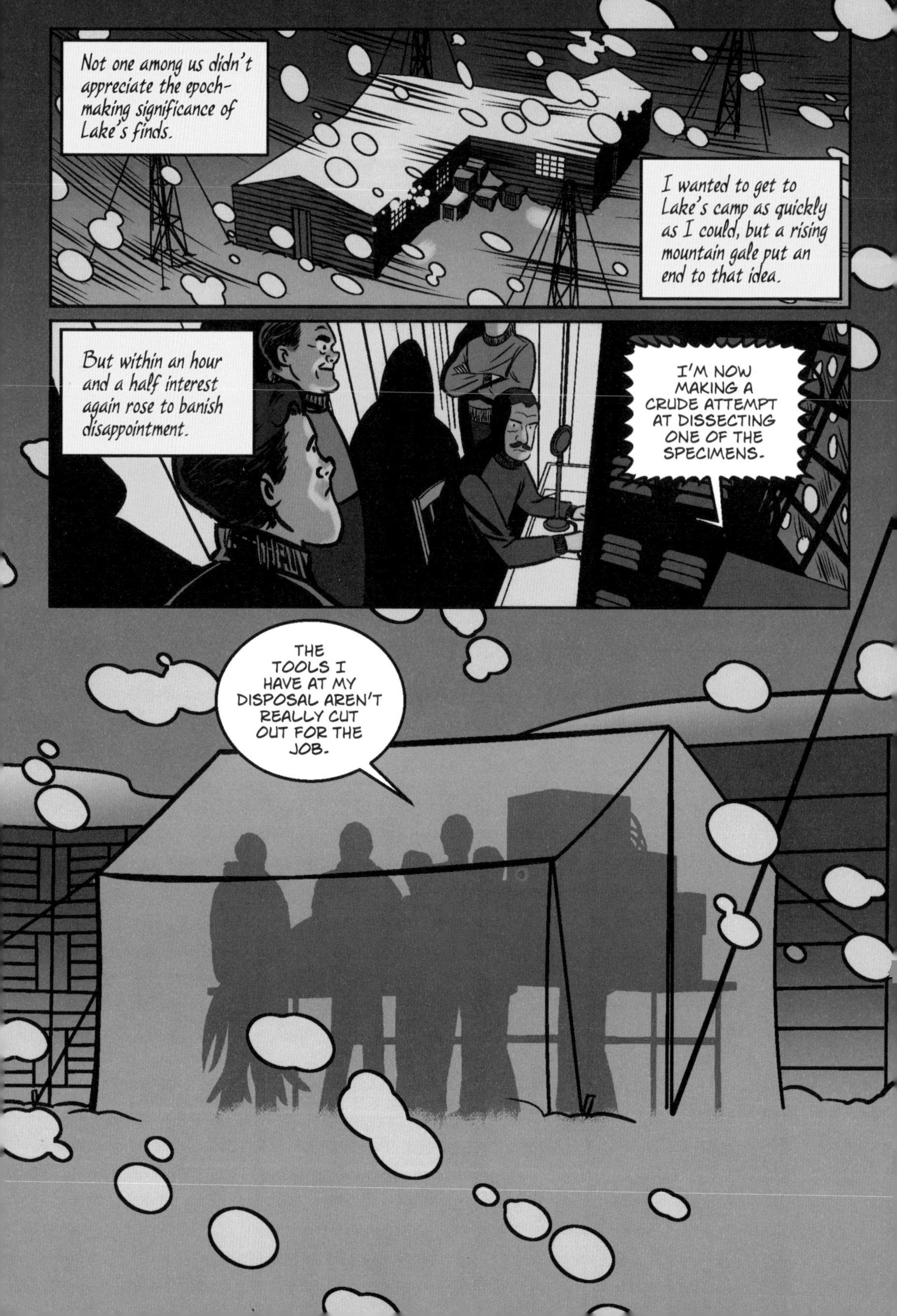
Not one among us didn't appreciate the epoch-making significance of Lake's finds.
I wanted to get to Lake's camp as quickly as I could, but a rising mountain gale put an end to that idea.
But within an hour and a half interest again rose to banish disappointment.
I'M NOW MAKING A CRUDE ATTEMPT AT DISSECTING ONE OF THE SPECIMENS.
THE TOOLS I HAVE AT MY DISPOSAL AREN'T REALLY CUT OUT FOR THE JOB.

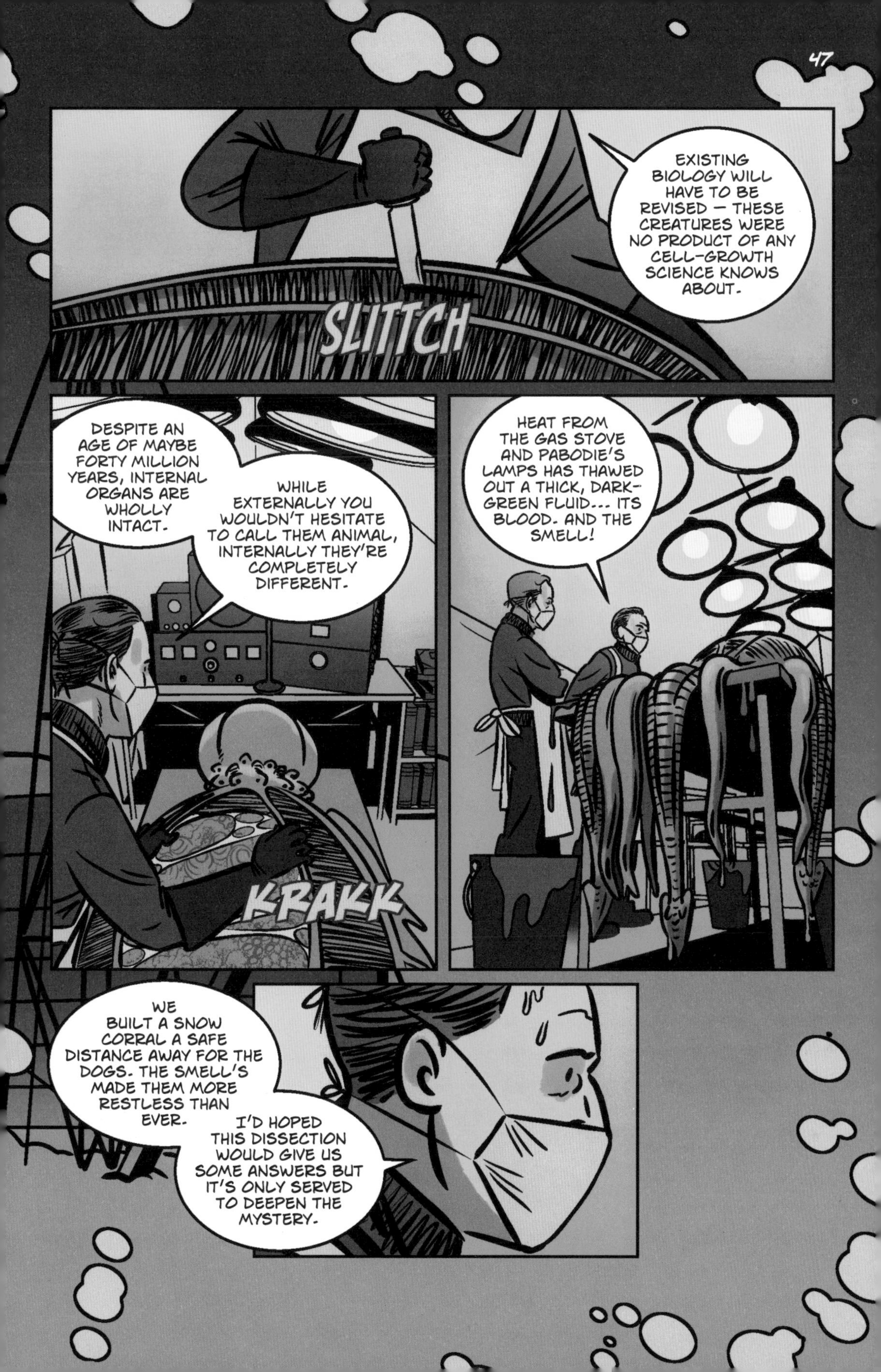
EXISTING BIOLOGY WILL HAVE TO BE REVISED — THESE CREATURES WERE NO PRODUCT OF ANY CELL-GROWTH SCIENCE KNOWS ABOUT.
SLITTCH
DESPITE AN AGE OF MAYBE FORTY MILLION YEARS, INTERNAL ORGANS ARE WHOLLY INTACT.
WHILE EXTERNALLY YOU WOULDN'T HESITATE TO CALL THEM ANIMAL, INTERNALLY THEY'RE COMPLETELY DIFFERENT.
KRAKK
HEAT FROM THE GAS STOVE AND PABODIE'S LAMPS HAS THAWED OUT A THICK, DARK-GREEN FLUID... ITS BLOOD. AND THE SMELL!
WE BUILT A SNOW CORRAL A SAFE DISTANCE AWAY FOR THE DOGS. THE SMELL'S MADE THEM MORE RESTLESS THAN EVER.
I'D HOPED THIS DISSECTION WOULD GIVE US SOME ANSWERS BUT IT'S ONLY SERVED TO DEEPEN THE MYSTERY.

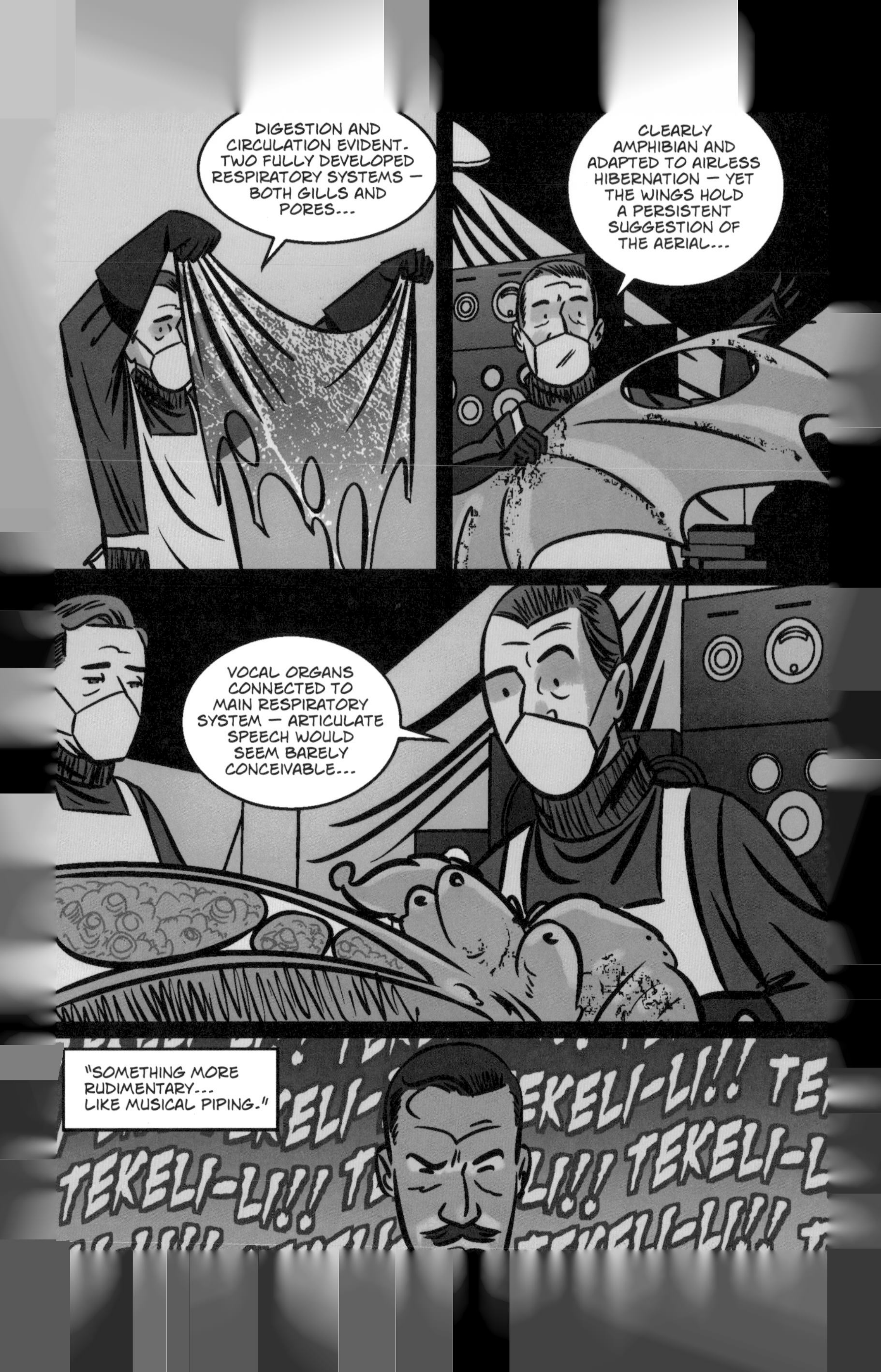
DIGESTION AND CIRCULATION EVIDENT. TWO FULLY DEVELOPED RESPIRATORY SYSTEMS — BOTH GILLS AND PORES...
CLEARLY AMPHIBIAN AND ADAPTED TO AIRLESS HIBERNATION — YET THE WINGS HOLD A PERSISTENT SUGGESTION OF THE AERIAL...
VOCAL ORGANS CONNECTED TO MAIN RESPIRATORY SYSTEM — ARTICULATE SPEECH WOULD SEEM BARELY CONCEIVABLE...
"SOMETHING MORE RUDIMENTARY... LIKE MUSICAL PIPING."
TEKELI-LI!! TEKELI-LI!! TEKELI-LI!!

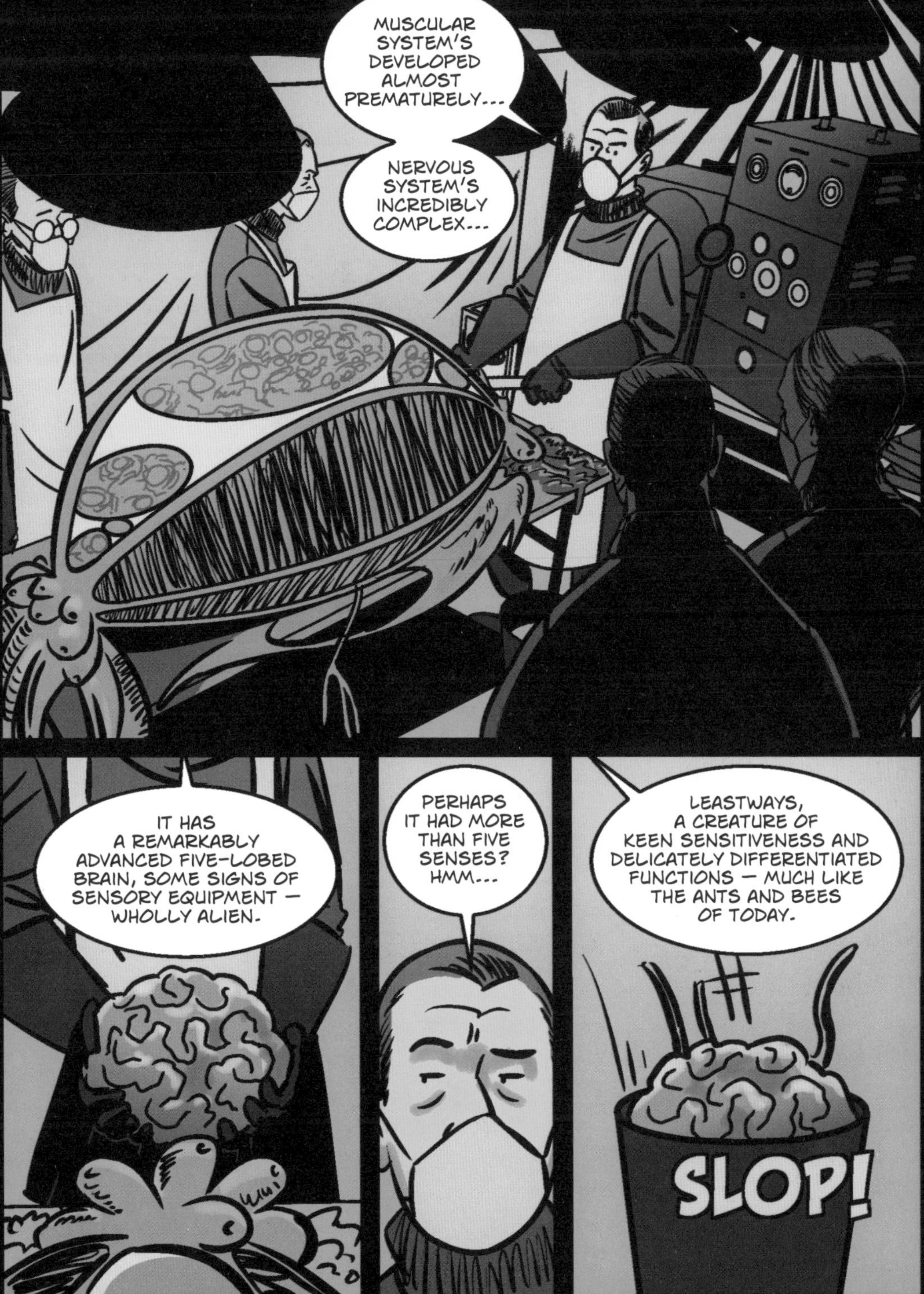
MUSCULAR SYSTEM'S DEVELOPED ALMOST PREMATURELY...
NERVOUS SYSTEM'S INCREDIBLY COMPLEX...
IT HAS A REMARKABLY ADVANCED FIVE-LOBED BRAIN, SOME SIGNS OF SENSORY EQUIPMENT — WHOLLY ALIEN.
PERHAPS IT HAD MORE THAN FIVE SENSES? HMM...
LEASTWAYS, A CREATURE OF KEEN SENSITIVENESS AND DELICATELY DIFFERENTIATED FUNCTIONS — MUCH LIKE THE ANTS AND BEES OF TODAY.
SLOP!

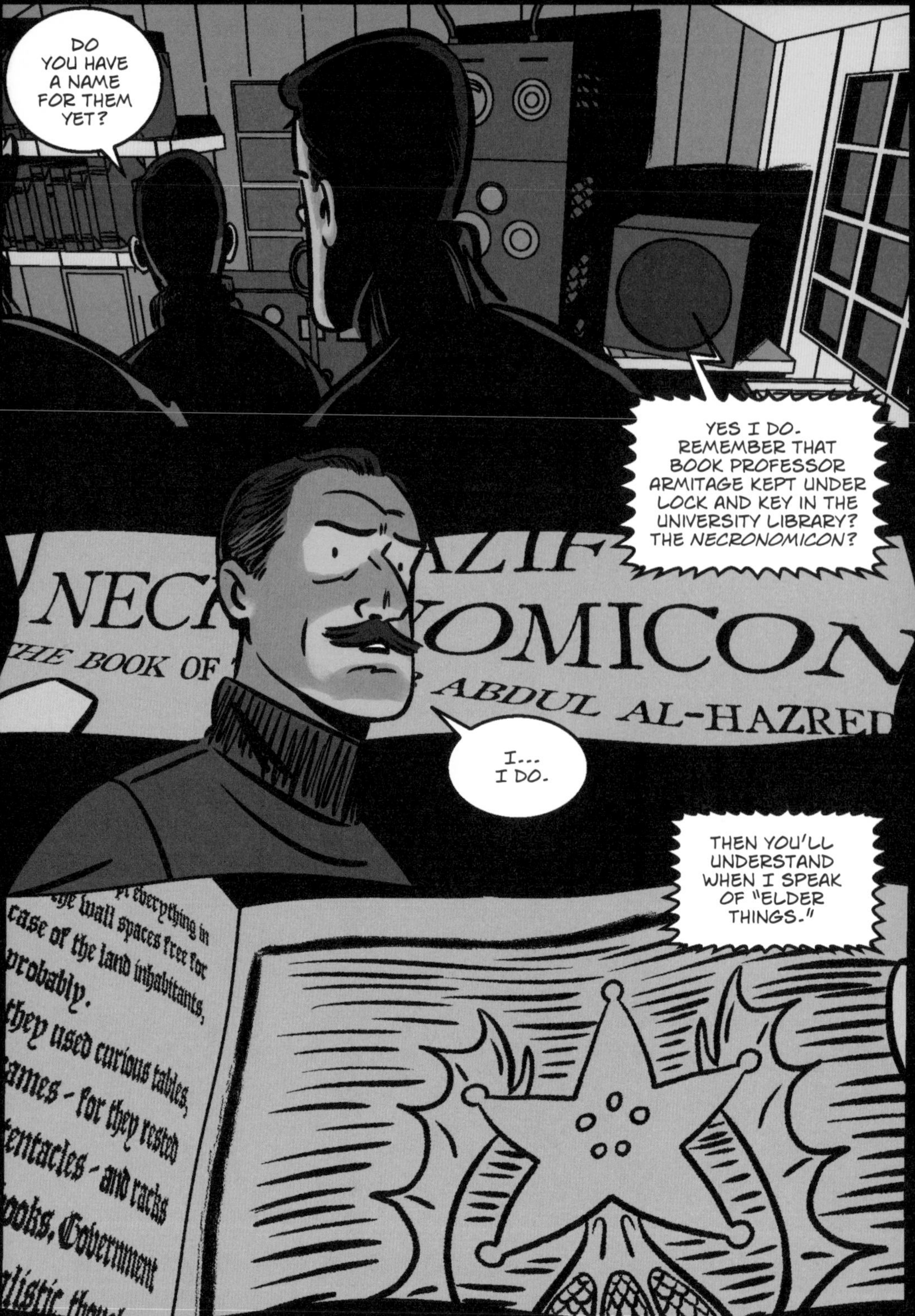
DO YOU HAVE A NAME FOR THEM YET?
YES I DO. REMEMBER THAT BOOK PROFESSOR ARMITAGE KEPT UNDER LOCK AND KEY IN THE UNIVERSITY LIBRARY? THE *NECRONOMICON*?
I... I DO.
THEN YOU'LL UNDERSTAND WHEN I SPEAK OF "ELDER THINGS."

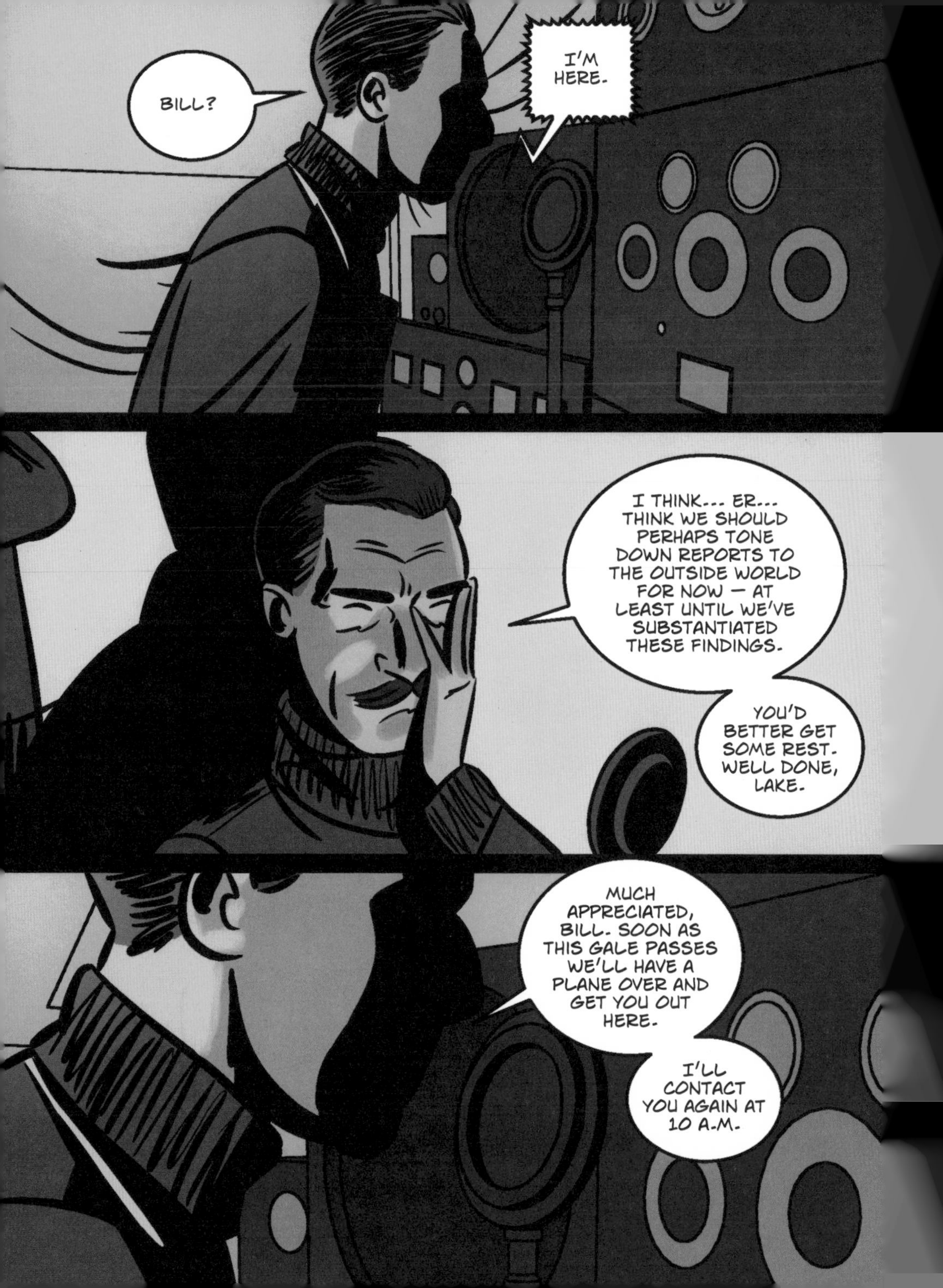
BILL?
I'M HERE.
I THINK... ER... THINK WE SHOULD PERHAPS TONE DOWN REPORTS TO THE OUTSIDE WORLD FOR NOW — AT LEAST UNTIL WE'VE SUBSTANTIATED THESE FINDINGS.
YOU'D BETTER GET SOME REST. WELL DONE, LAKE.
MUCH APPRECIATED, BILL. SOON AS THIS GALE PASSES WE'LL HAVE A PLANE OVER AND GET YOU OUT HERE.
I'LL CONTACT YOU AGAIN AT 10 A.M.

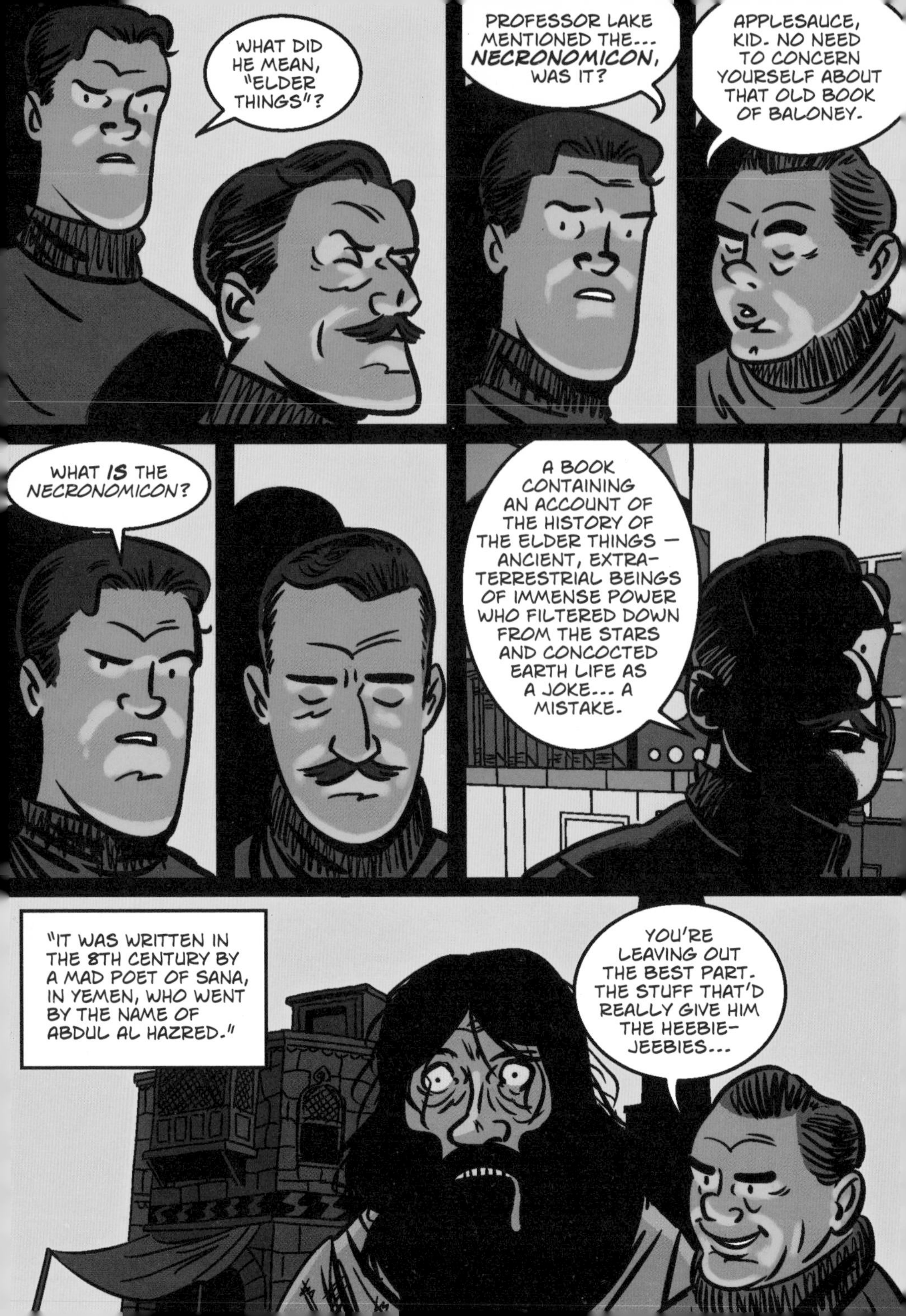
WHAT DID HE MEAN, "ELDER THINGS"?
PROFESSOR LAKE MENTIONED THE... NECRONOMICON, WAS IT?
APPLESAUCE, KID. NO NEED TO CONCERN YOURSELF ABOUT THAT OLD BOOK OF BALONEY.
WHAT IS THE NECRONOMICON?
A BOOK CONTAINING AN ACCOUNT OF THE HISTORY OF THE ELDER THINGS — ANCIENT, EXTRA-TERRESTRIAL BEINGS OF IMMENSE POWER WHO FILTERED DOWN FROM THE STARS AND CONCOCTED EARTH LIFE AS A JOKE... A MISTAKE.
"IT WAS WRITTEN IN THE 8TH CENTURY BY A MAD POET OF SANA, IN YEMEN, WHO WENT BY THE NAME OF ABDUL AL HAZRED."
YOU'RE LEAVING OUT THE BEST PART. THE STUFF THAT'D REALLY GIVE HIM THE HEEBIE-JEEBIES...

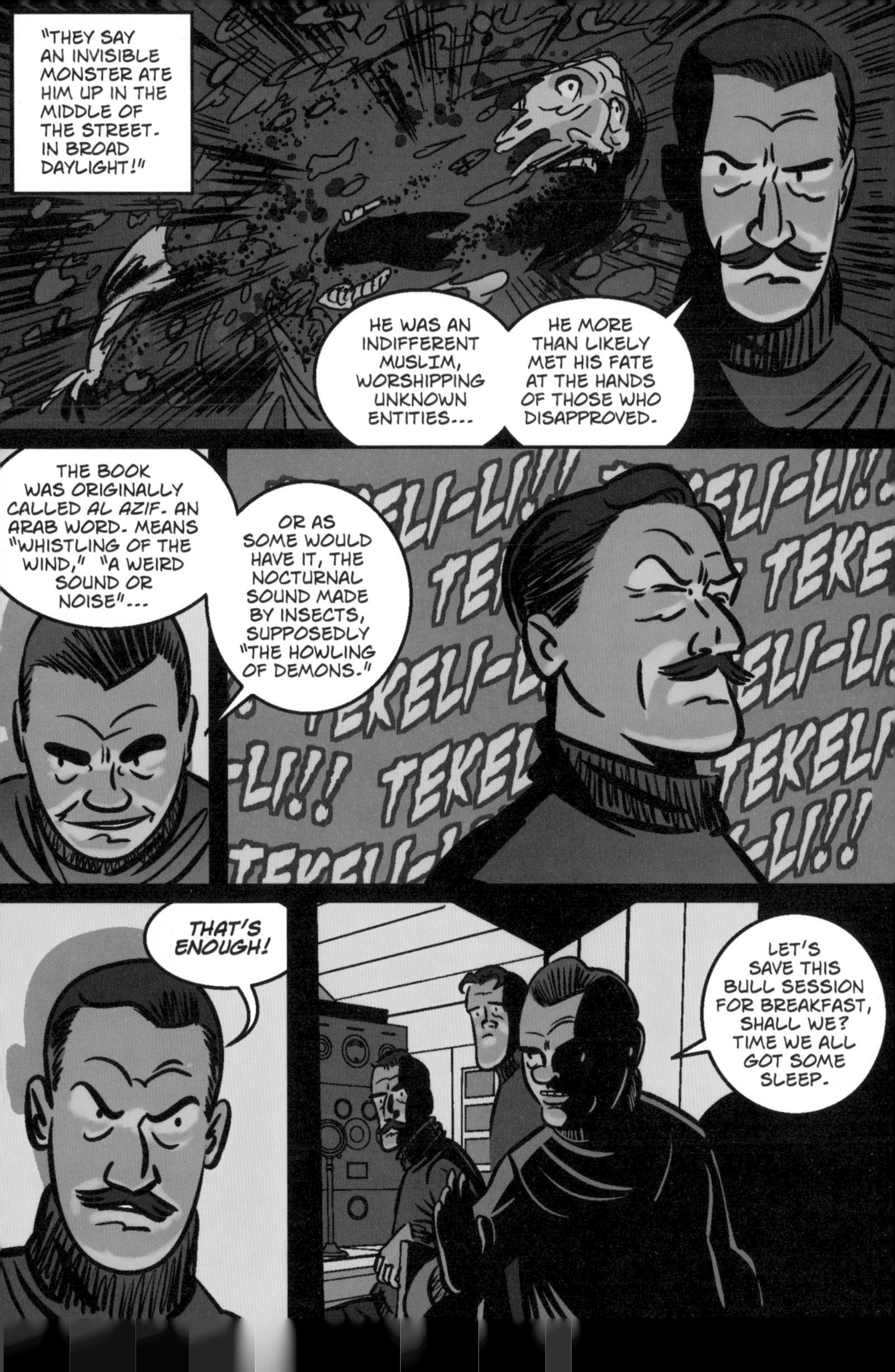
"THEY SAY AN INVISIBLE MONSTER ATE HIM UP IN THE MIDDLE OF THE STREET. IN BROAD DAYLIGHT!"
HE WAS AN INDIFFERENT MUSLIM, WORSHIPPING UNKNOWN ENTITIES...
HE MORE THAN LIKELY MET HIS FATE AT THE HANDS OF THOSE WHO DISAPPROVED.
THE BOOK WAS ORIGINALLY CALLED AL AZIF. AN ARAB WORD. MEANS "WHISTLING OF THE WIND," "A WEIRD SOUND OR NOISE"...
OR AS SOME WOULD HAVE IT, THE NOCTURNAL SOUND MADE BY INSECTS, SUPPOSEDLY "THE HOWLING OF DEMONS."
TEKELI-LI!! TEKELI-LI!!
THAT'S ENOUGH!
LET'S SAVE THIS BULL SESSION FOR BREAKFAST, SHALL WE? TIME WE ALL GOT SOME SLEEP.

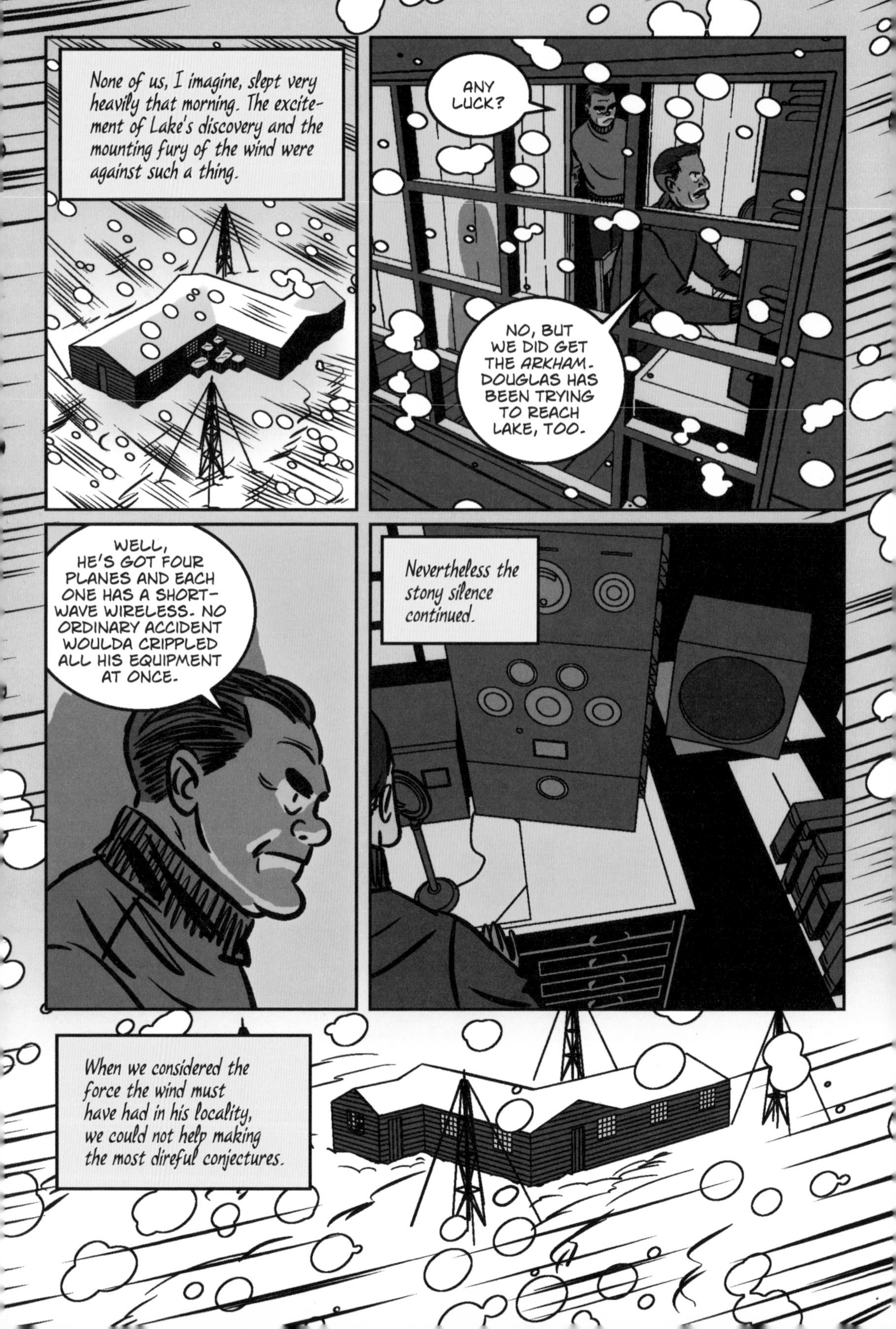
None of us, I imagine, slept very heavily that morning. The excitement of Lake's discovery and the mounting fury of the wind were against such a thing.
ANY LUCK?
NO, BUT WE DID GET THE ARKHAM. DOUGLAS HAS BEEN TRYING TO REACH LAKE, TOO.
WELL, HE'S GOT FOUR PLANES AND EACH ONE HAS A SHORT-WAVE WIRELESS. NO ORDINARY ACCIDENT WOULDA CRIPPLED ALL HIS EQUIPMENT AT ONCE.
Nevertheless the stony silence continued.
When we considered the force the wind must have had in his locality, we could not help making the most direful conjectures.

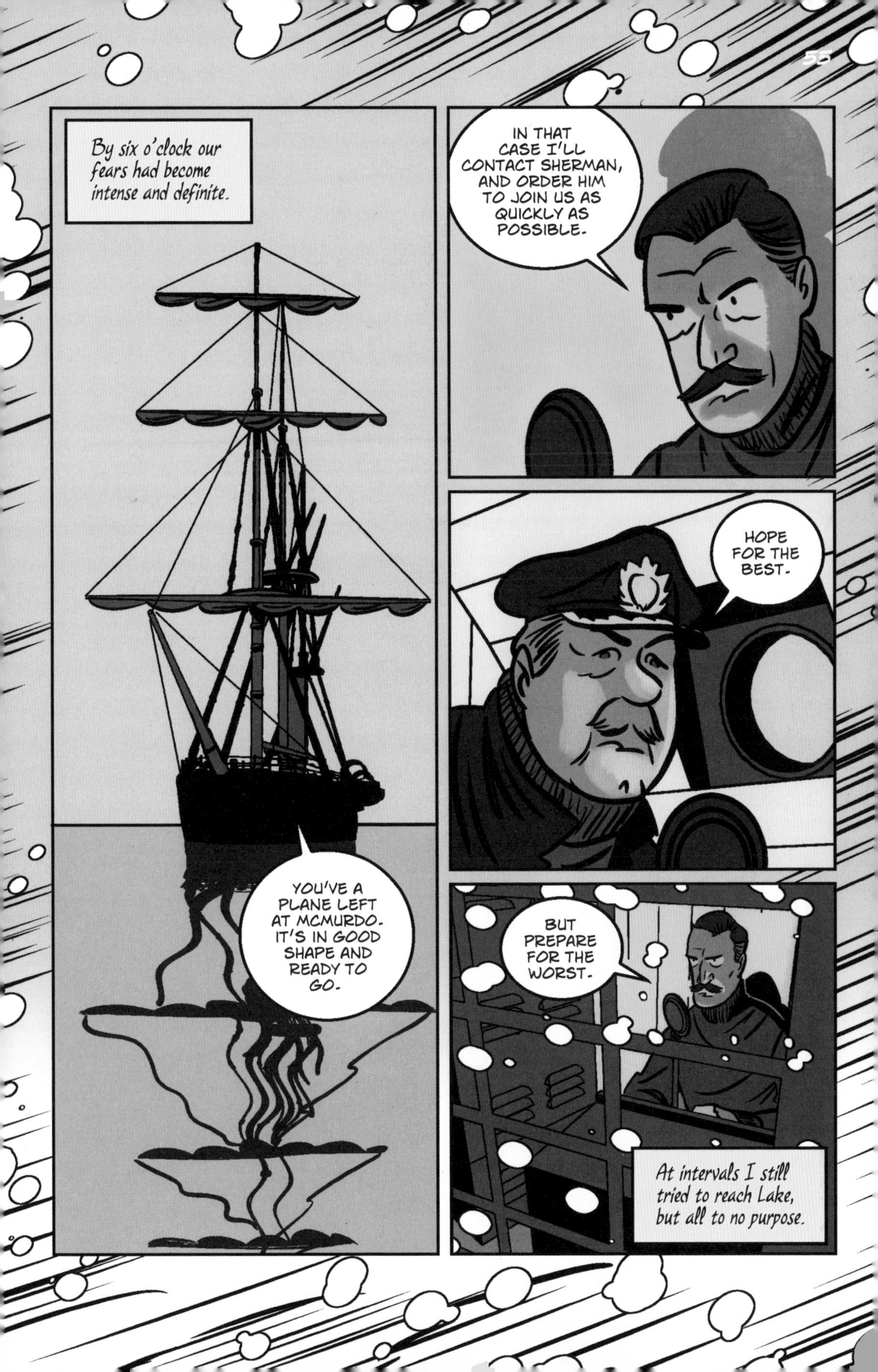
By six o'clock our fears had become intense and definite.
YOU'VE A PLANE LEFT AT MCMURDO. IT'S IN GOOD SHAPE AND READY TO GO.
IN THAT CASE I'LL CONTACT SHERMAN, AND ORDER HIM TO JOIN US AS QUICKLY AS POSSIBLE.
HOPE FOR THE BEST.
BUT PREPARE FOR THE WORST.
At intervals I still tried to reach Lake, but all to no purpose.

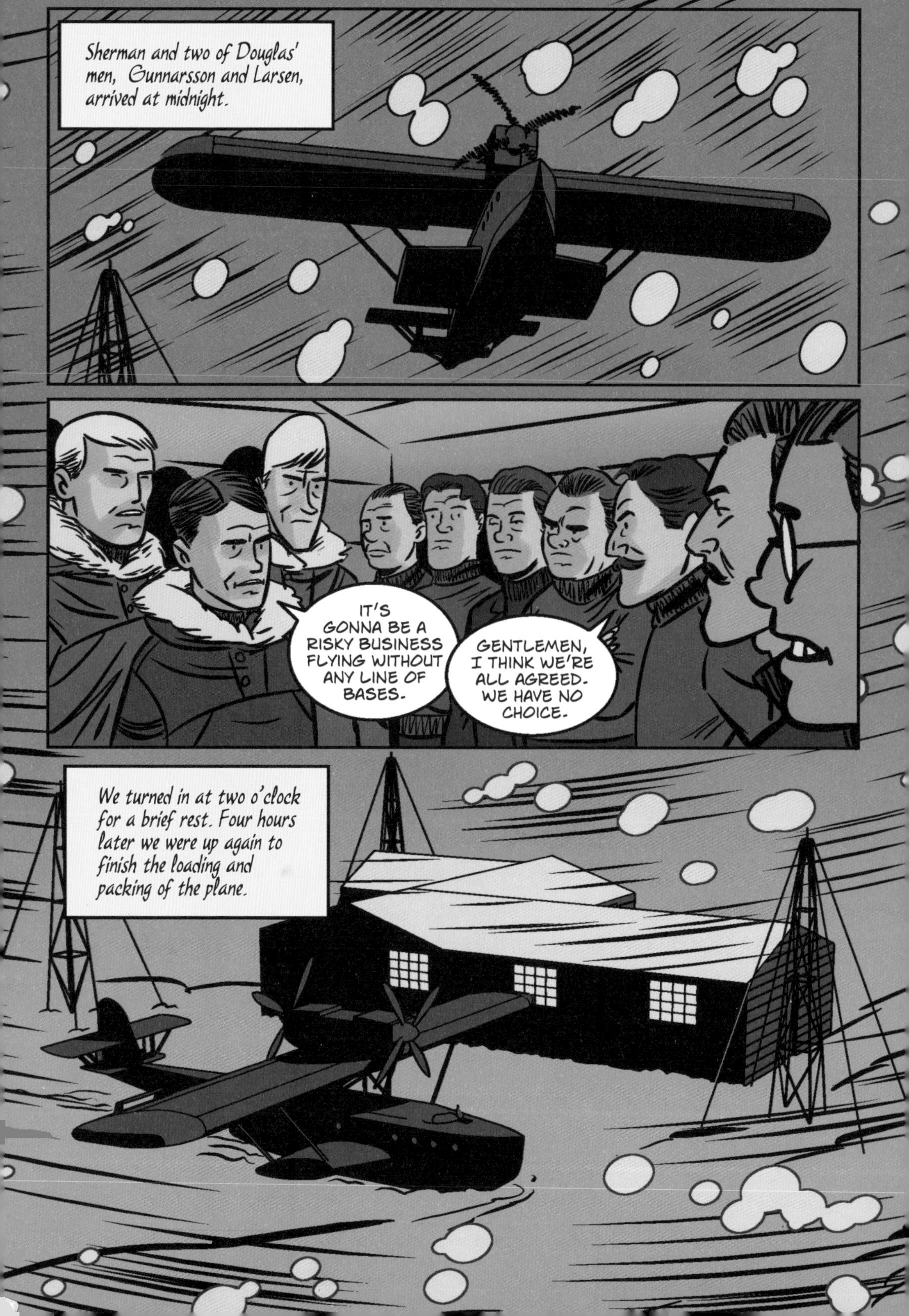
Sherman and two of Douglas' men, Gunnarsson and Larsen, arrived at midnight.
IT'S GONNA BE A RISKY BUSINESS FLYING WITHOUT ANY LINE OF BASES.
GENTLEMEN, I THINK WE'RE ALL AGREED. WE HAVE NO CHOICE.
We turned in at two o'clock for a brief rest. Four hours later we were up again to finish the loading and packing of the plane.

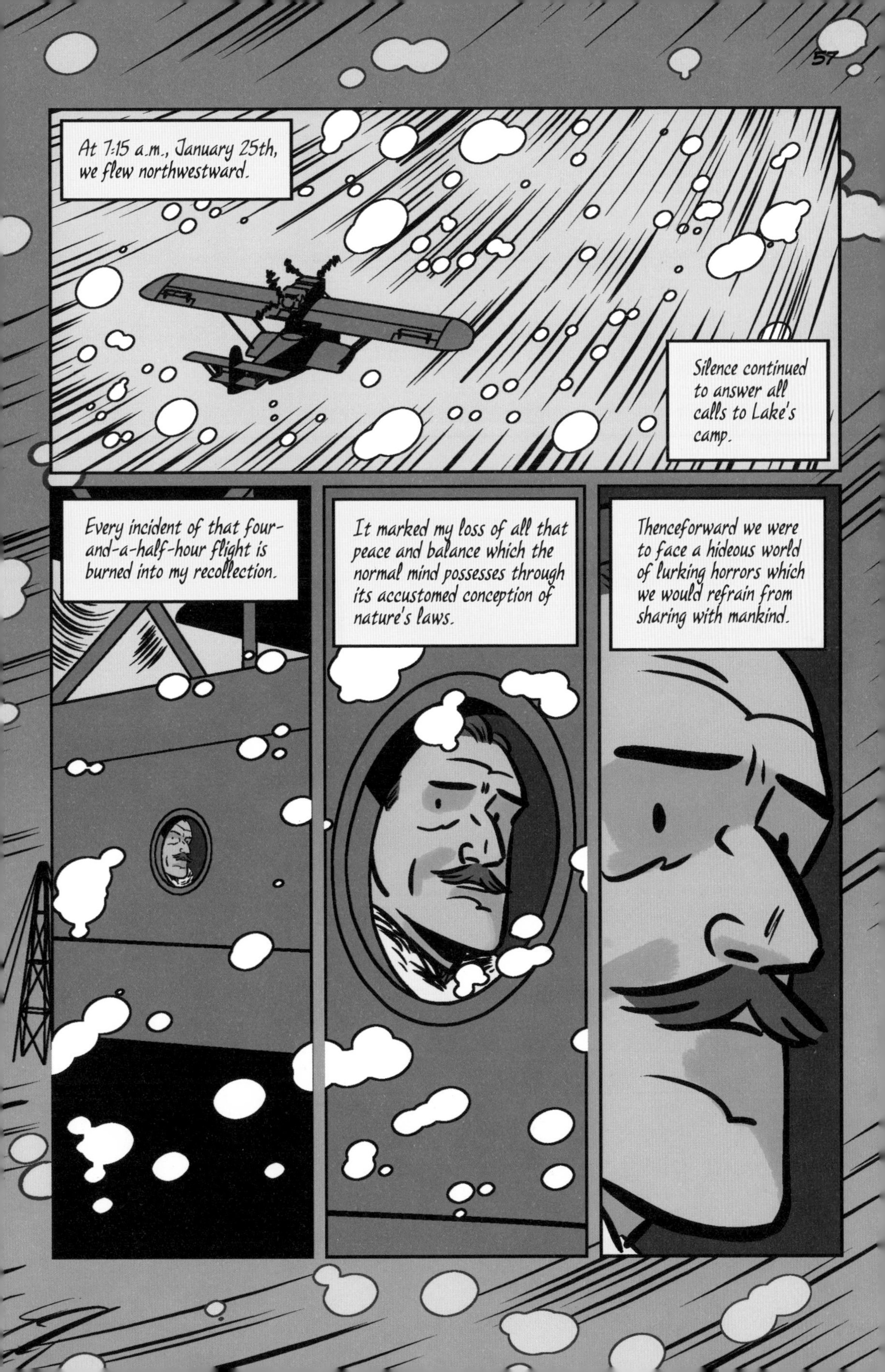
At 7:15 a.m., January 25th, we flew northwestward.
Silence continued to answer all calls to Lake's camp.
Every incident of that four-and-a-half-hour flight is burned into my recollection.
It marked my loss of all that peace and balance which the normal mind possesses through its accustomed conception of nature's laws.
Thenceforward we were to face a hideous world of lurking horrors which we would refrain from sharing with mankind.

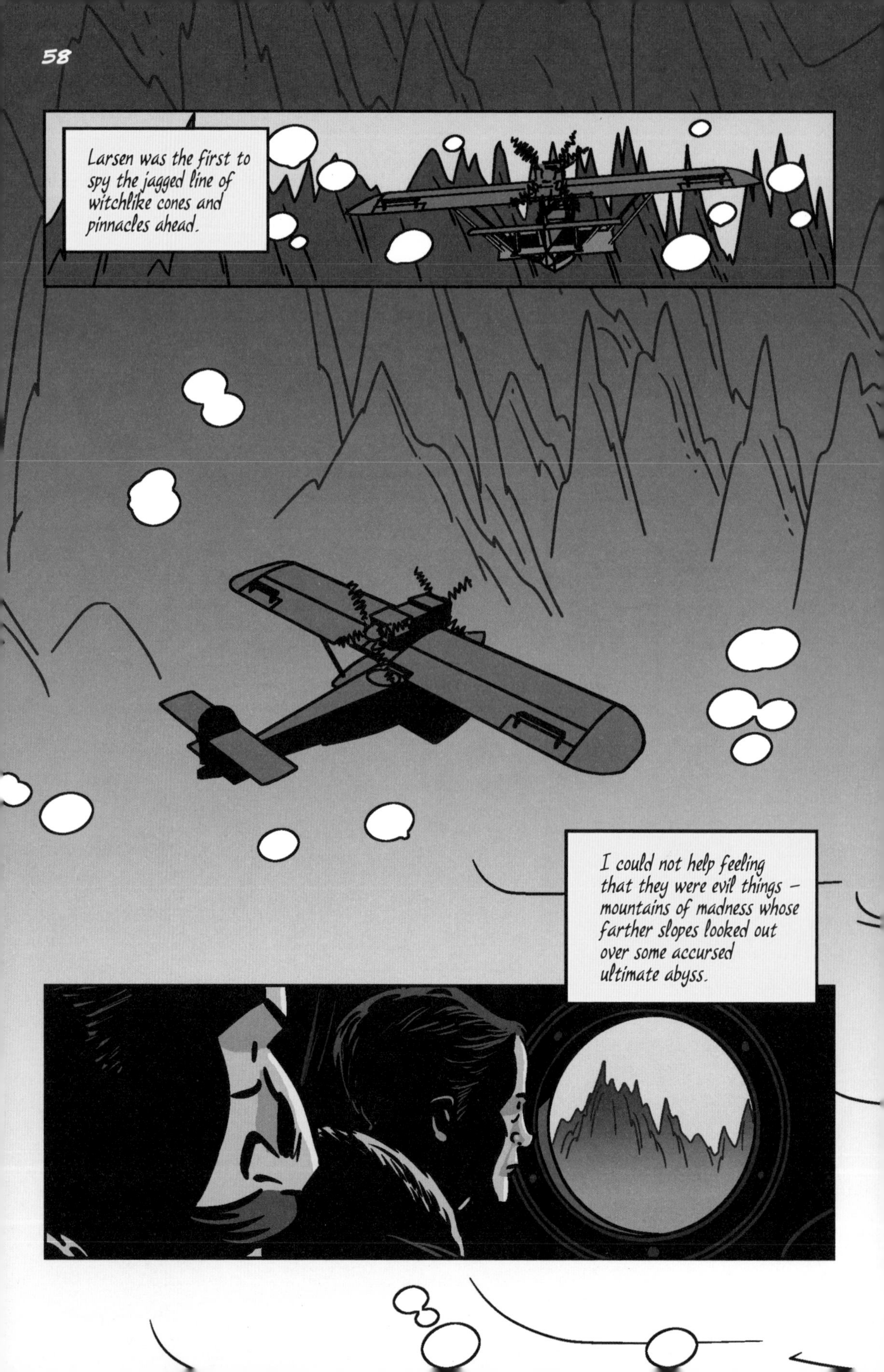
Larsen was the first to spy the jagged line of witchlike cones and pinnacles ahead.
I could not help feeling that they were evil things – mountains of madness whose farther slopes looked out over some accursed ultimate abyss.

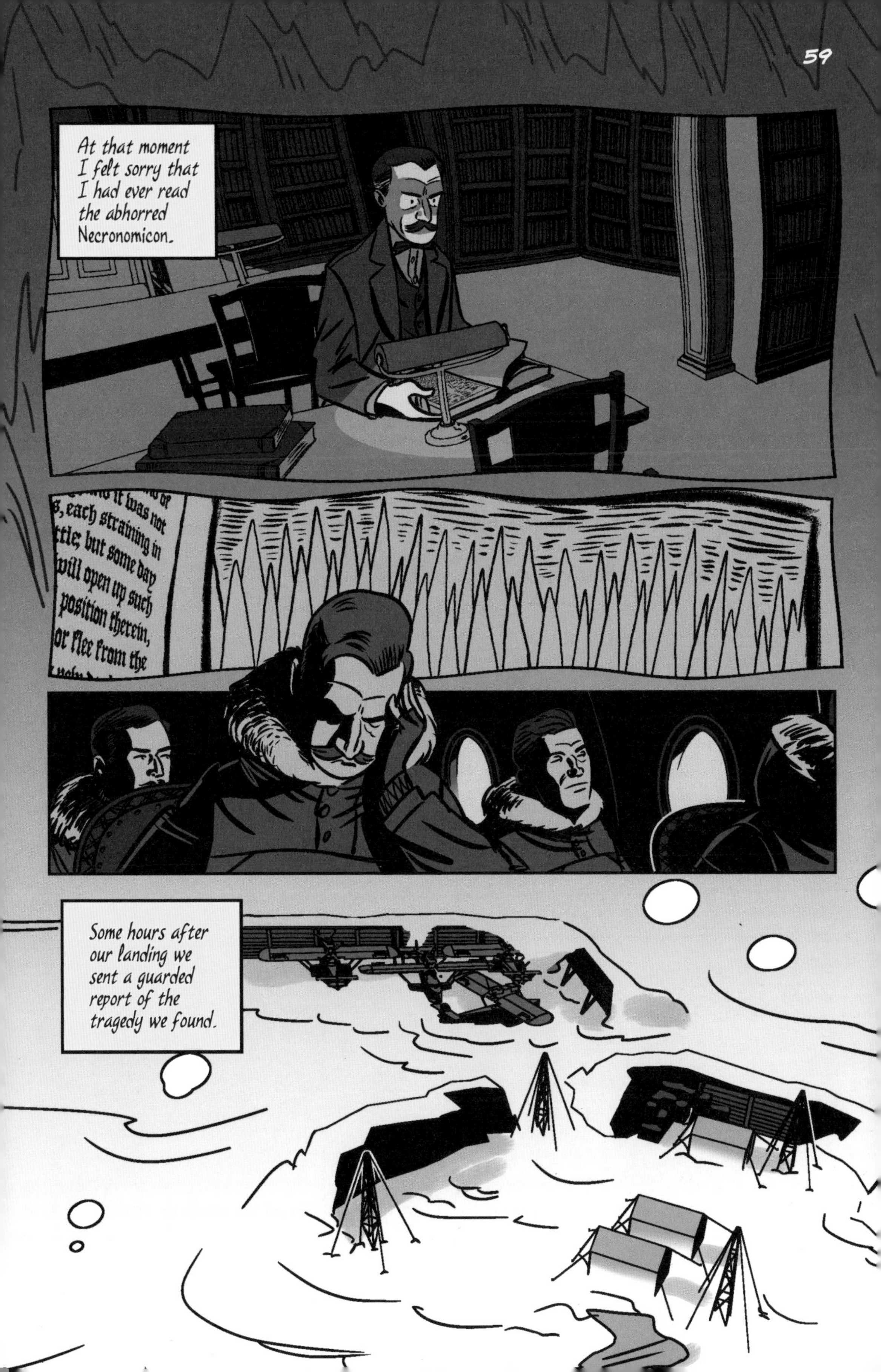
At that moment I felt sorry that I had ever read the abhorred Necronomicon.
it was not
each straining in
ttle; but some day
will open up such
position therein,
or flee from the
Some hours after our landing we sent a guarded report of the tragedy we found.

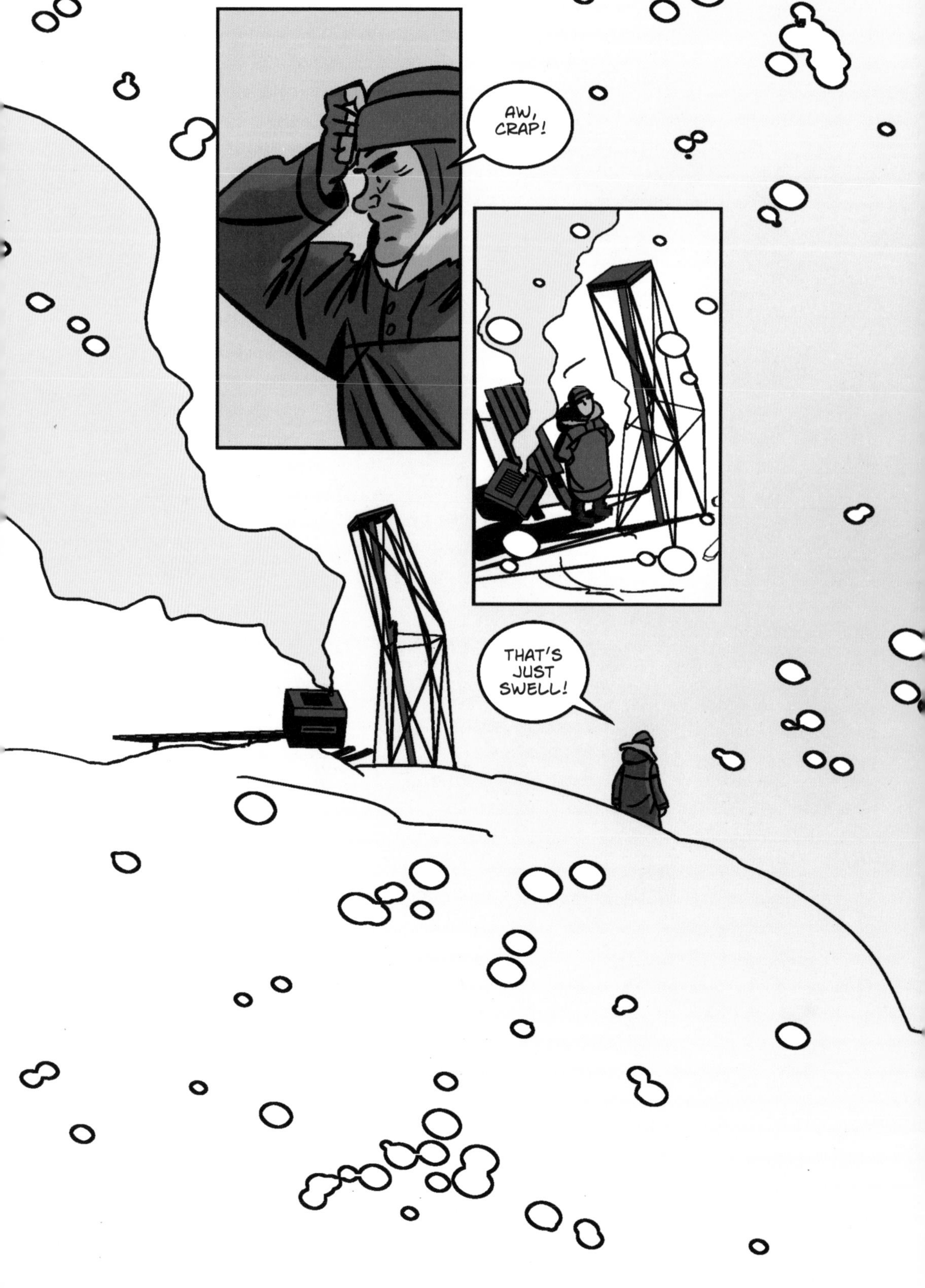
AW, CRAP!
THAT'S JUST SWELL!

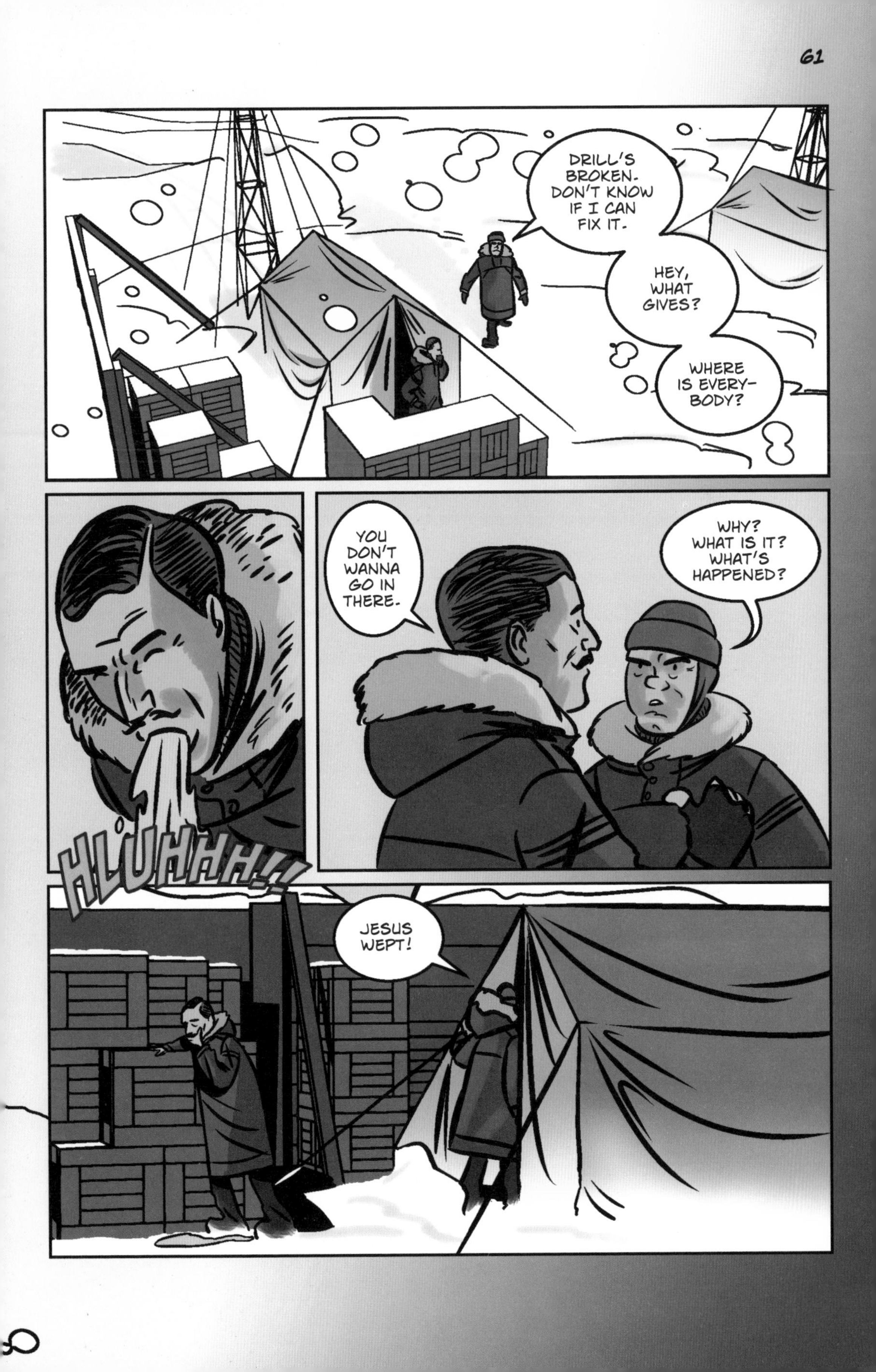
DRILL'S BROKEN. DON'T KNOW IF I CAN FIX IT.
HEY, WHAT GIVES?
WHERE IS EVERY-BODY?
HLUHHH!!
YOU DON'T WANNA GO IN THERE.
WHY? WHAT IS IT? WHAT'S HAPPENED?
JESUS WEPT!

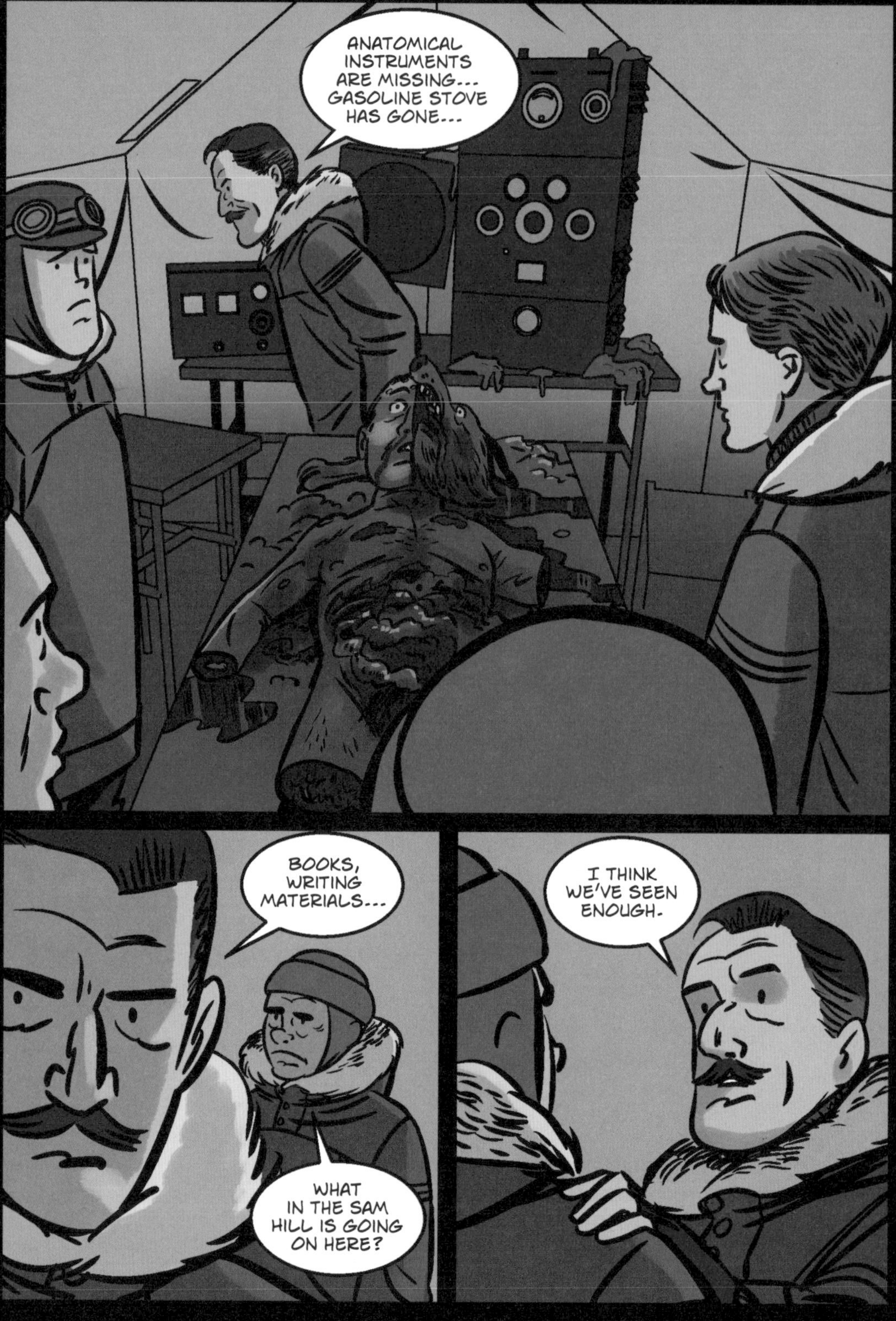
ANATOMICAL INSTRUMENTS ARE MISSING... GASOLINE STOVE HAS GONE...
BOOKS, WRITING MATERIALS...
WHAT IN THE SAM HILL IS GOING ON HERE?
I THINK WE'VE SEEN ENOUGH.

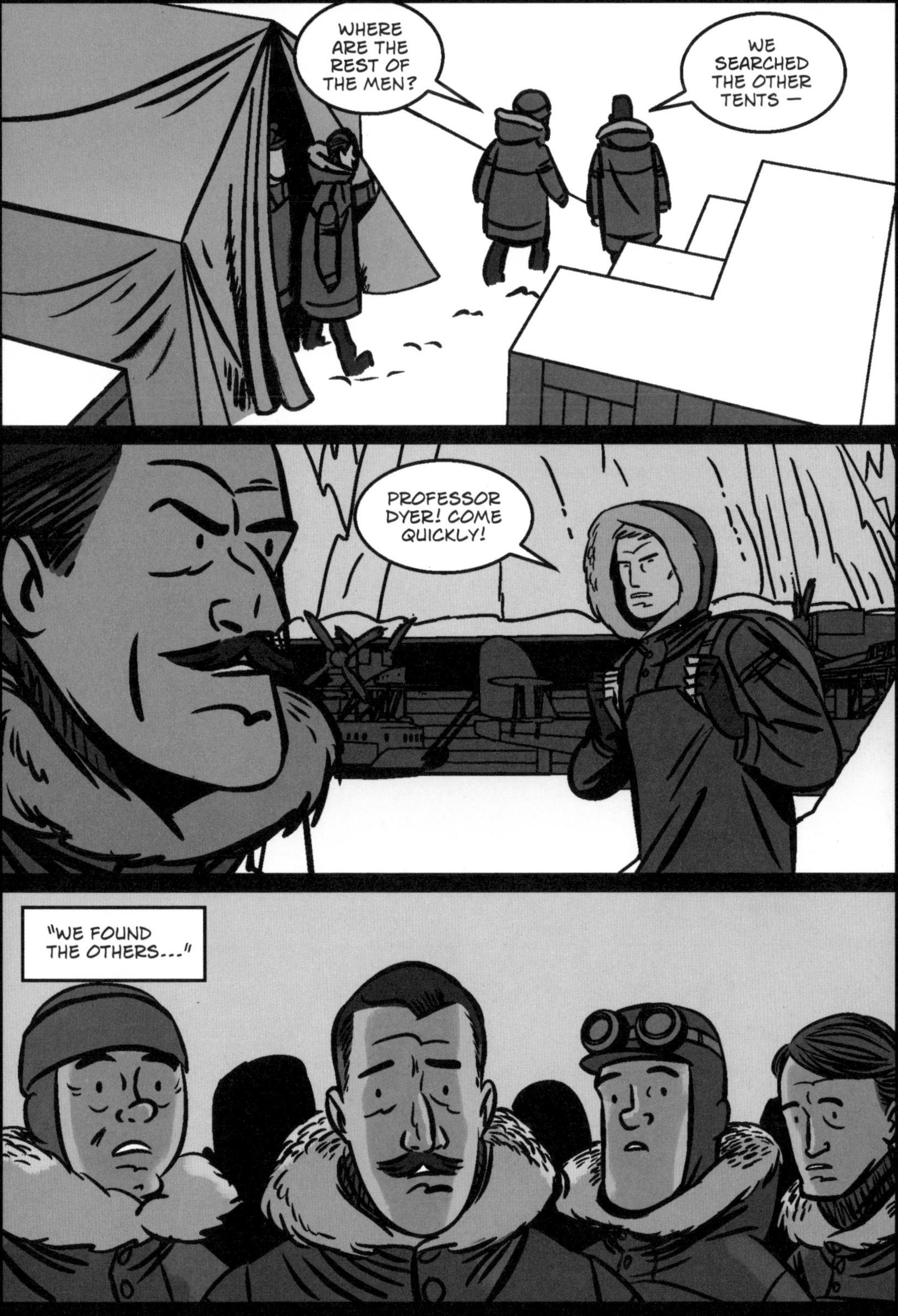
WHERE ARE THE REST OF THE MEN?
WE SEARCHED THE OTHER TENTS —
PROFESSOR DYER! COME QUICKLY!
"WE FOUND THE OTHERS..."

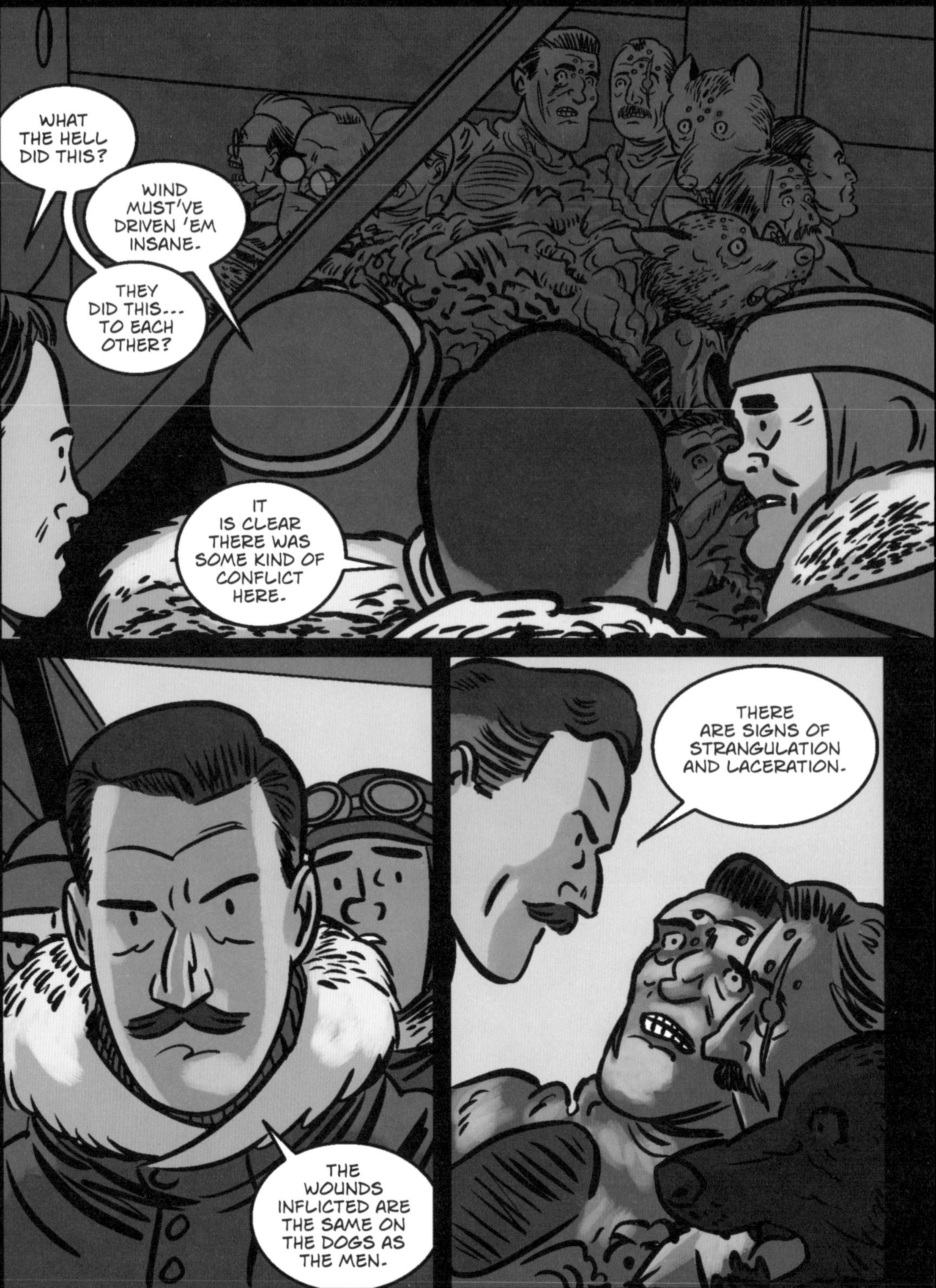
WHAT THE HELL DID THIS?
WIND MUST'VE DRIVEN 'EM INSANE.
THEY DID THIS... TO EACH OTHER?
IT IS CLEAR THERE WAS SOME KIND OF CONFLICT HERE.
THERE ARE SIGNS OF STRANGULATION AND LACERATION.
THE WOUNDS INFLICTED ARE THE SAME ON THE DOGS AS THE MEN.

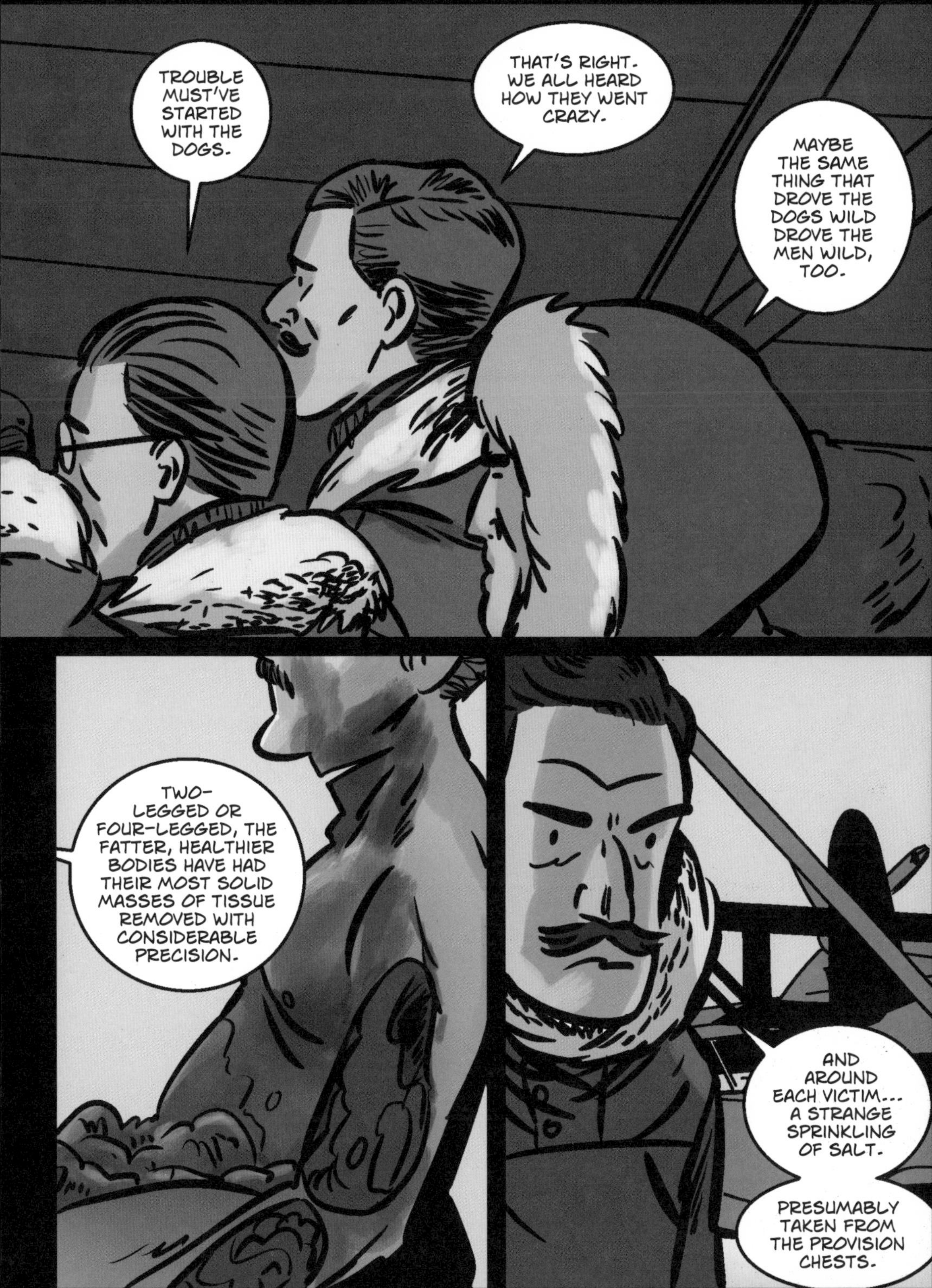
TROUBLE MUST'VE STARTED WITH THE DOGS.
THAT'S RIGHT. WE ALL HEARD HOW THEY WENT CRAZY.
MAYBE THE SAME THING THAT DROVE THE DOGS WILD DROVE THE MEN WILD, TOO.
TWO-LEGGED OR FOUR-LEGGED, THE FATTER, HEALTHIER BODIES HAVE HAD THEIR MOST SOLID MASSES OF TISSUE REMOVED WITH CONSIDERABLE PRECISION.
AND AROUND EACH VICTIM... A STRANGE SPRINKLING OF SALT.
PRESUMABLY TAKEN FROM THE PROVISION CHESTS.

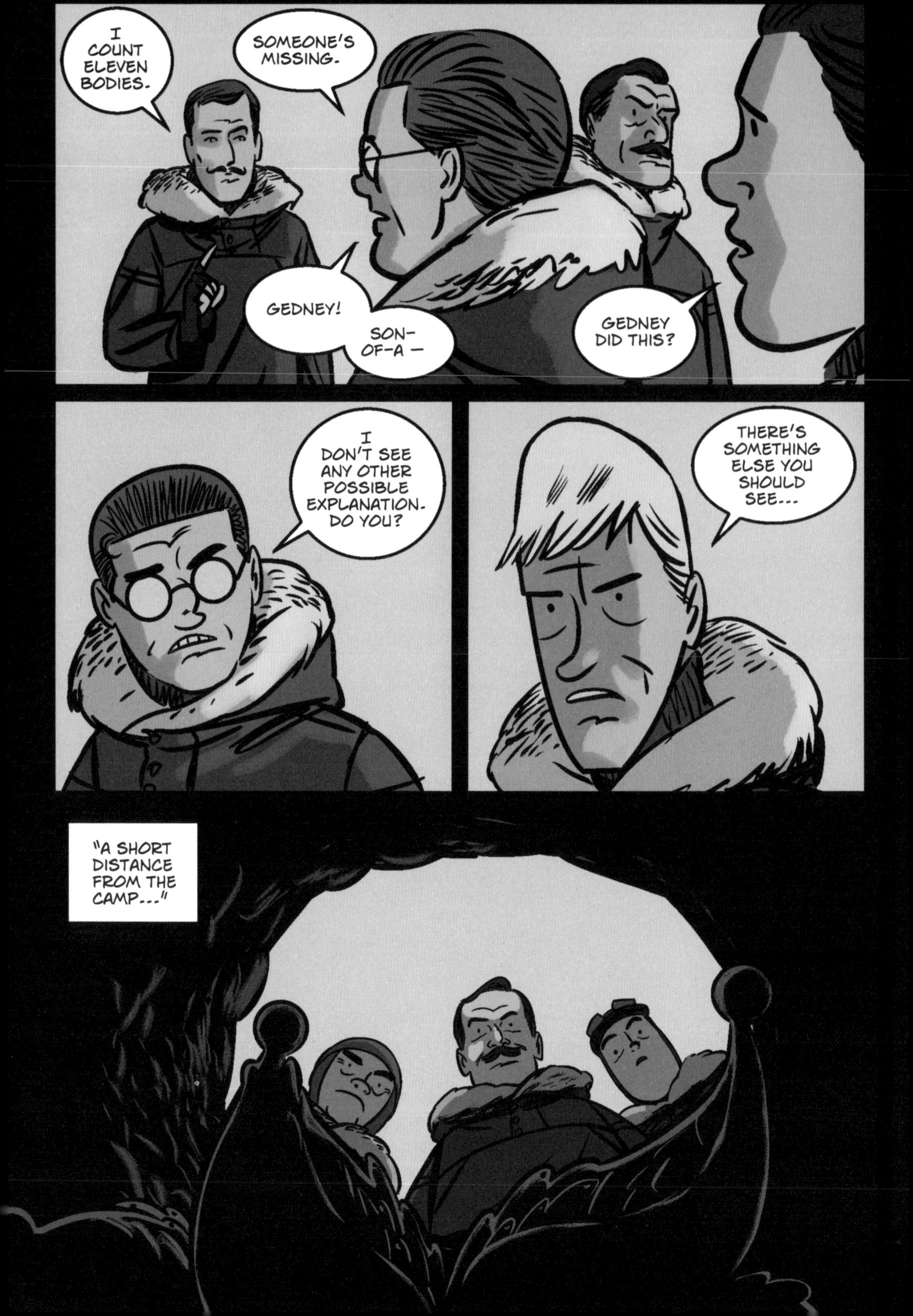
I COUNT ELEVEN BODIES.
SOMEONE'S MISSING.
GEDNEY!
SON-OF-A —
GEDNEY DID THIS?
I DON'T SEE ANY OTHER POSSIBLE EXPLANATION. DO YOU?
THERE'S SOMETHING ELSE YOU SHOULD SEE...
"A SHORT DISTANCE FROM THE CAMP..."

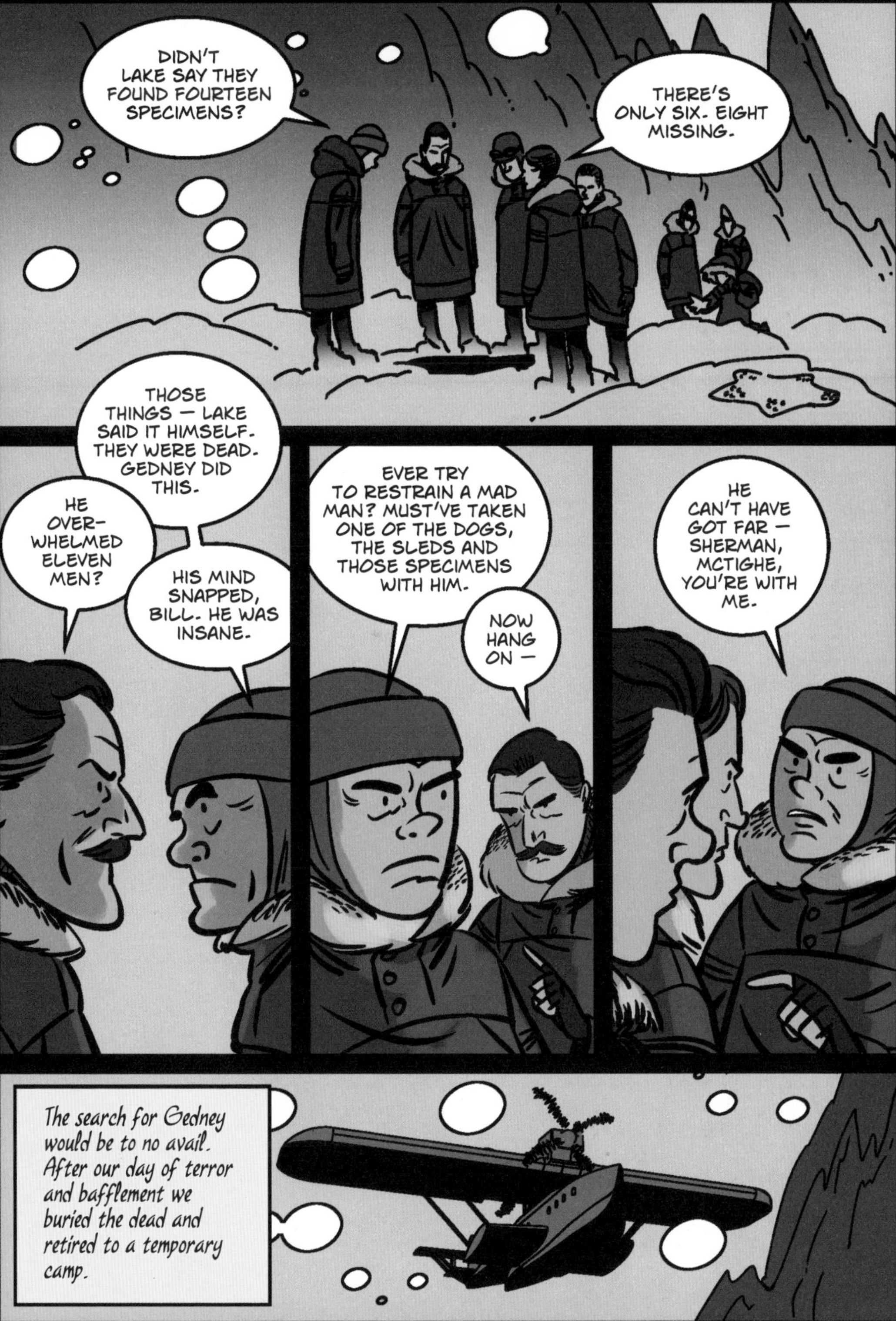
DIDN'T LAKE SAY THEY FOUND FOURTEEN SPECIMENS?
THERE'S ONLY SIX. EIGHT MISSING.
THOSE THINGS — LAKE SAID IT HIMSELF. THEY WERE DEAD. GEDNEY DID THIS.
HE OVER-WHELMED ELEVEN MEN?
HIS MIND SNAPPED, BILL. HE WAS INSANE.
EVER TRY TO RESTRAIN A MAD MAN? MUST'VE TAKEN ONE OF THE DOGS, THE SLEDS AND THOSE SPECIMENS WITH HIM.
NOW HANG ON —
HE CAN'T HAVE GOT FAR — SHERMAN, MCTIGHE, YOU'RE WITH ME.
The search for Gedney would be to no avail. After our day of terror and bafflement we buried the dead and retired to a temporary camp.

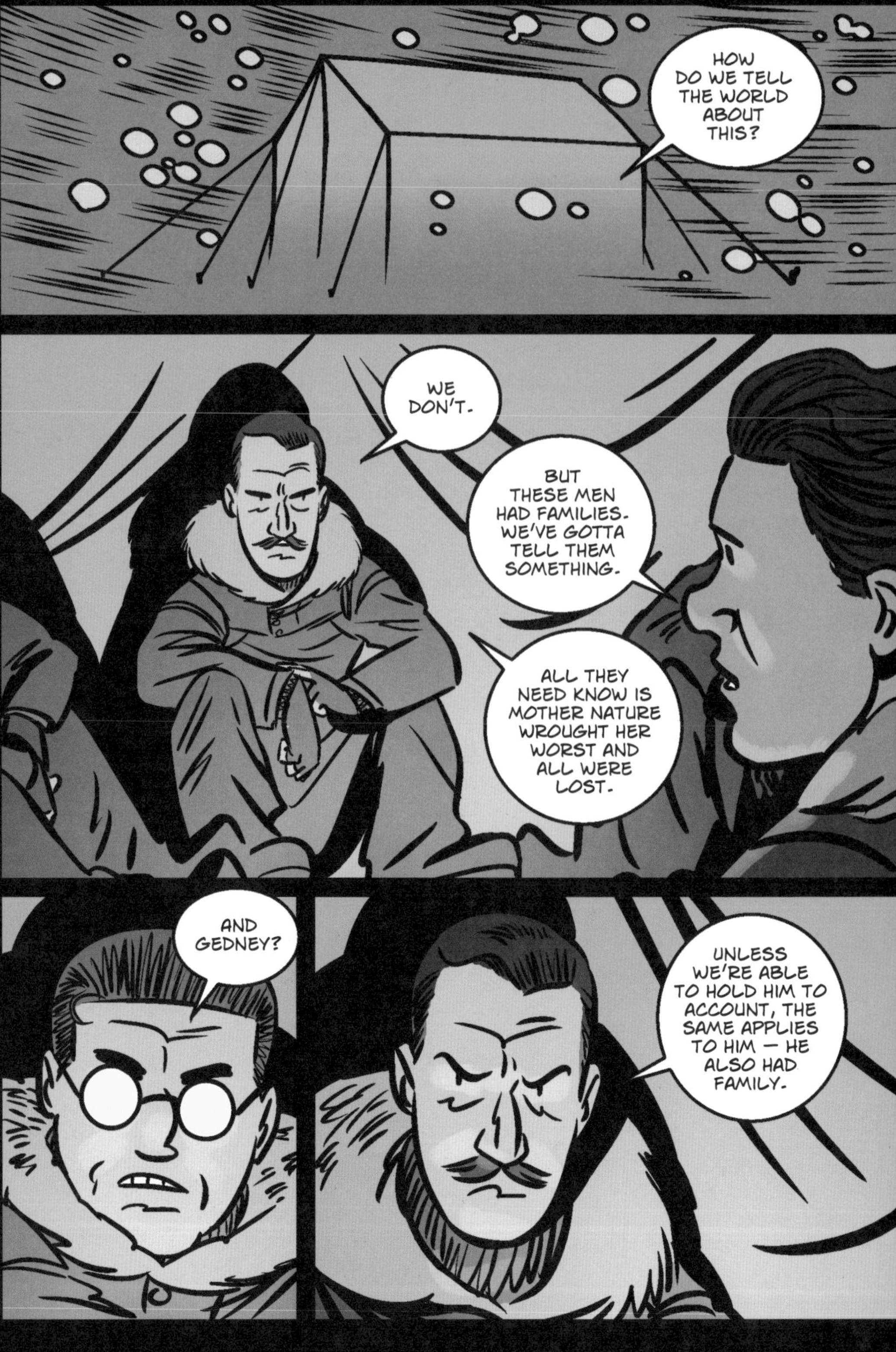
HOW DO WE TELL THE WORLD ABOUT THIS?
WE DON'T.
BUT THESE MEN HAD FAMILIES. WE'VE GOTTA TELL THEM SOMETHING.
ALL THEY NEED KNOW IS MOTHER NATURE WROUGHT HER WORST AND ALL WERE LOST.
AND GEDNEY?
UNLESS WE'RE ABLE TO HOLD HIM TO ACCOUNT, THE SAME APPLIES TO HIM — HE ALSO HAD FAMILY.

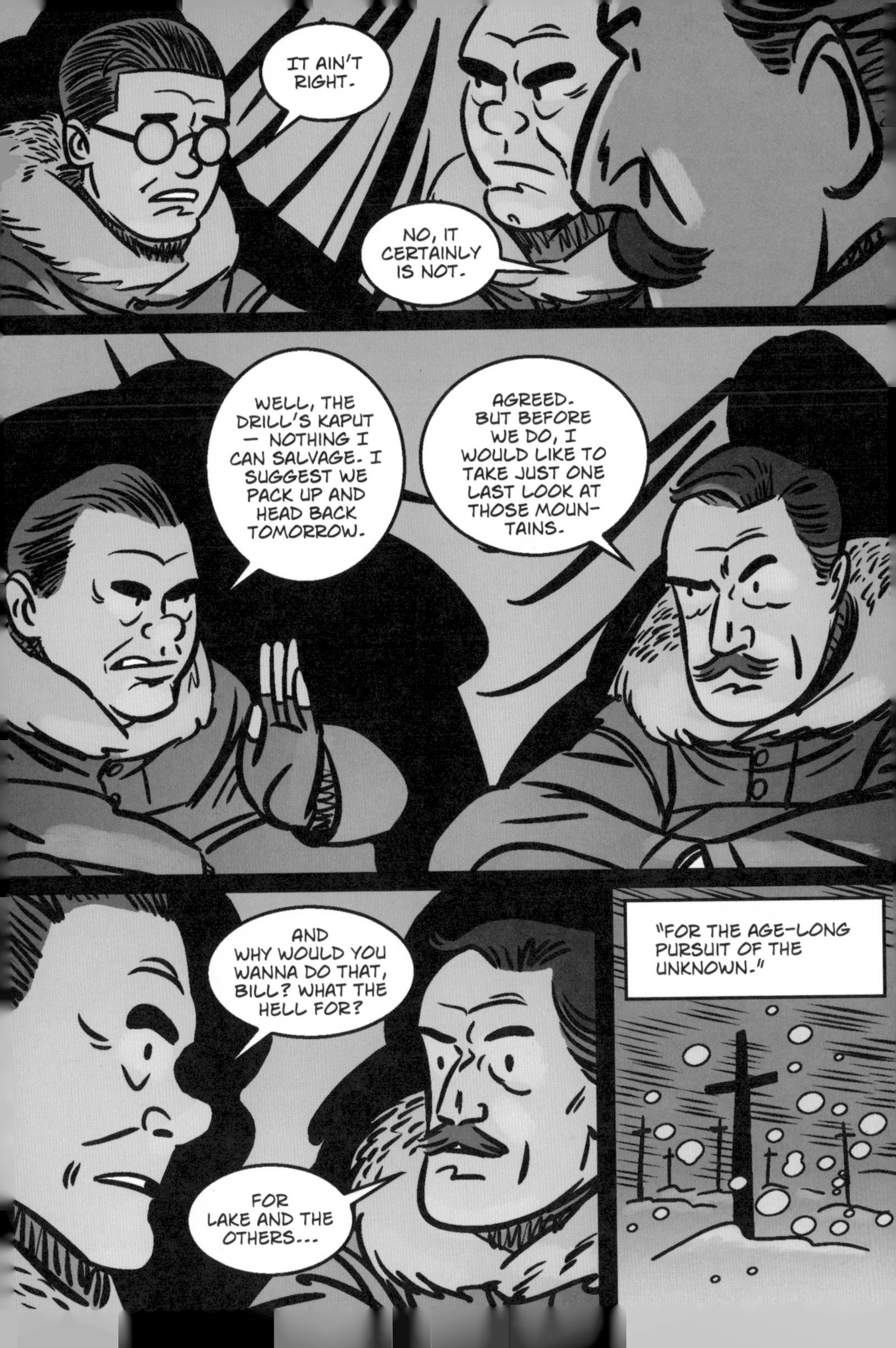
IT AIN'T RIGHT.
NO, IT CERTAINLY IS NOT.
WELL, THE DRILL'S KAPUT — NOTHING I CAN SALVAGE. I SUGGEST WE PACK UP AND HEAD BACK TOMORROW.
AGREED. BUT BEFORE WE DO, I WOULD LIKE TO TAKE JUST ONE LAST LOOK AT THOSE MOUNTAINS.
AND WHY WOULD YOU WANNA DO THAT, BILL? WHAT THE HELL FOR?
FOR LAKE AND THE OTHERS...
"FOR THE AGE-LONG PURSUIT OF THE UNKNOWN."

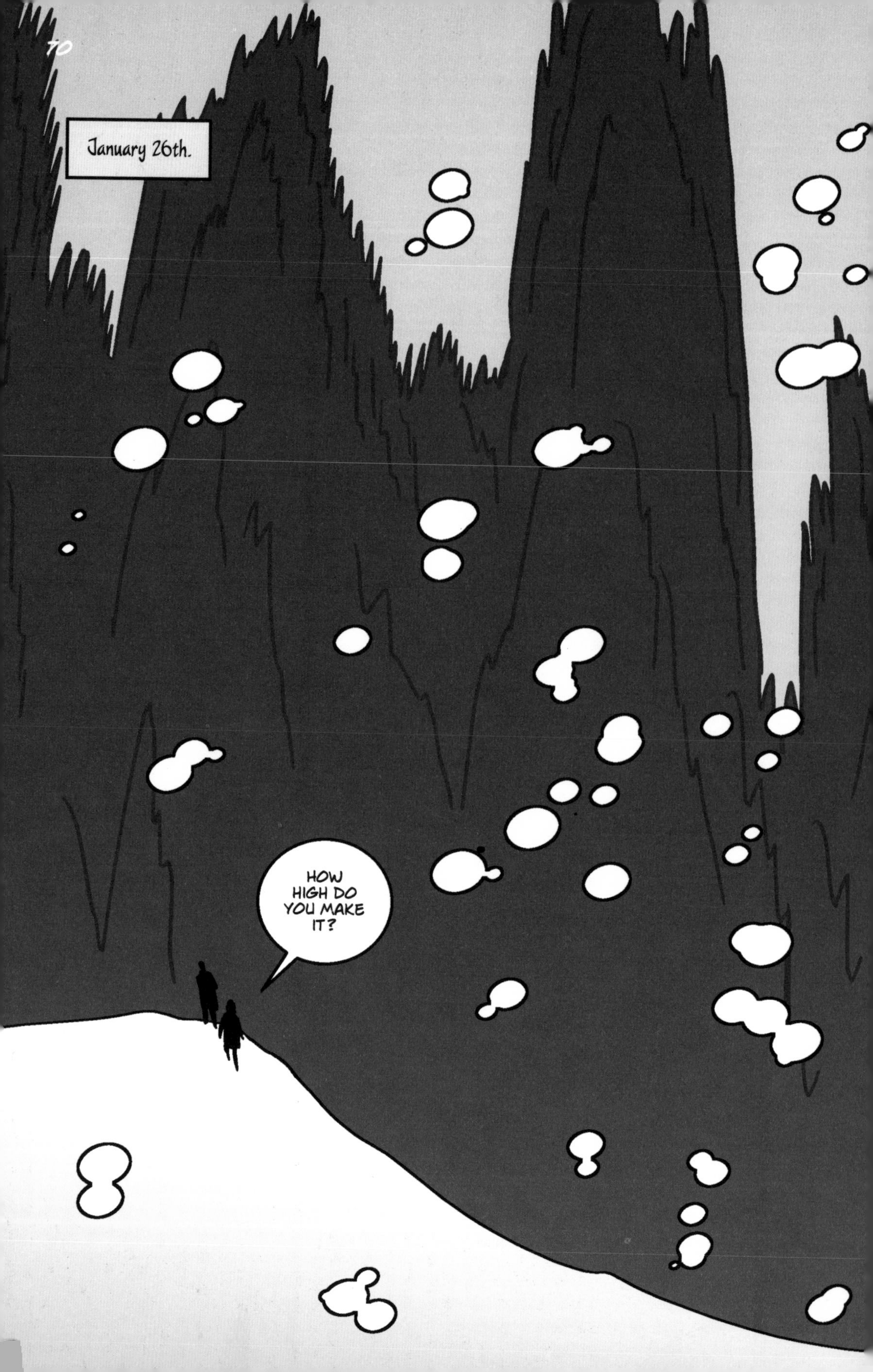
January 26th.
HOW HIGH DO YOU MAKE IT?

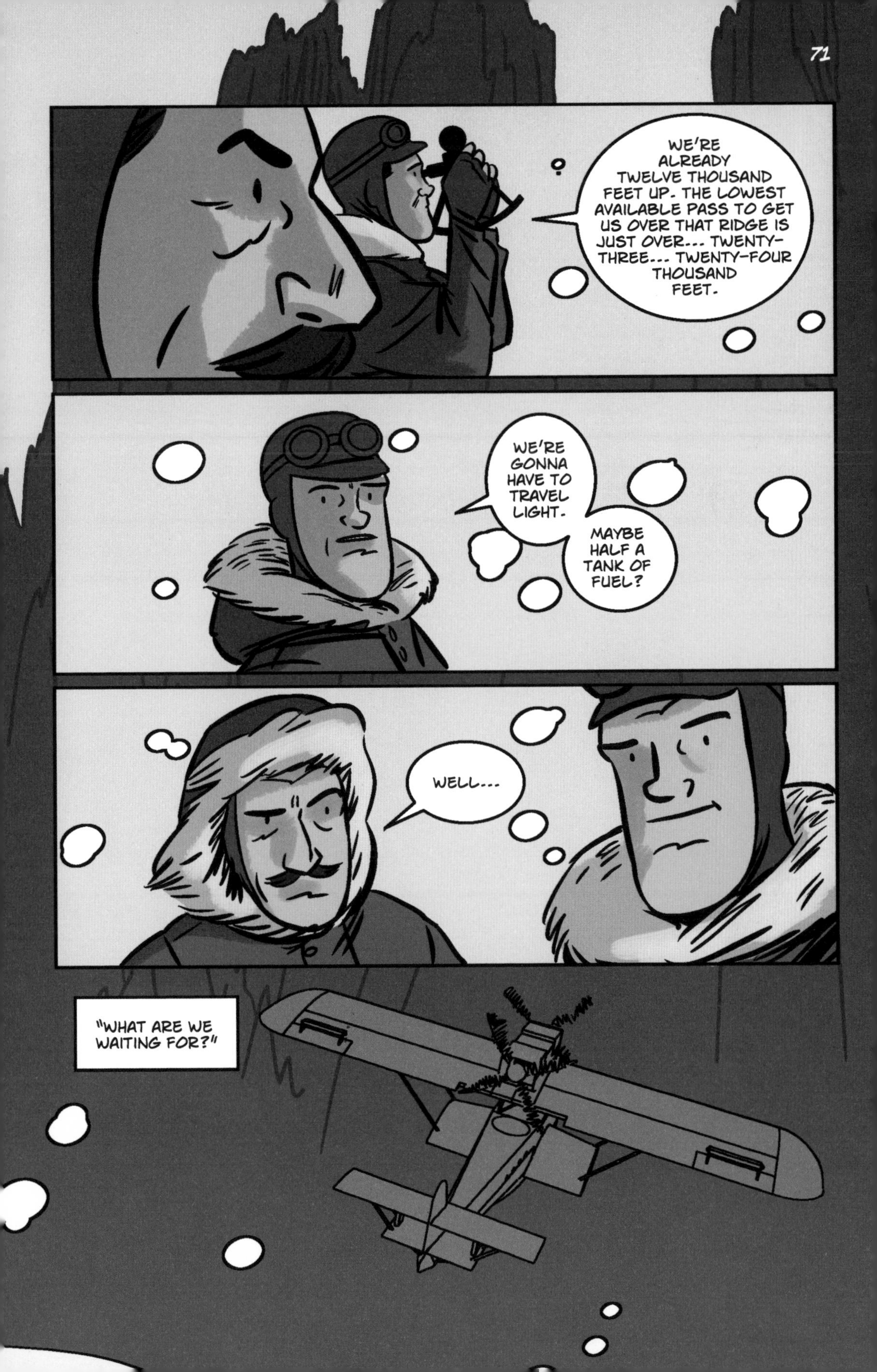

WE'RE ALREADY TWELVE THOUSAND FEET UP. THE LOWEST AVAILABLE PASS TO GET US OVER THAT RIDGE IS JUST OVER... TWENTY-THREE... TWENTY-FOUR THOUSAND FEET.
WE'RE GONNA HAVE TO TRAVEL LIGHT.
MAYBE HALF A TANK OF FUEL?
WELL...
"WHAT ARE WE WAITING FOR?"

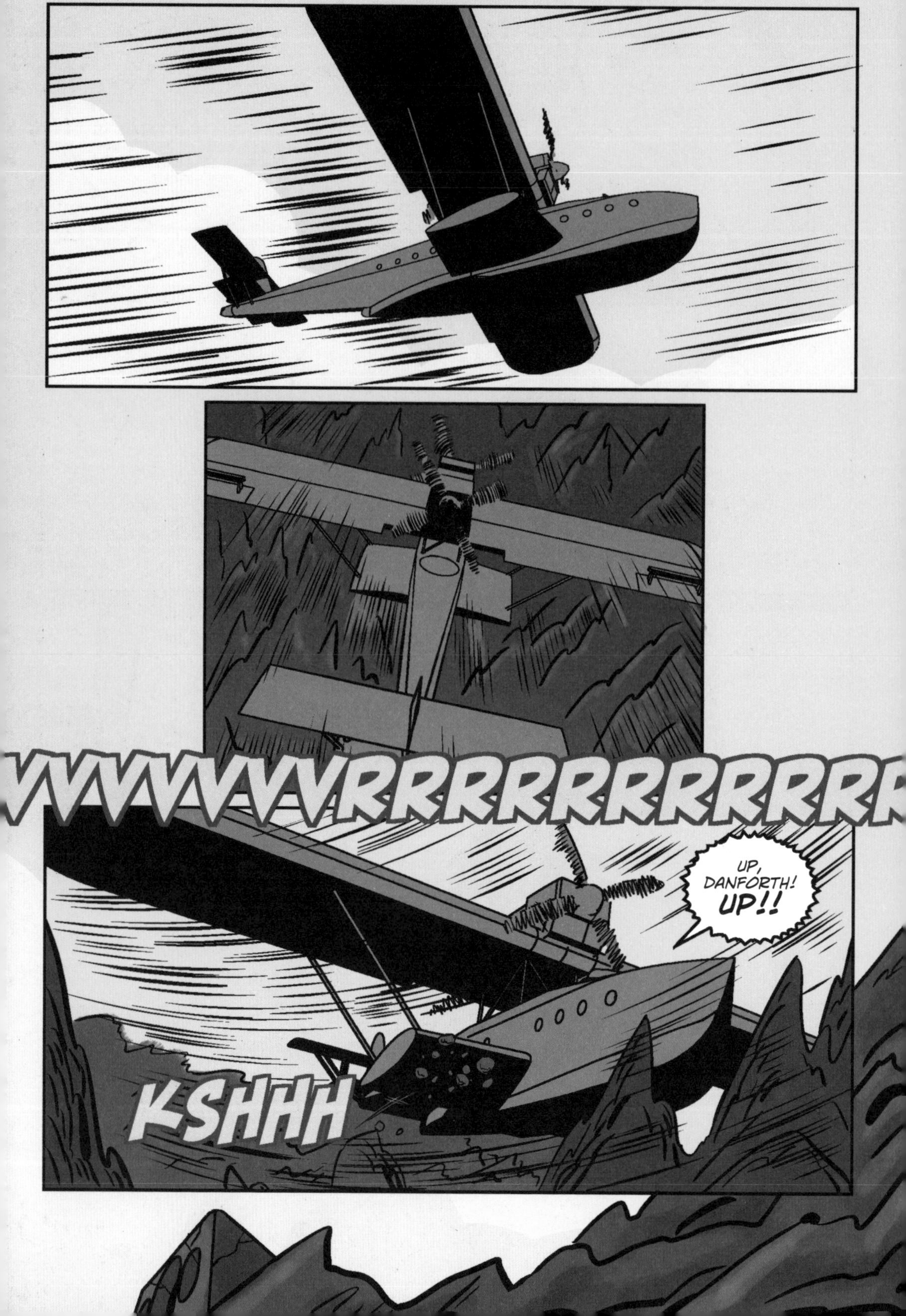
VVVVVVVRRRRRRRRRRRR
UP, DANFORTH! UP!!
KSHHH

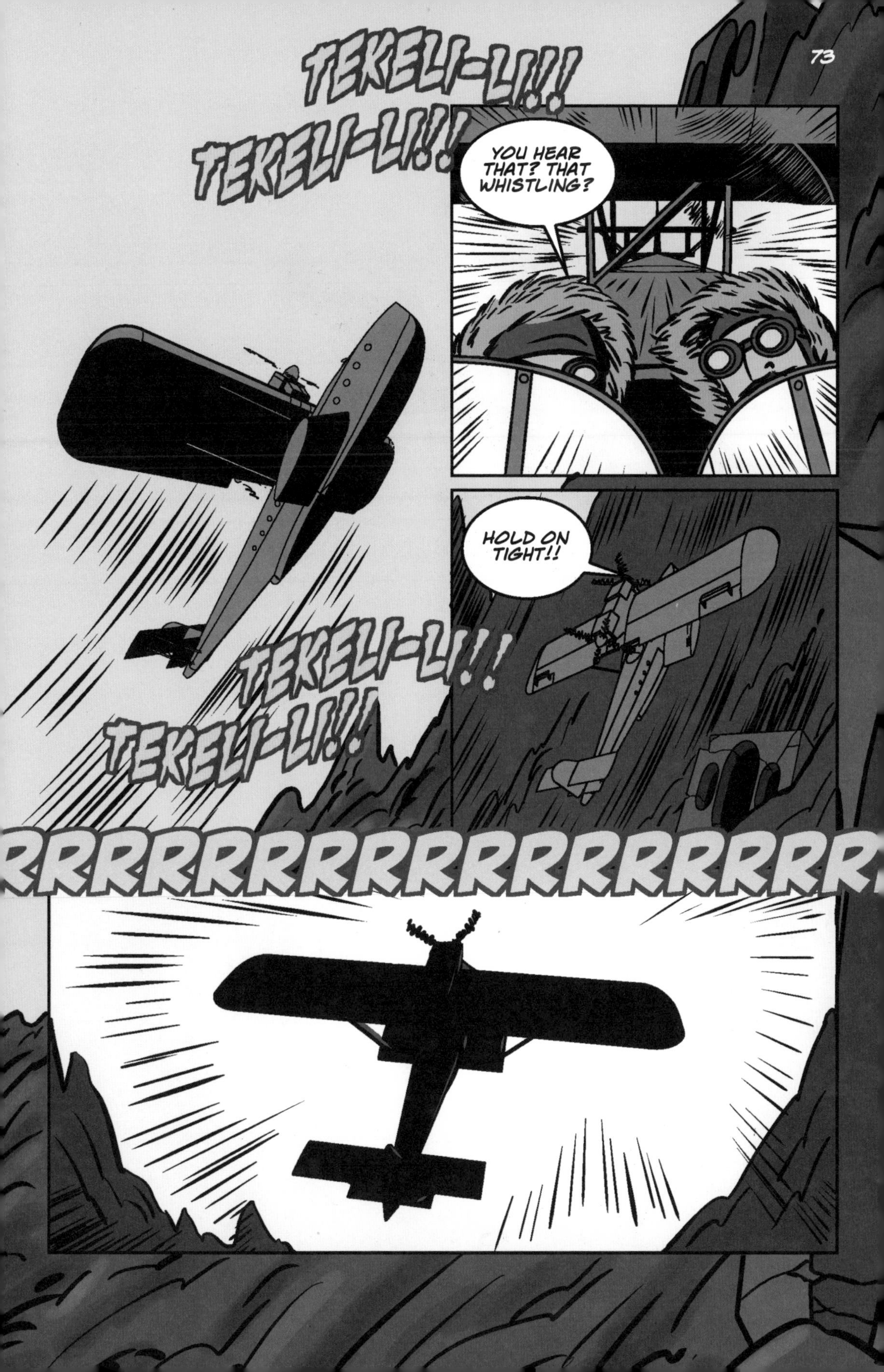
TEKELI-LI!!
TEKELI-LI!!
YOU HEAR THAT? THAT WHISTLING?
TEKELI-LI!!
TEKELI-LI!!
HOLD ON TIGHT!!
RRRRRRRRRRRRRRRRRR

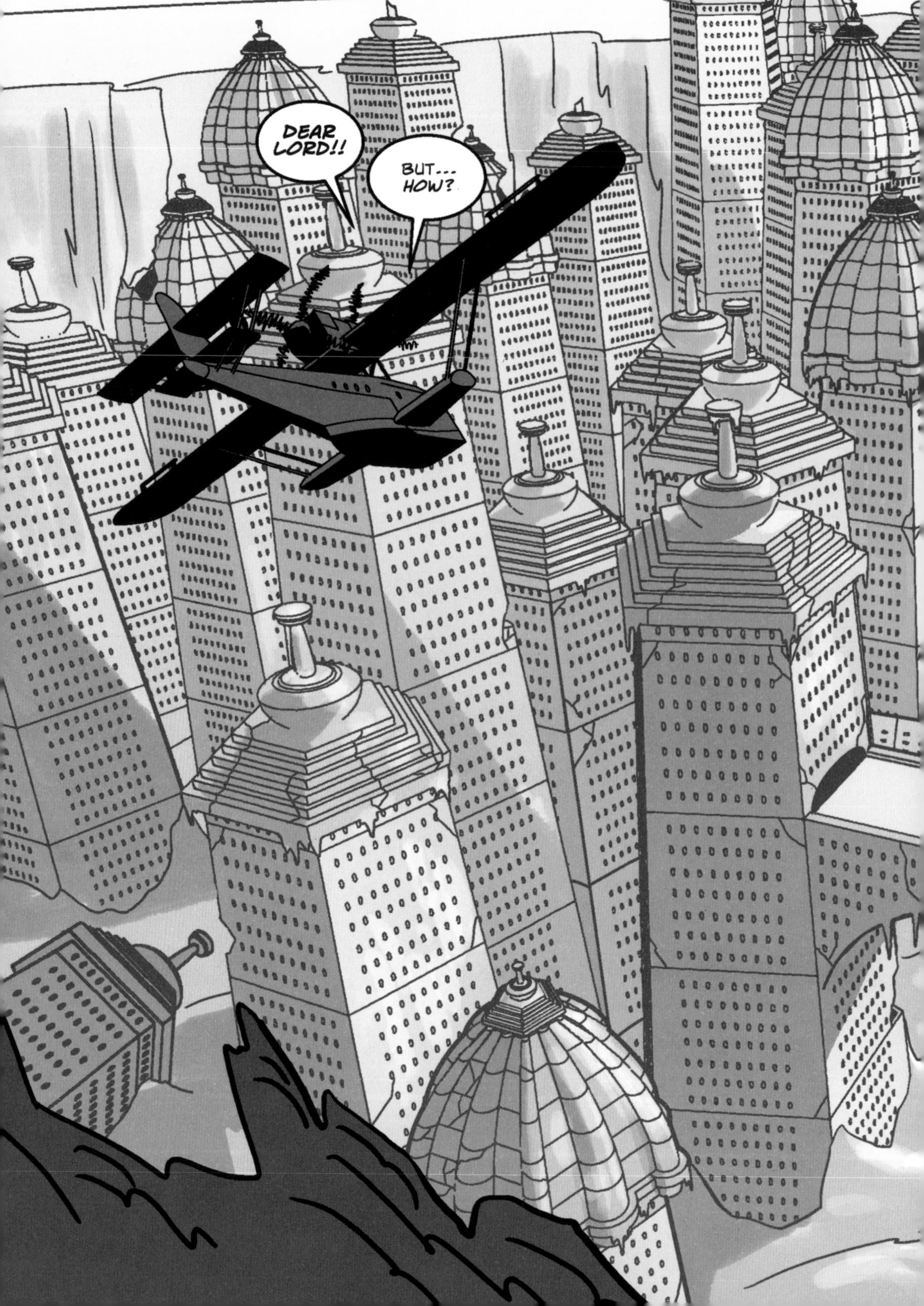
DEAR LORD!!
BUT... HOW?

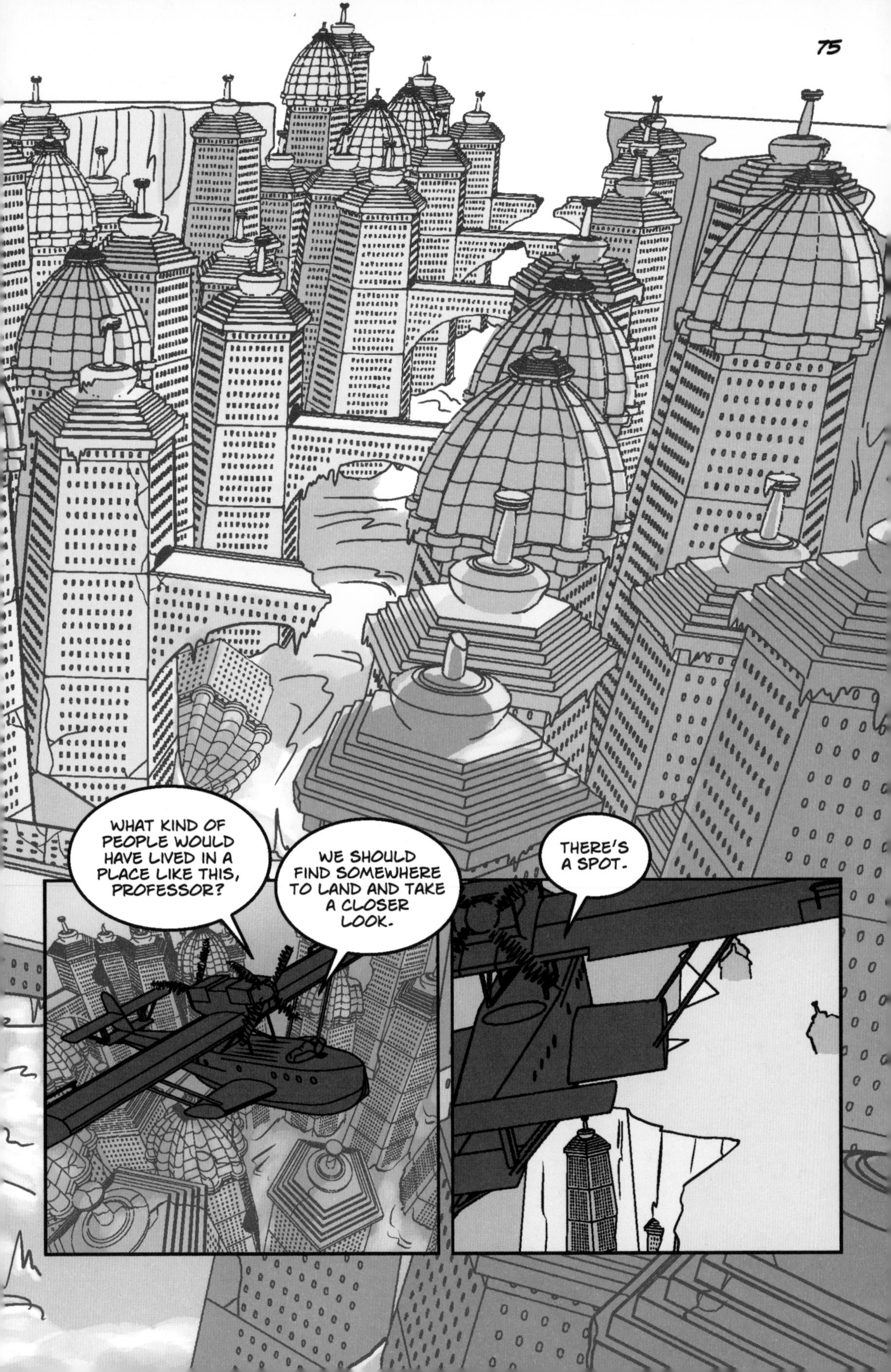
WHAT KIND OF PEOPLE WOULD HAVE LIVED IN A PLACE LIKE THIS, PROFESSOR?
WE SHOULD FIND SOMEWHERE TO LAND AND TAKE A CLOSER LOOK.
THERE'S A SPOT.

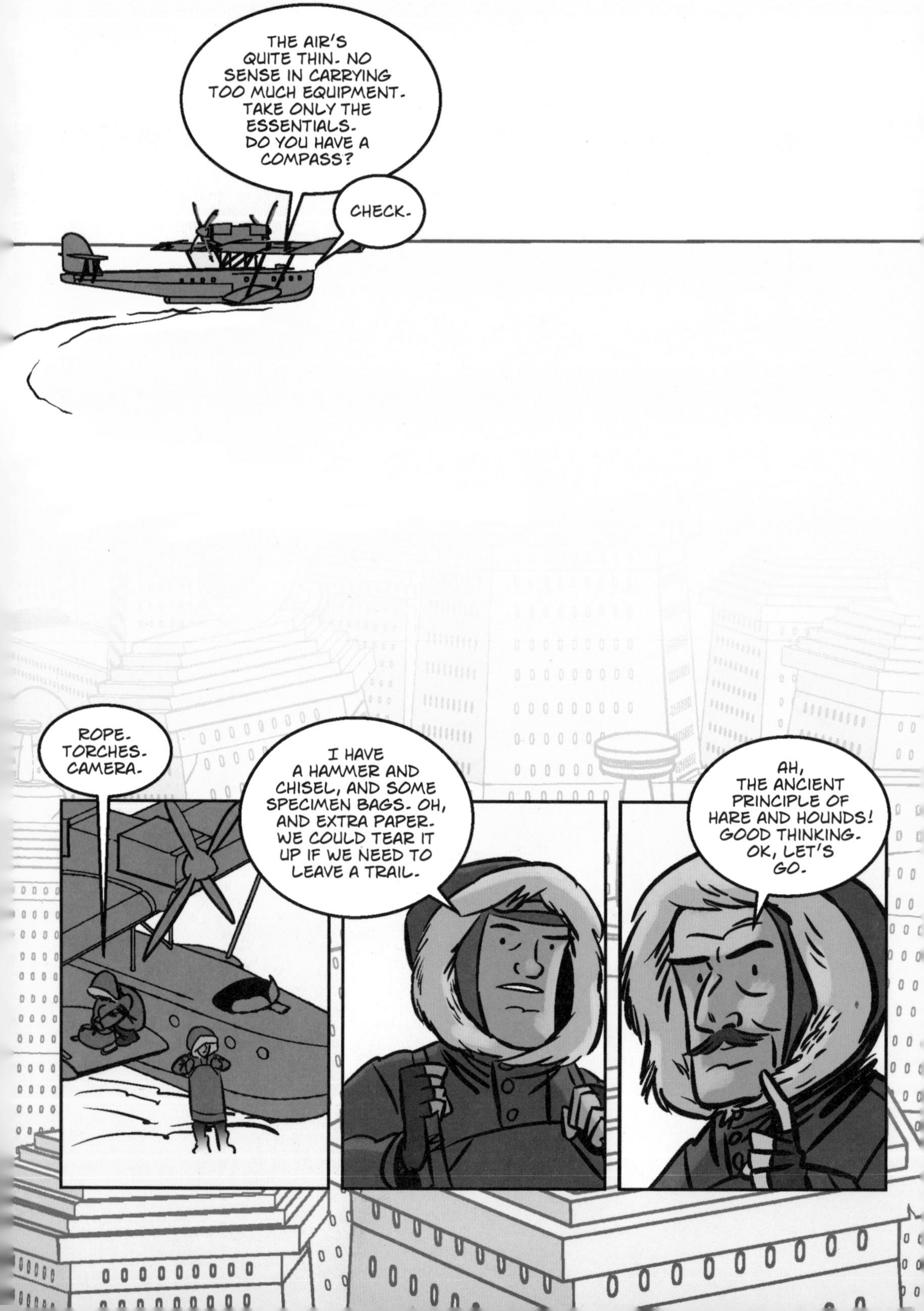
THE AIR'S QUITE THIN. NO SENSE IN CARRYING TOO MUCH EQUIPMENT. TAKE ONLY THE ESSENTIALS. DO YOU HAVE A COMPASS?
CHECK.
ROPE. TORCHES. CAMERA.
I HAVE A HAMMER AND CHISEL, AND SOME SPECIMEN BAGS. OH, AND EXTRA PAPER. WE COULD TEAR IT UP IF WE NEED TO LEAVE A TRAIL.
AH, THE ANCIENT PRINCIPLE OF HARE AND HOUNDS! GOOD THINKING. OK, LET'S GO.

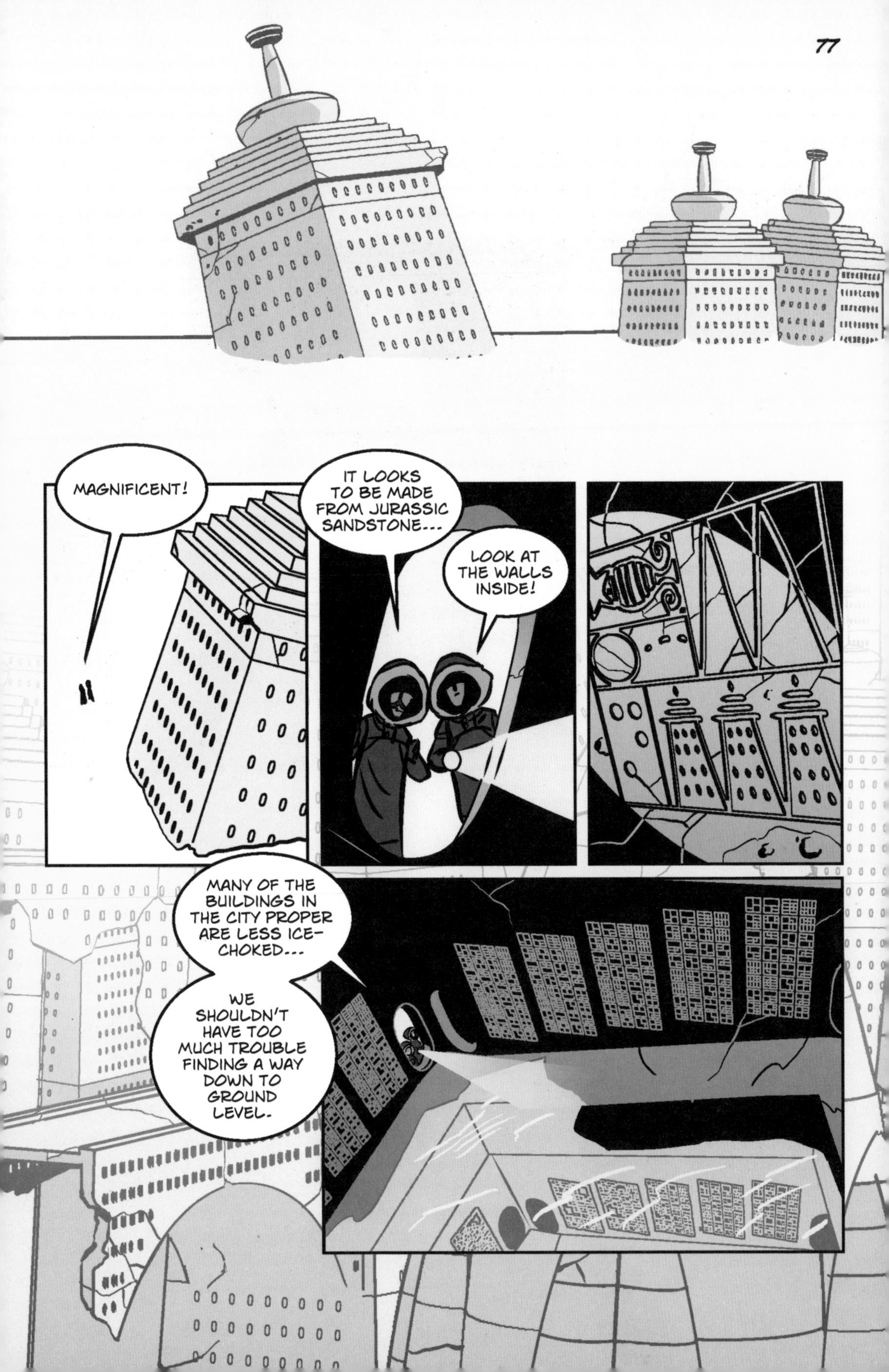
MAGNIFICENT!
IT LOOKS TO BE MADE FROM JURASSIC SANDSTONE...
LOOK AT THE WALLS INSIDE!
MANY OF THE BUILDINGS IN THE CITY PROPER ARE LESS ICE-CHOKED...
WE SHOULDN'T HAVE TOO MUCH TROUBLE FINDING A WAY DOWN TO GROUND LEVEL.

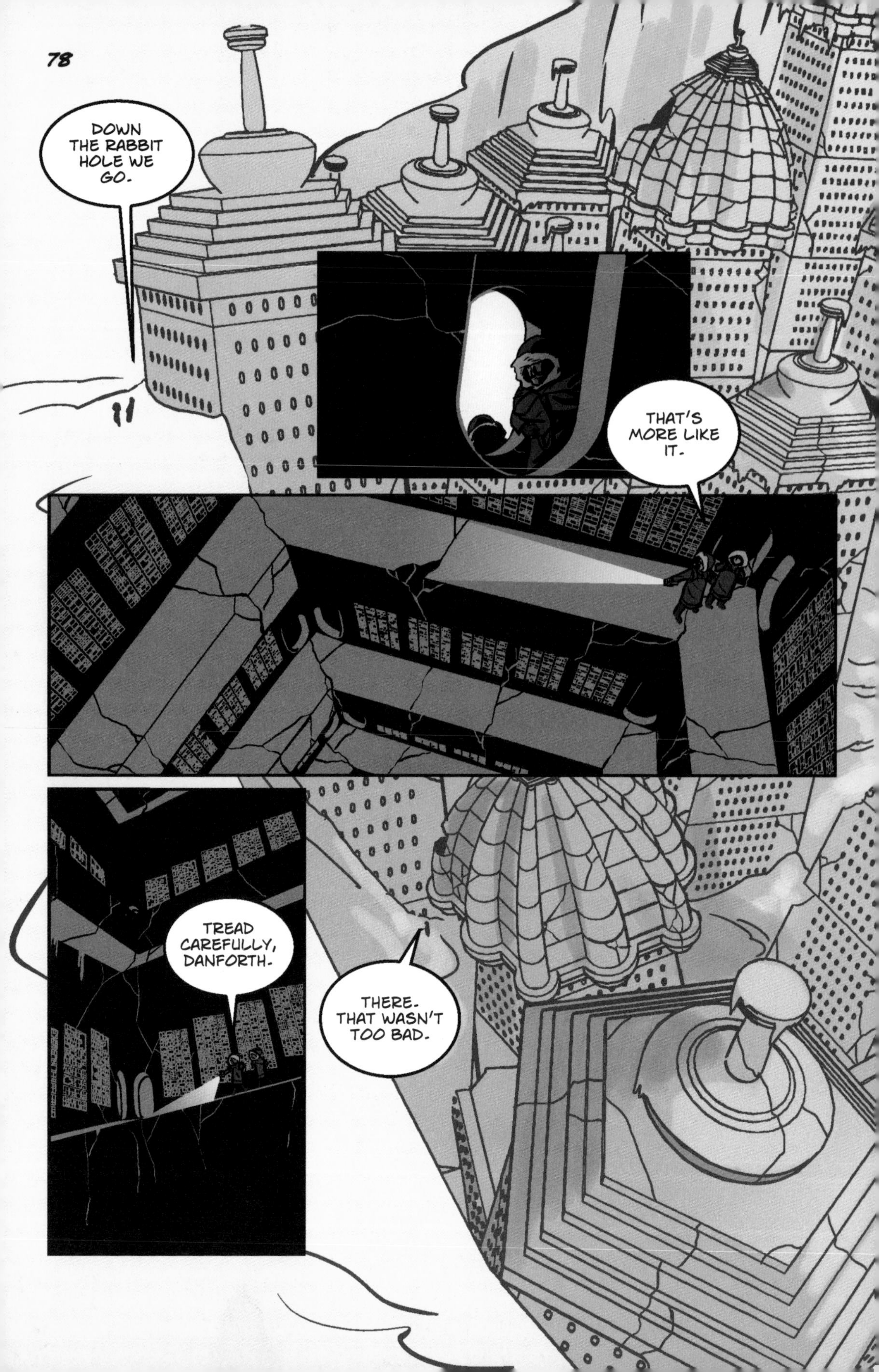
DOWN THE RABBIT HOLE WE GO.
THAT'S MORE LIKE IT.
TREAD CAREFULLY, DANFORTH.
THERE. THAT WASN'T TOO BAD.

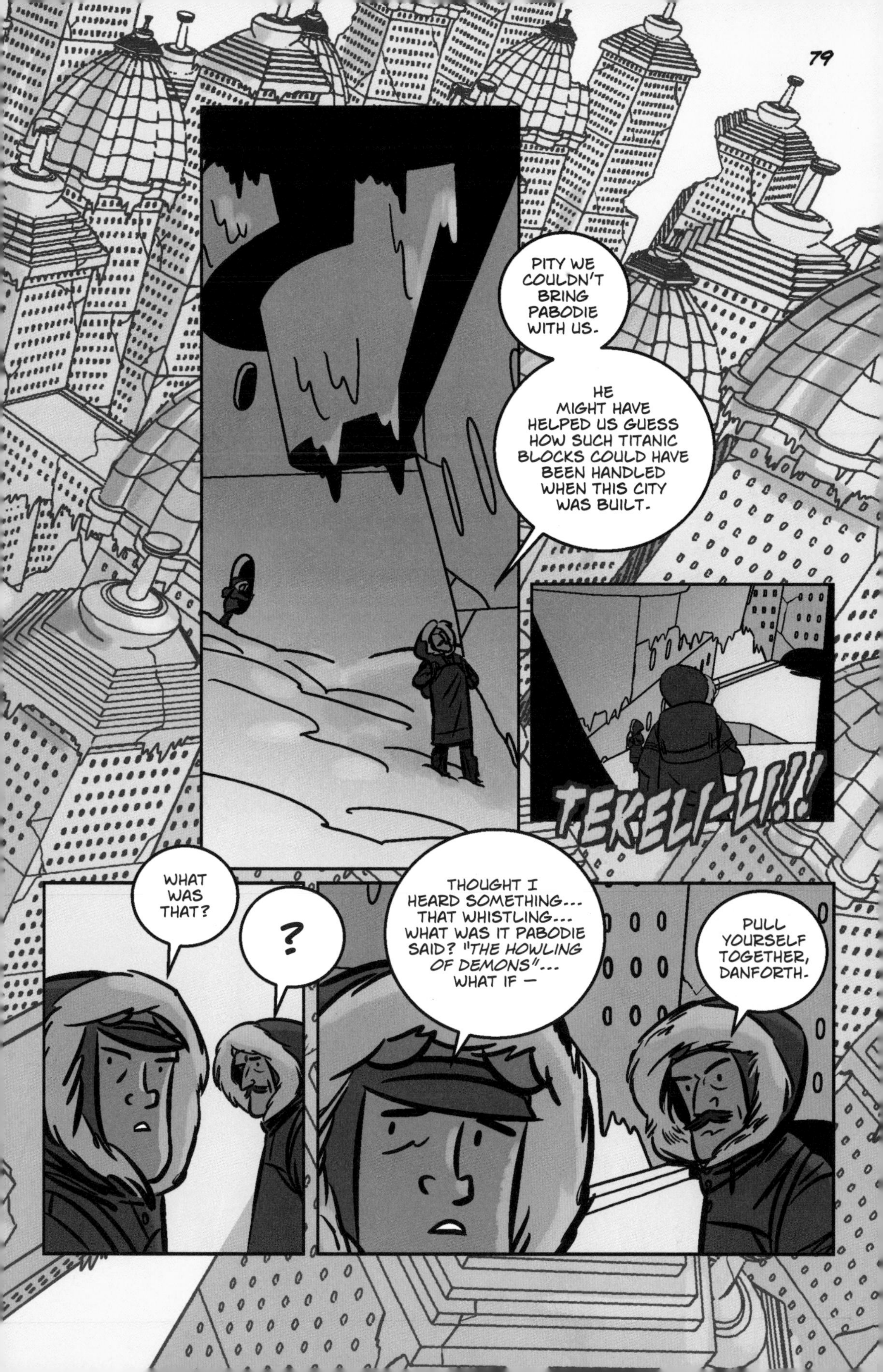
PITY WE COULDN'T BRING PABODIE WITH US.
HE MIGHT HAVE HELPED US GUESS HOW SUCH TITANIC BLOCKS COULD HAVE BEEN HANDLED WHEN THIS CITY WAS BUILT.
TEKELI-LI!!
WHAT WAS THAT?
?
THOUGHT I HEARD SOMETHING... THAT WHISTLING... WHAT WAS IT PABODIE SAID? "*THE HOWLING OF DEMONS*"... WHAT IF —
PULL YOURSELF TOGETHER, DANFORTH.

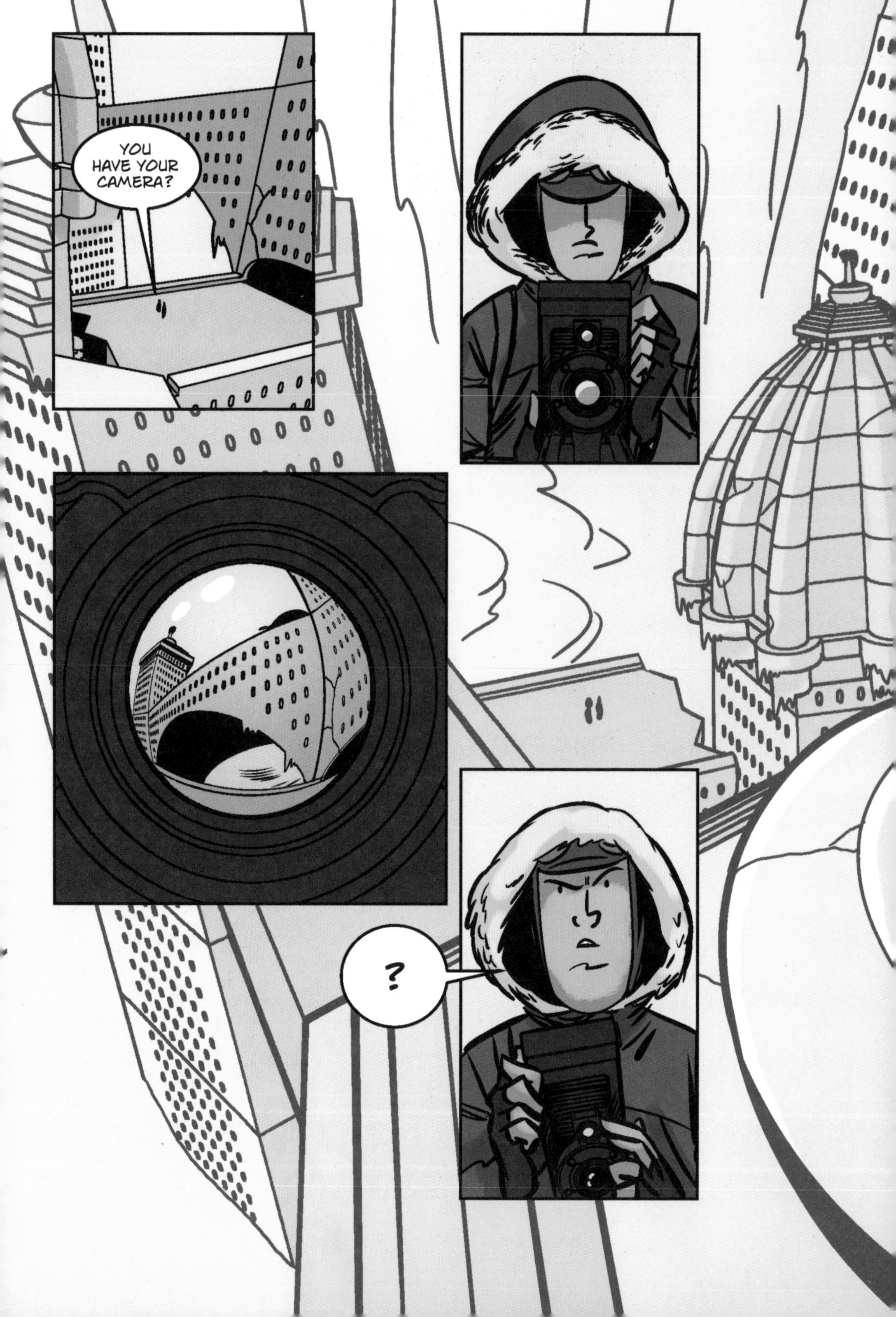
YOU HAVE YOUR CAMERA?
?

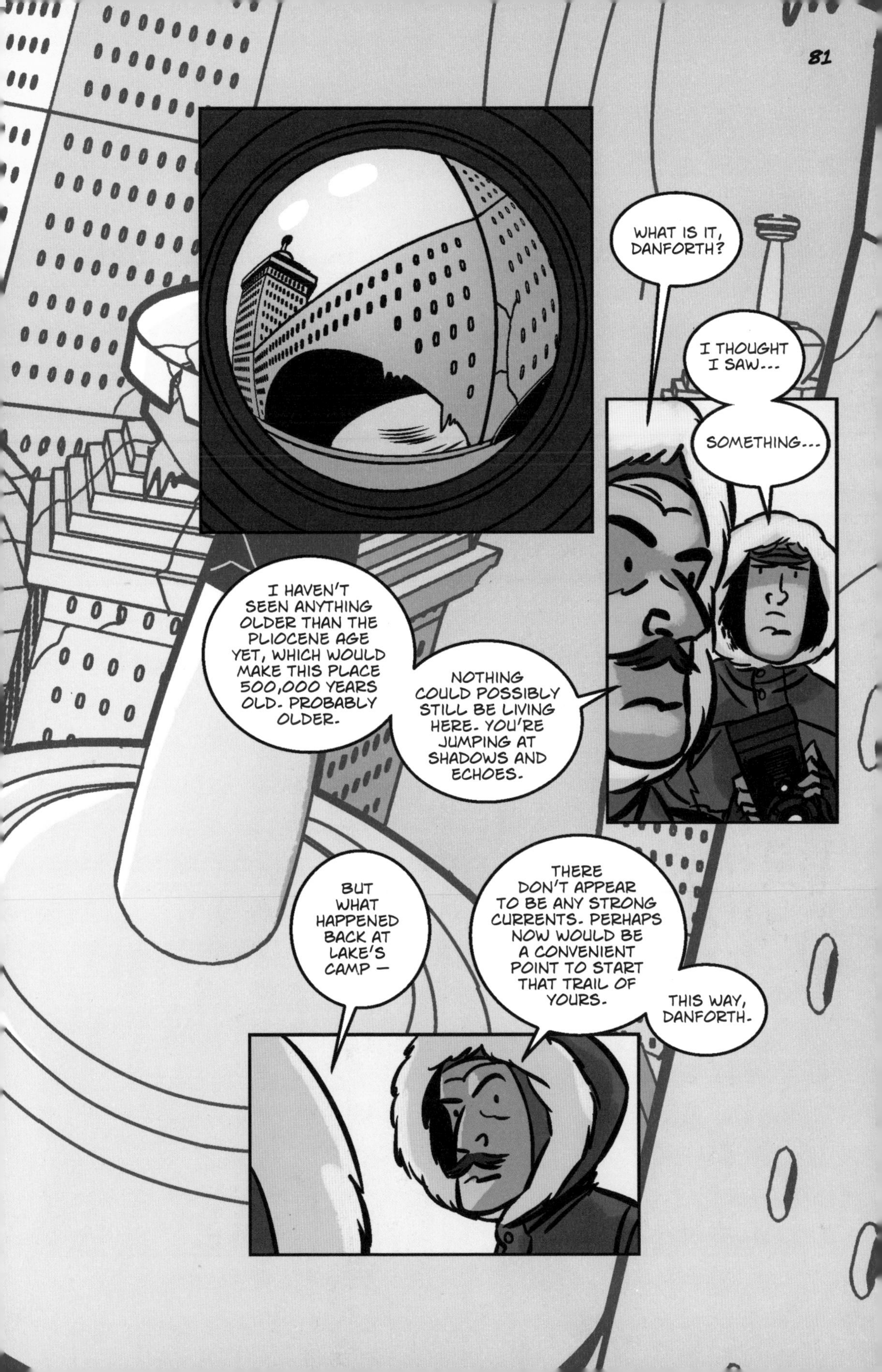

WHAT IS IT, DANFORTH?
I THOUGHT I SAW...
SOMETHING...
I HAVEN'T SEEN ANYTHING OLDER THAN THE PLIOCENE AGE YET, WHICH WOULD MAKE THIS PLACE 500,000 YEARS OLD. PROBABLY OLDER.
NOTHING COULD POSSIBLY STILL BE LIVING HERE. YOU'RE JUMPING AT SHADOWS AND ECHOES.
BUT WHAT HAPPENED BACK AT LAKE'S CAMP —
THERE DON'T APPEAR TO BE ANY STRONG CURRENTS. PERHAPS NOW WOULD BE A CONVENIENT POINT TO START THAT TRAIL OF YOURS.
THIS WAY, DANFORTH.

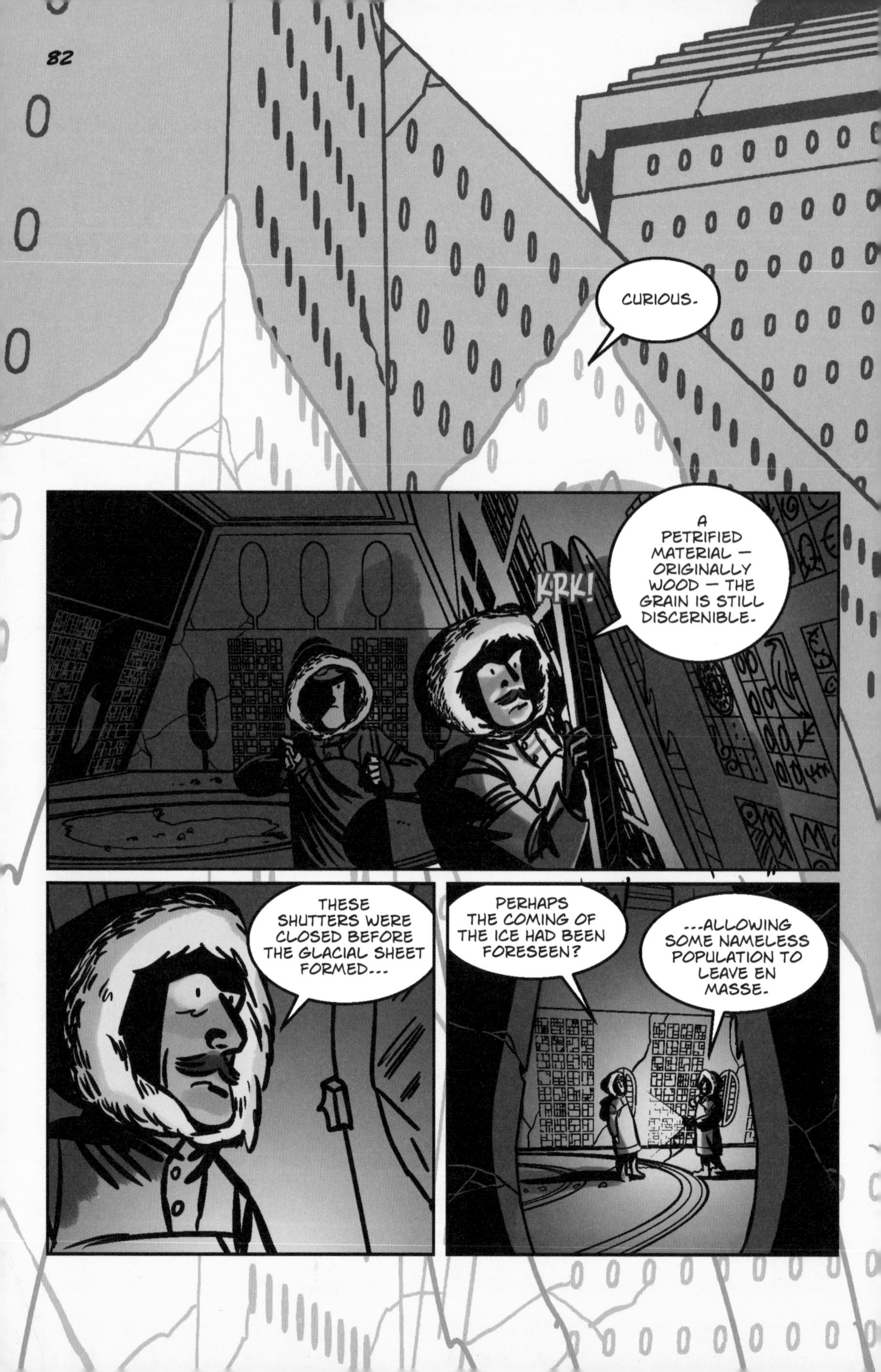
CURIOUS.
KRK!
A PETRIFIED MATERIAL — ORIGINALLY WOOD — THE GRAIN IS STILL DISCERNIBLE.
THESE SHUTTERS WERE CLOSED BEFORE THE GLACIAL SHEET FORMED...
PERHAPS THE COMING OF THE ICE HAD BEEN FORESEEN?
...ALLOWING SOME NAMELESS POPULATION TO LEAVE EN MASSE.

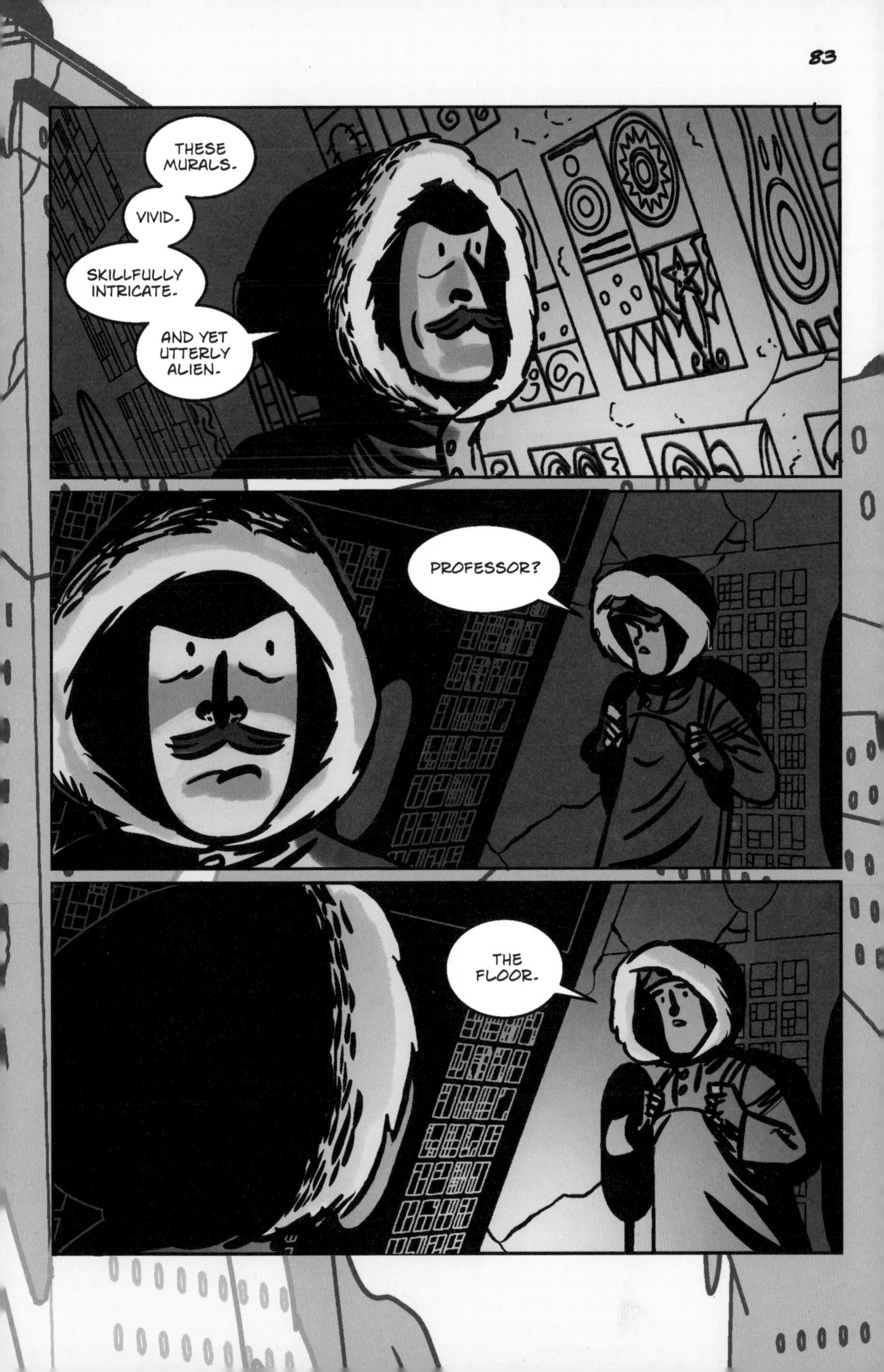
THESE MURALS.
VIVID.
SKILLFULLY INTRICATE.
AND YET UTTERLY ALIEN.
PROFESSOR?
THE FLOOR.

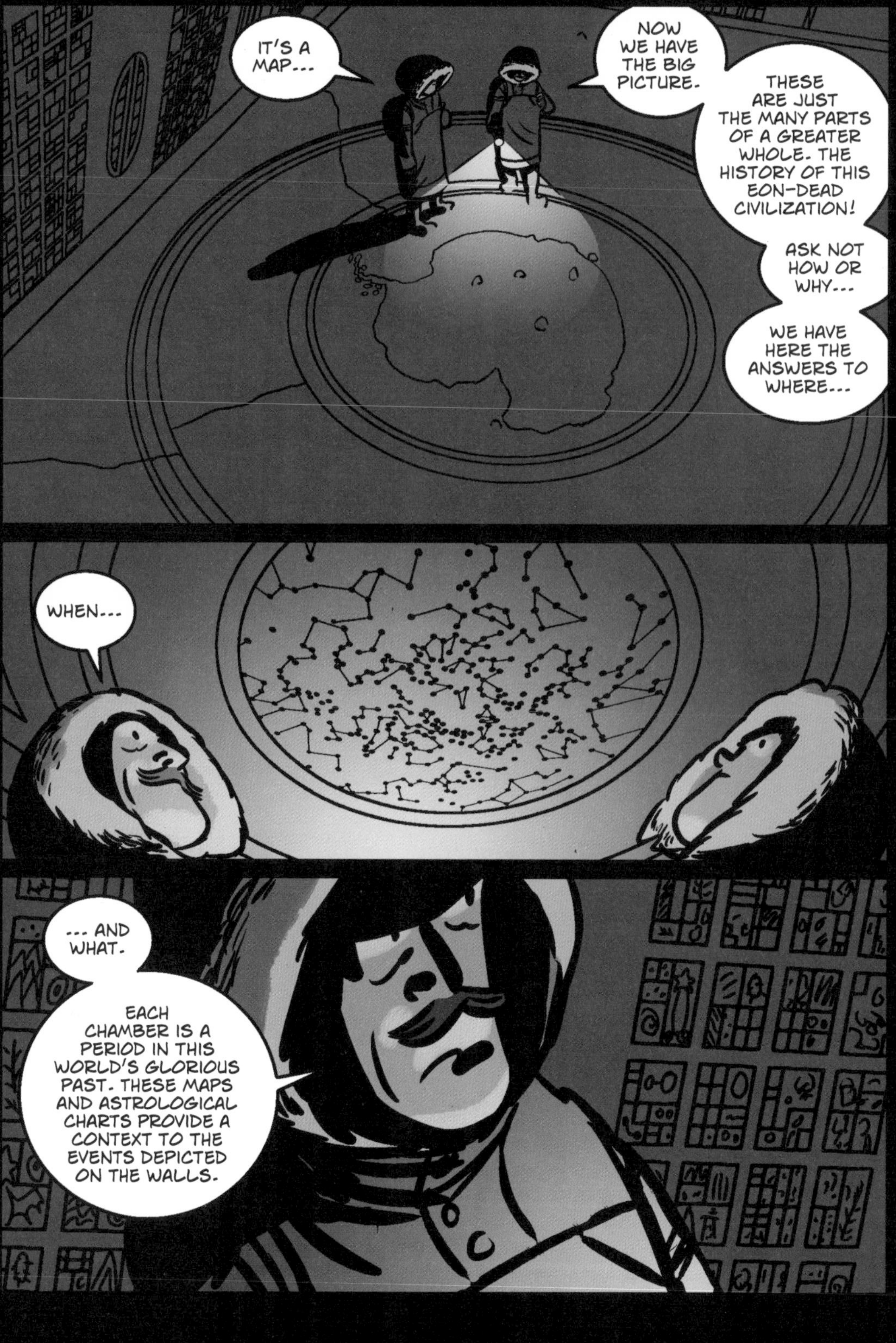
IT'S A MAP...
NOW WE HAVE THE BIG PICTURE.
THESE ARE JUST THE MANY PARTS OF A GREATER WHOLE. THE HISTORY OF THIS EON-DEAD CIVILIZATION!
ASK NOT HOW OR WHY...
WE HAVE HERE THE ANSWERS TO WHERE...
WHEN...
... AND WHAT.
EACH CHAMBER IS A PERIOD IN THIS WORLD'S GLORIOUS PAST. THESE MAPS AND ASTROLOGICAL CHARTS PROVIDE A CONTEXT TO THE EVENTS DEPICTED ON THE WALLS.

COME ALONG, DANFORTH, WE HAVE MUCH TO LEARN.

LOOK. THE TALE TOLD HERE IS NOW OF A PRE-TERRESTRIAL HISTORY.

HOW SO?

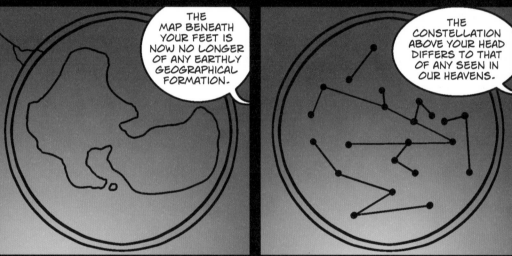

THE MAP BENEATH YOUR FEET IS NOW NO LONGER OF ANY EARTHLY GEOGRAPHICAL FORMATION.

THE CONSTELLATION ABOVE YOUR HEAD DIFFERS TO THAT OF ANY SEEN IN OUR HEAVENS.

THE THINGS WHICH ONCE LIVED HERE... THEY WERE NOT BRAINLESS DINOSAURS.

THEY WERE WISE AND ANCIENT — FILTERED DOWN FROM THE STARS WHEN THE EARTH WAS YOUNG...

BEINGS WHOSE SUBSTANCE AN ALIEN EVOLUTION HAD SHAPED, AND WHOSE POWERS WERE SUCH AS THIS PLANET HAD NEVER BRED.

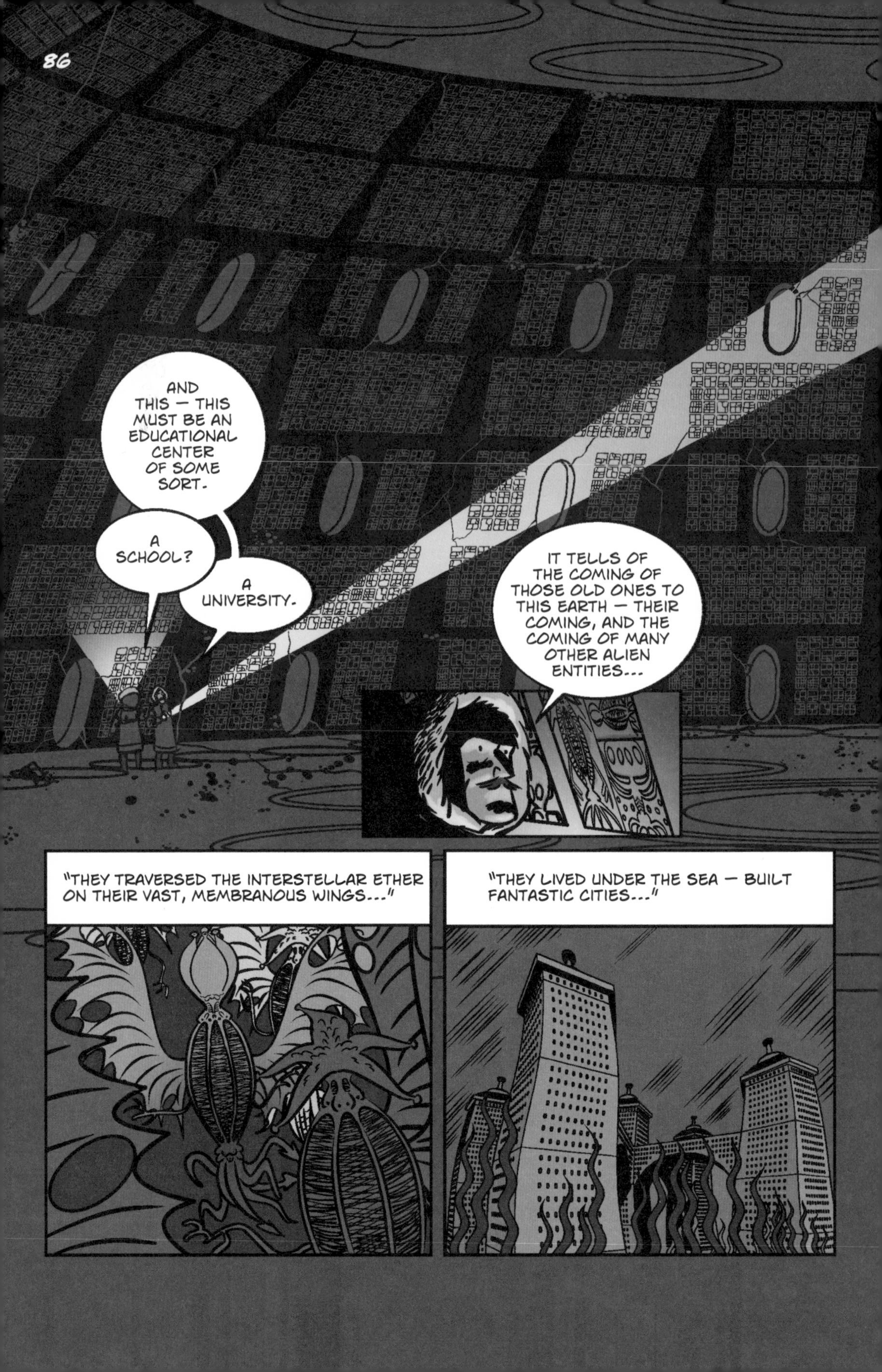
AND THIS — THIS MUST BE AN EDUCATIONAL CENTER OF SOME SORT.
A SCHOOL?
A UNIVERSITY.
IT TELLS OF THE COMING OF THOSE OLD ONES TO THIS EARTH — THEIR COMING, AND THE COMING OF MANY OTHER ALIEN ENTITIES...
"THEY TRAVERSED THE INTERSTELLAR ETHER ON THEIR VAST, MEMBRANOUS WINGS..."
"THEY LIVED UNDER THE SEA — BUILT FANTASTIC CITIES..."

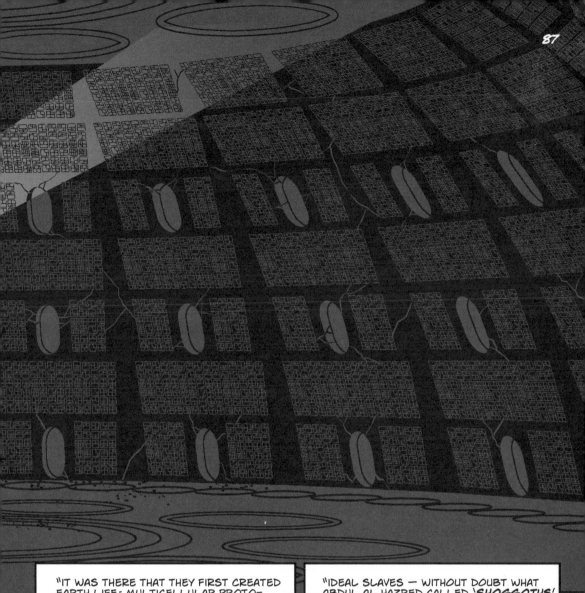

"IT WAS THERE THAT THEY FIRST CREATED EARTH LIFE: MULTICELLULAR PROTO-PLASMIC VISCOUS MASSES..."

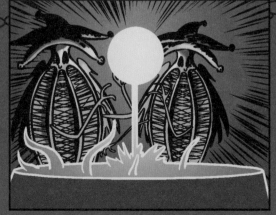

"IDEAL SLAVES — WITHOUT DOUBT WHAT ABDUL AL HAZRED CALLED *'SHOGGOTHS'* IN HIS FRIGHTFUL *NECRONOMICON*..."

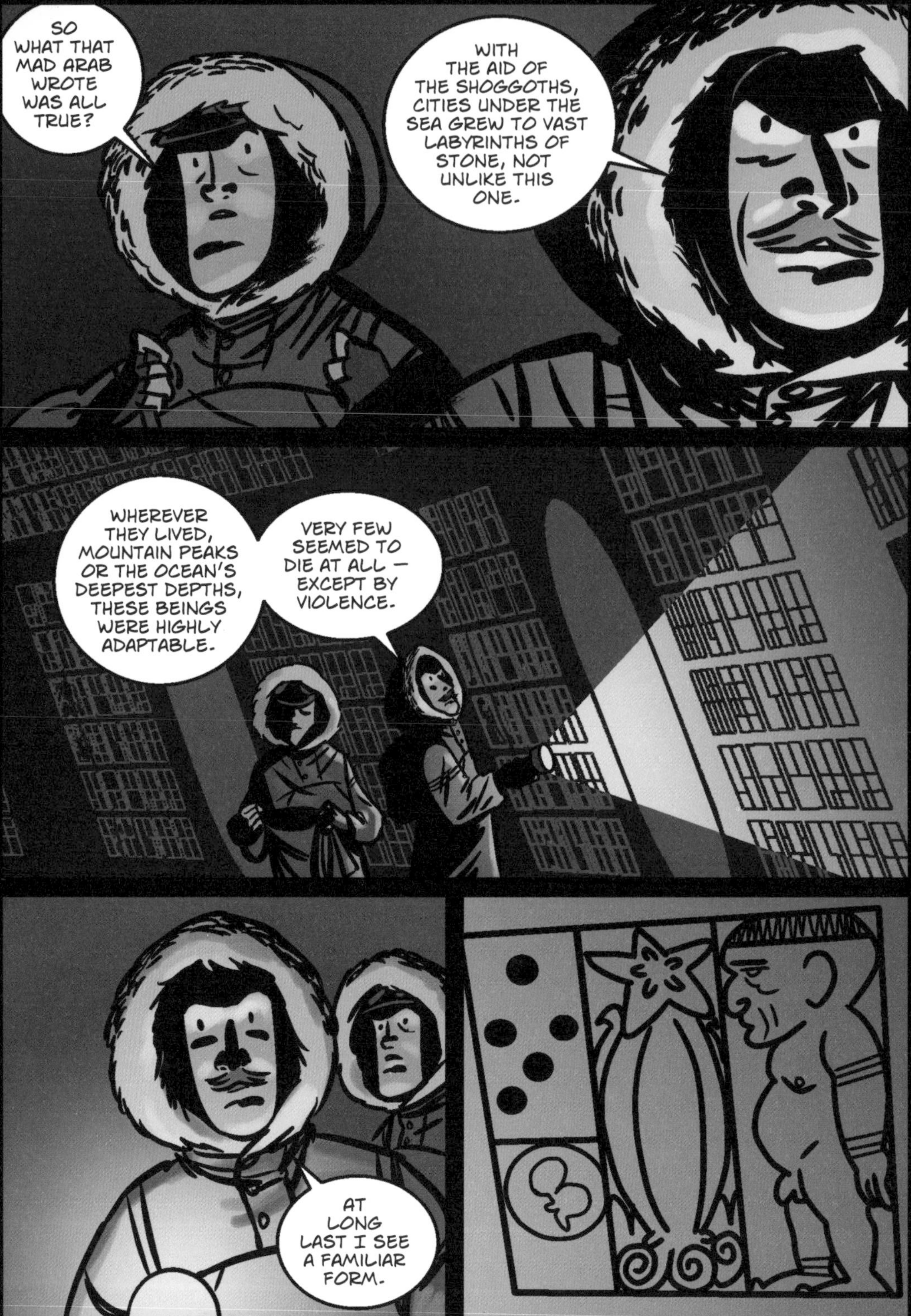
SO WHAT THAT MAD ARAB WROTE WAS ALL TRUE?
WITH THE AID OF THE SHOGGOTHS, CITIES UNDER THE SEA GREW TO VAST LABYRINTHS OF STONE, NOT UNLIKE THIS ONE.
WHEREVER THEY LIVED, MOUNTAIN PEAKS OR THE OCEAN'S DEEPEST DEPTHS, THESE BEINGS WERE HIGHLY ADAPTABLE.
VERY FEW SEEMED TO DIE AT ALL — EXCEPT BY VIOLENCE.
AT LONG LAST I SEE A FAMILIAR FORM.

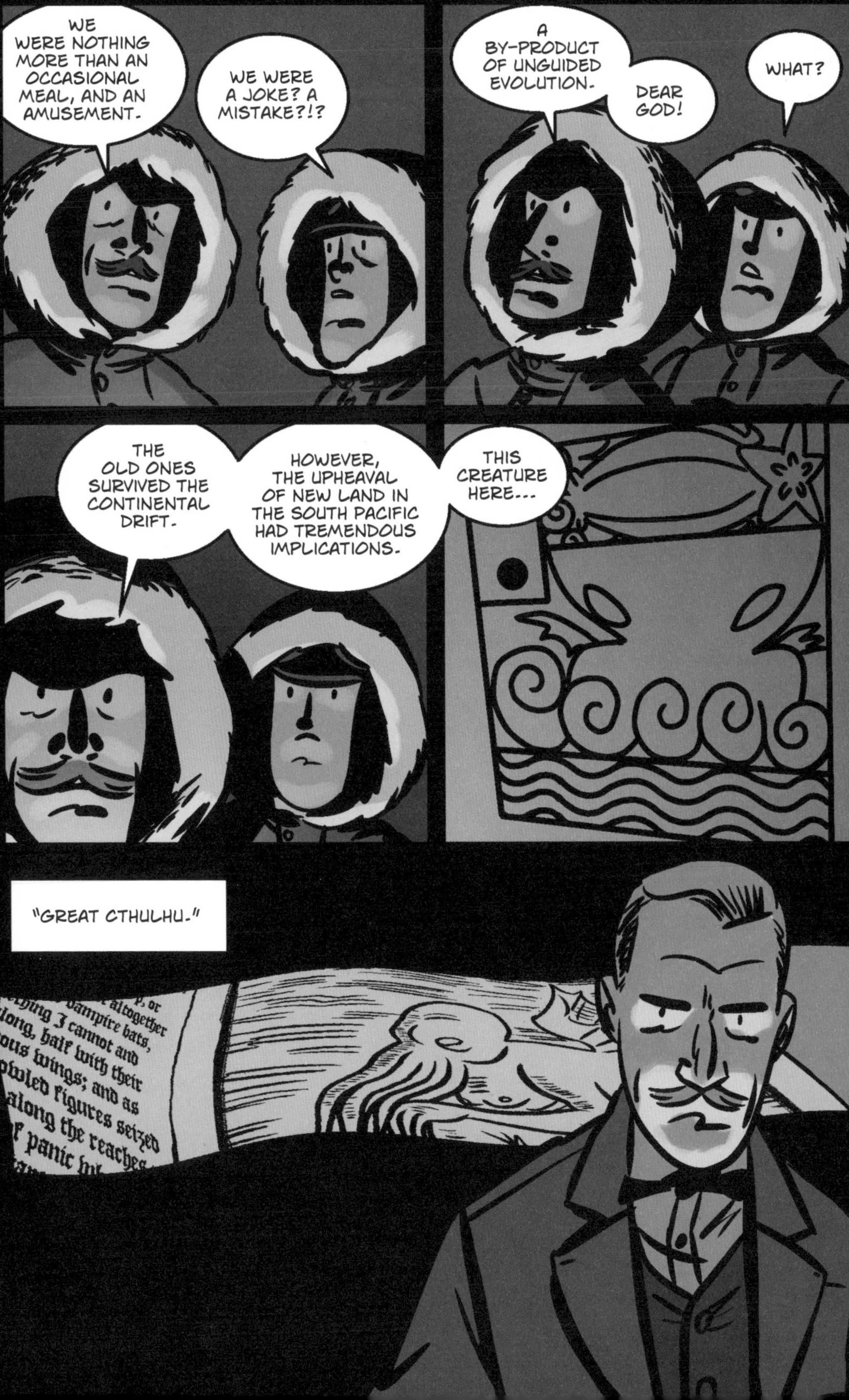
WE WERE NOTHING MORE THAN AN OCCASIONAL MEAL, AND AN AMUSEMENT.
WE WERE A JOKE? A MISTAKE?!?
A BY-PRODUCT OF UNGUIDED EVOLUTION.
DEAR GOD!
WHAT?
THE OLD ONES SURVIVED THE CONTINENTAL DRIFT.
HOWEVER, THE UPHEAVAL OF NEW LAND IN THE SOUTH PACIFIC HAD TREMENDOUS IMPLICATIONS.
THIS CREATURE HERE...
"GREAT CTHULHU."

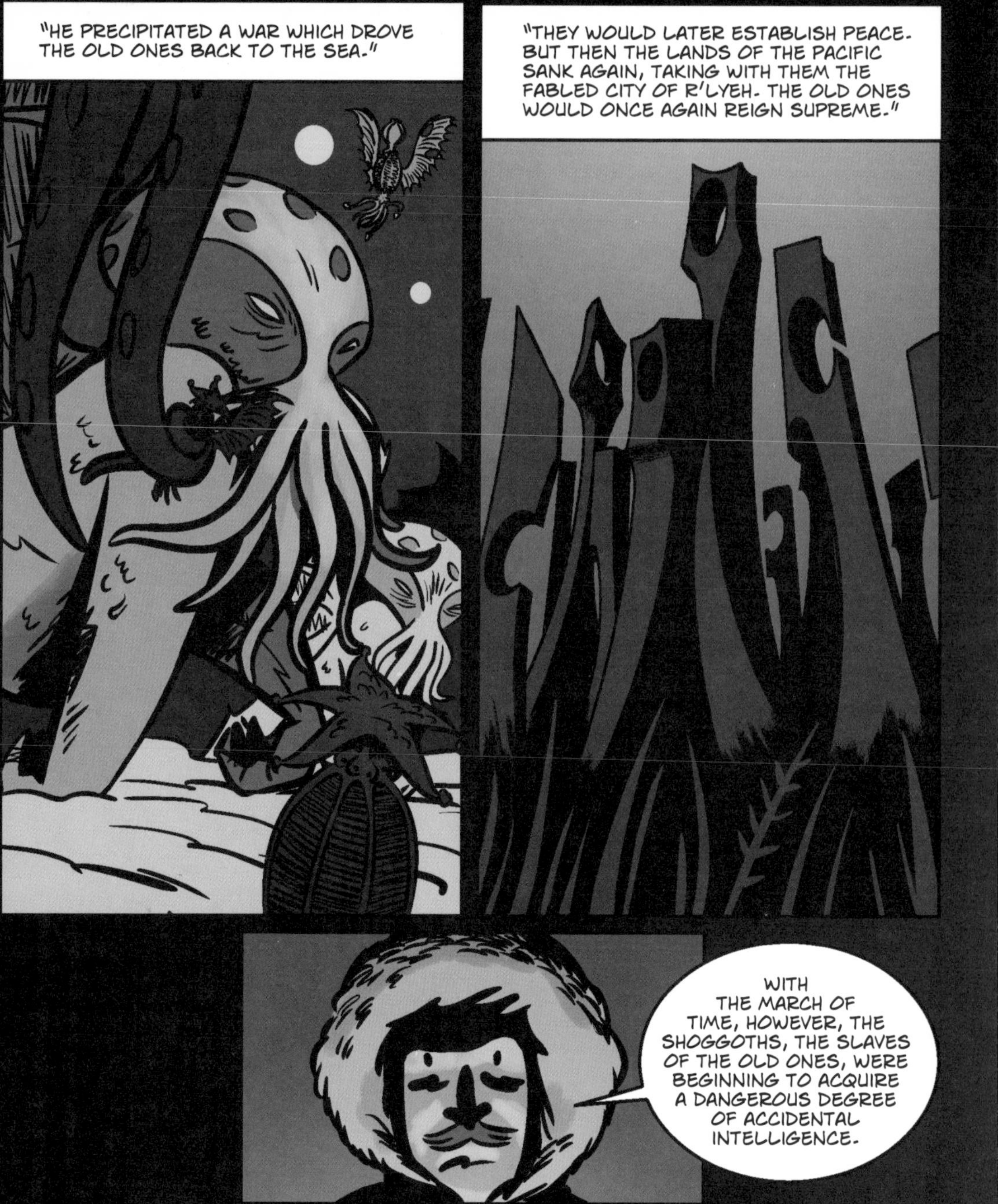
"HE PRECIPITATED A WAR WHICH DROVE THE OLD ONES BACK TO THE SEA."
"THEY WOULD LATER ESTABLISH PEACE. BUT THEN THE LANDS OF THE PACIFIC SANK AGAIN, TAKING WITH THEM THE FABLED CITY OF R'LYEH. THE OLD ONES WOULD ONCE AGAIN REIGN SUPREME."
WITH THE MARCH OF TIME, HOWEVER, THE SHOGGOTHS, THE SLAVES OF THE OLD ONES, WERE BEGINNING TO ACQUIRE A DANGEROUS DEGREE OF ACCIDENTAL INTELLIGENCE.

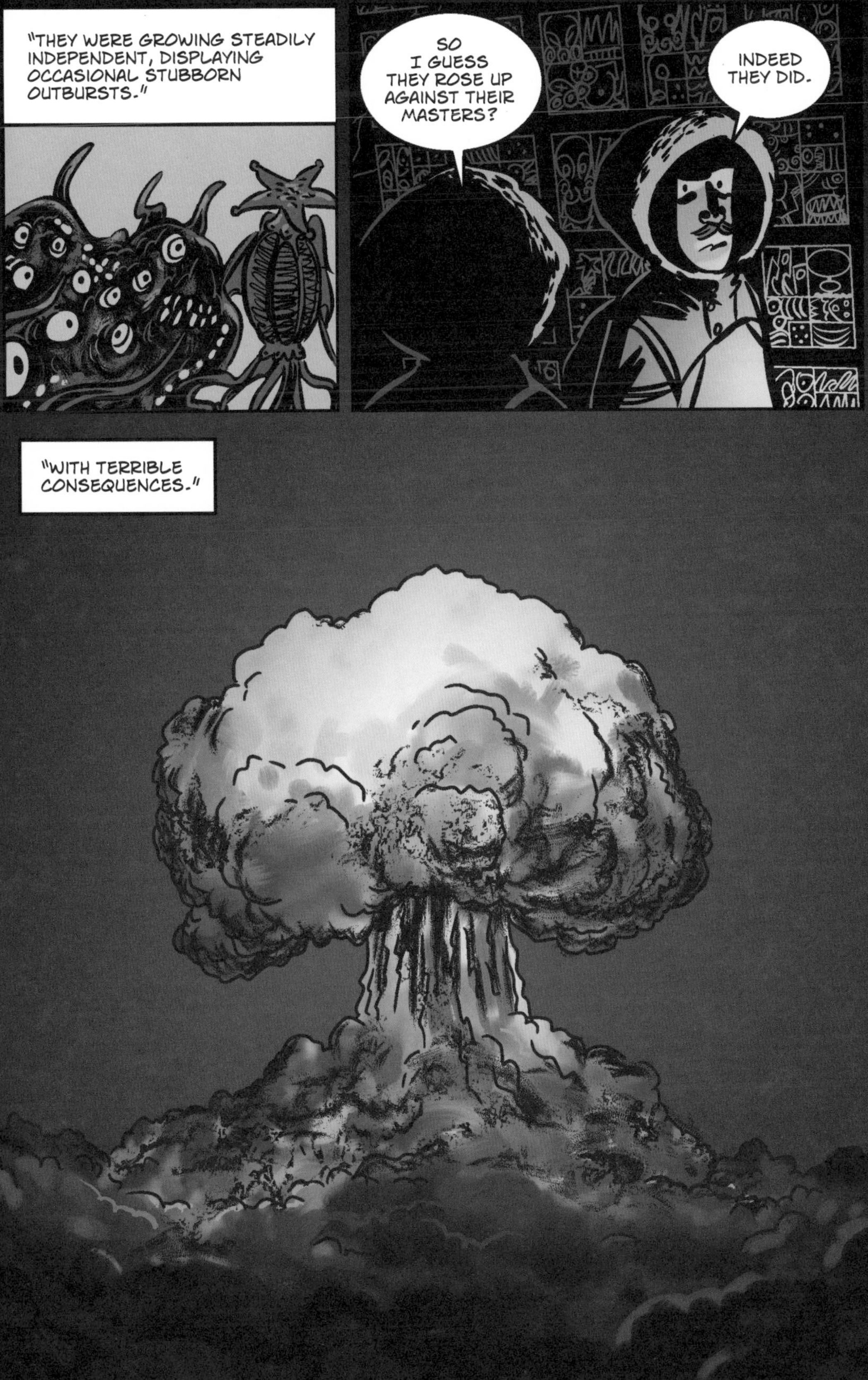
"THEY WERE GROWING STEADILY INDEPENDENT, DISPLAYING OCCASIONAL STUBBORN OUTBURSTS."
SO I GUESS THEY ROSE UP AGAINST THEIR MASTERS?
INDEED THEY DID.
"WITH TERRIBLE CONSEQUENCES."

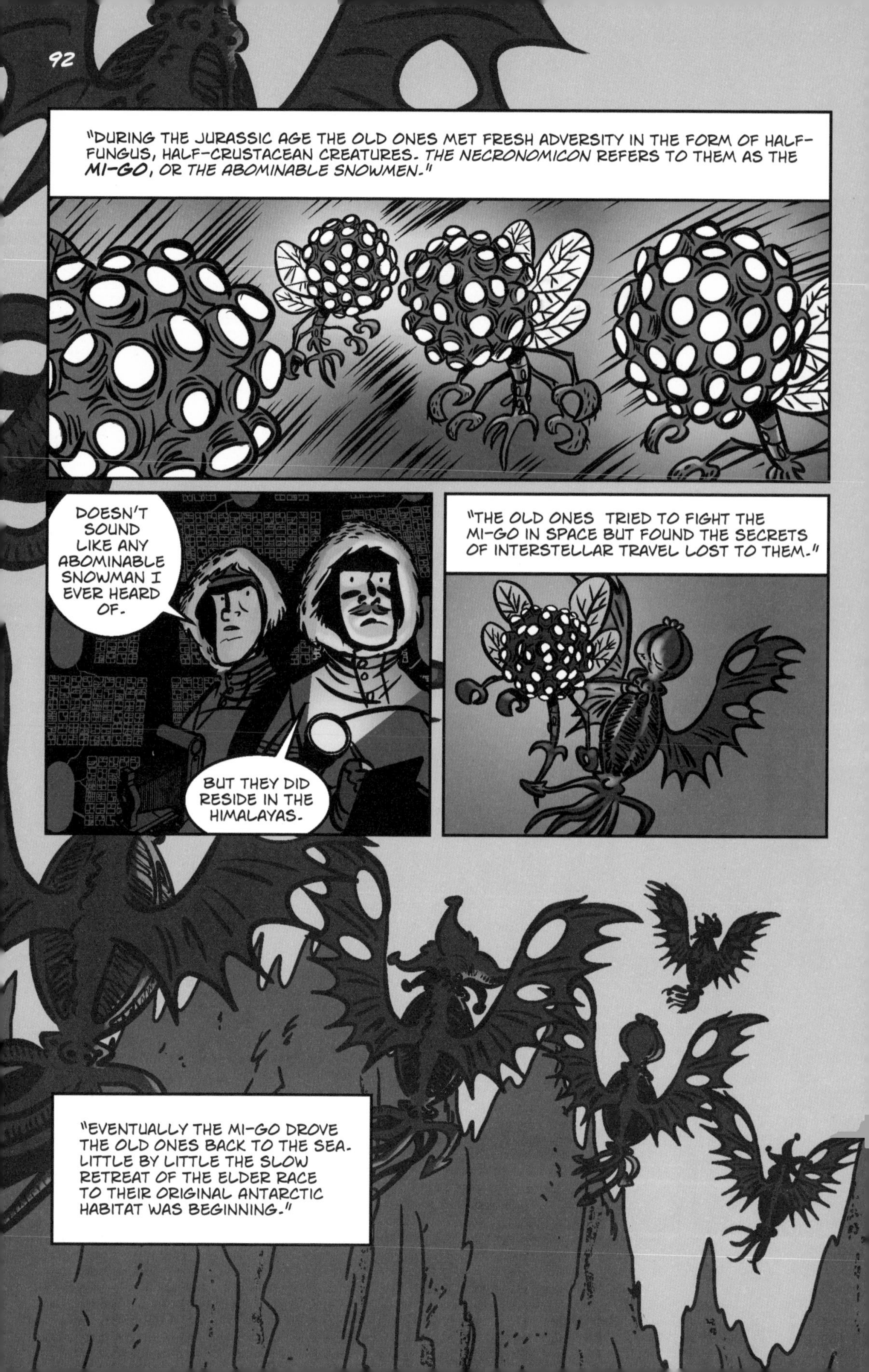
"DURING THE JURASSIC AGE THE OLD ONES MET FRESH ADVERSITY IN THE FORM OF HALF-FUNGUS, HALF-CRUSTACEAN CREATURES. *THE NECRONOMICON* REFERS TO THEM AS THE ***MI-GO***, OR THE ABOMINABLE SNOWMEN."
DOESN'T SOUND LIKE ANY ABOMINABLE SNOWMAN I EVER HEARD OF.
BUT THEY DID RESIDE IN THE HIMALAYAS.
"THE OLD ONES TRIED TO FIGHT THE MI-GO IN SPACE BUT FOUND THE SECRETS OF INTERSTELLAR TRAVEL LOST TO THEM."
"EVENTUALLY THE MI-GO DROVE THE OLD ONES BACK TO THE SEA. LITTLE BY LITTLE THE SLOW RETREAT OF THE ELDER RACE TO THEIR ORIGINAL ANTARCTIC HABITAT WAS BEGINNING."

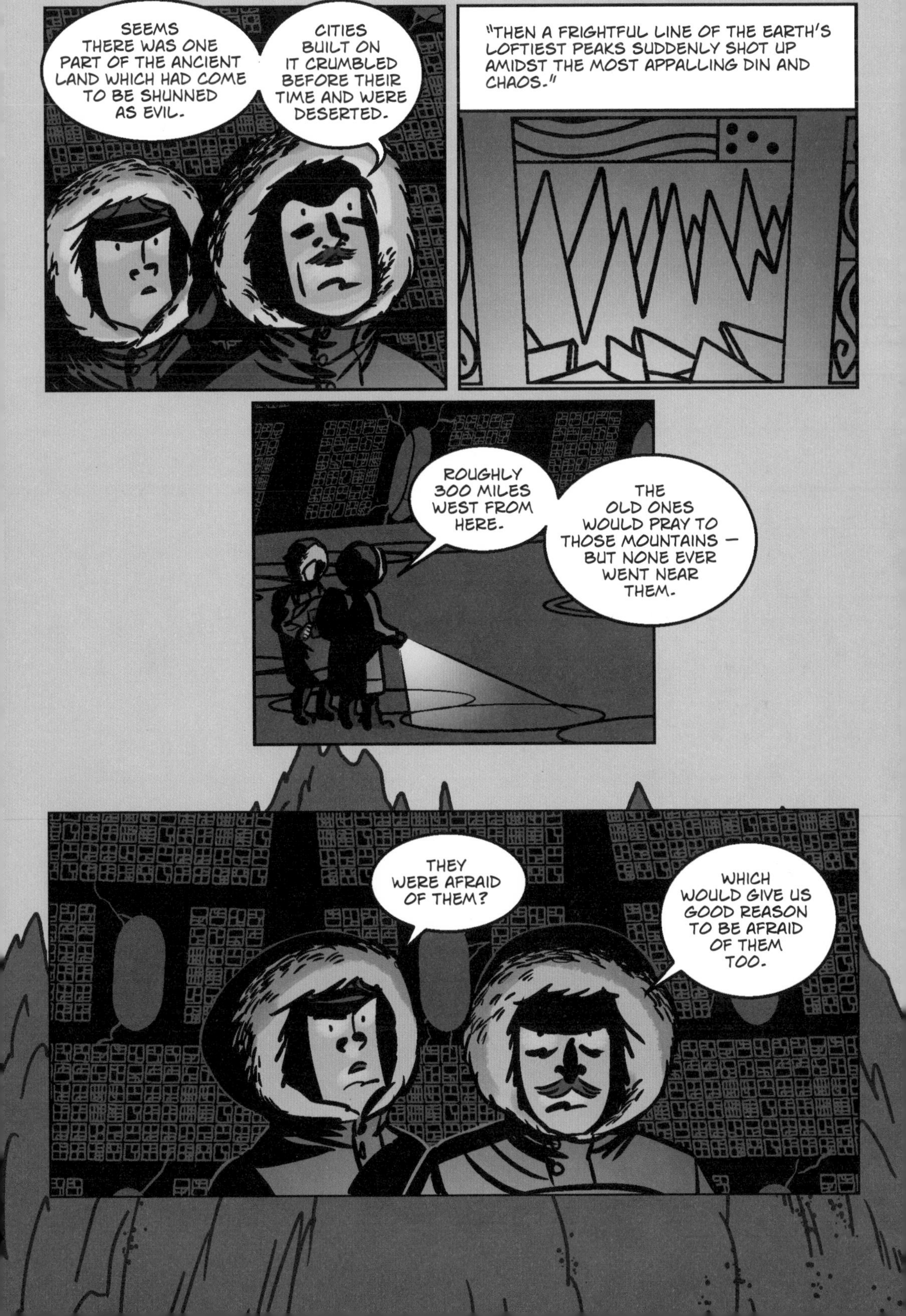
SEEMS THERE WAS ONE PART OF THE ANCIENT LAND WHICH HAD COME TO BE SHUNNED AS EVIL.
CITIES BUILT ON IT CRUMBLED BEFORE THEIR TIME AND WERE DESERTED.
"THEN A FRIGHTFUL LINE OF THE EARTH'S LOFTIEST PEAKS SUDDENLY SHOT UP AMIDST THE MOST APPALLING DIN AND CHAOS."
ROUGHLY 300 MILES WEST FROM HERE.
THE OLD ONES WOULD PRAY TO THOSE MOUNTAINS — BUT NONE EVER WENT NEAR THEM.
THEY WERE AFRAID OF THEM?
WHICH WOULD GIVE US GOOD REASON TO BE AFRAID OF THEM TOO.

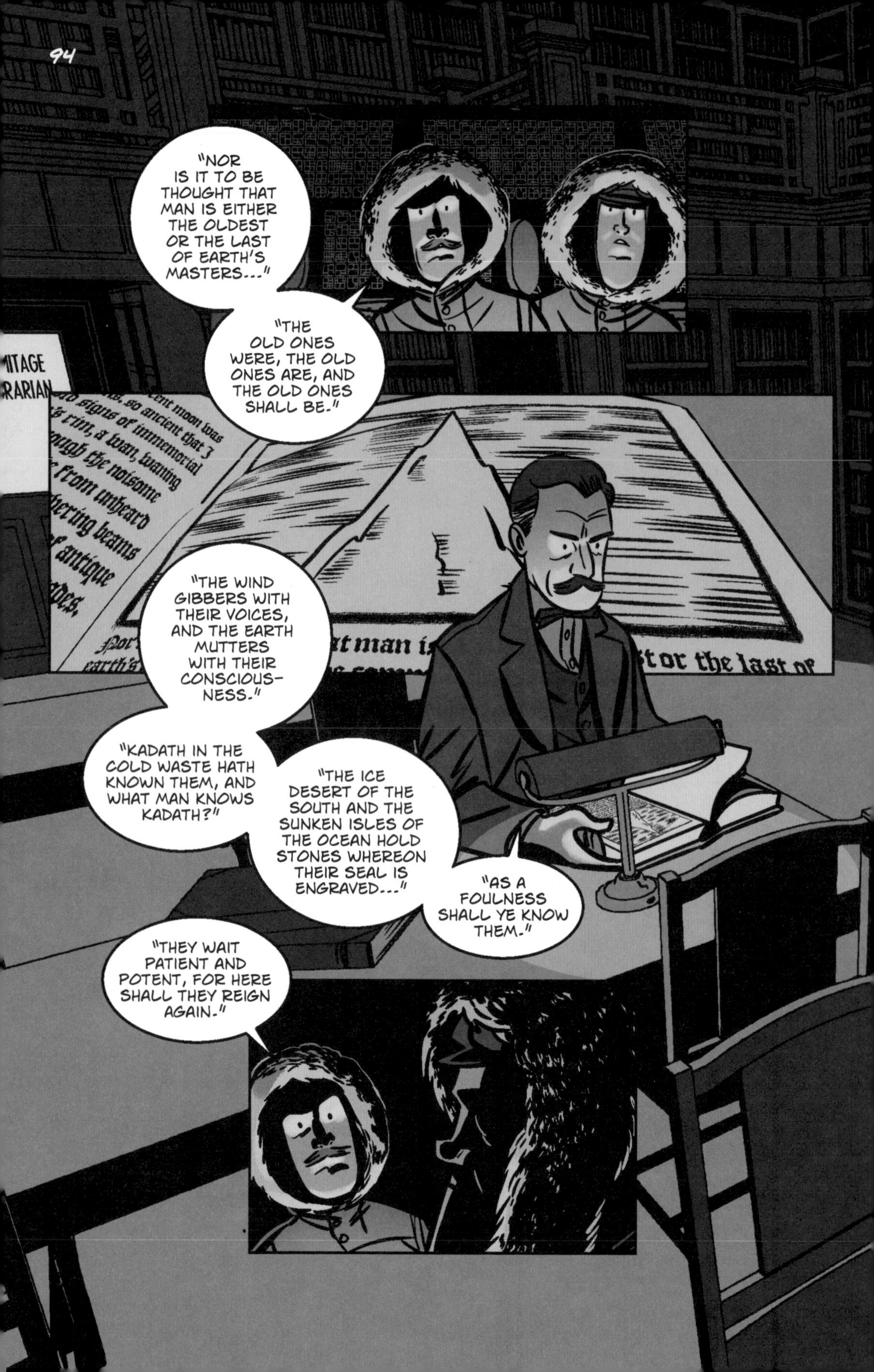
"NOR IS IT TO BE THOUGHT THAT MAN IS EITHER THE OLDEST OR THE LAST OF EARTH'S MASTERS..."
"THE OLD ONES WERE, THE OLD ONES ARE, AND THE OLD ONES SHALL BE."
"THE WIND GIBBERS WITH THEIR VOICES, AND THE EARTH MUTTERS WITH THEIR CONSCIOUS-NESS."
"KADATH IN THE COLD WASTE HATH KNOWN THEM, AND WHAT MAN KNOWS KADATH?"
"THE ICE DESERT OF THE SOUTH AND THE SUNKEN ISLES OF THE OCEAN HOLD STONES WHEREON THEIR SEAL IS ENGRAVED..."
"AS A FOULNESS SHALL YE KNOW THEM."
"THEY WAIT PATIENT AND POTENT, FOR HERE SHALL THEY REIGN AGAIN."

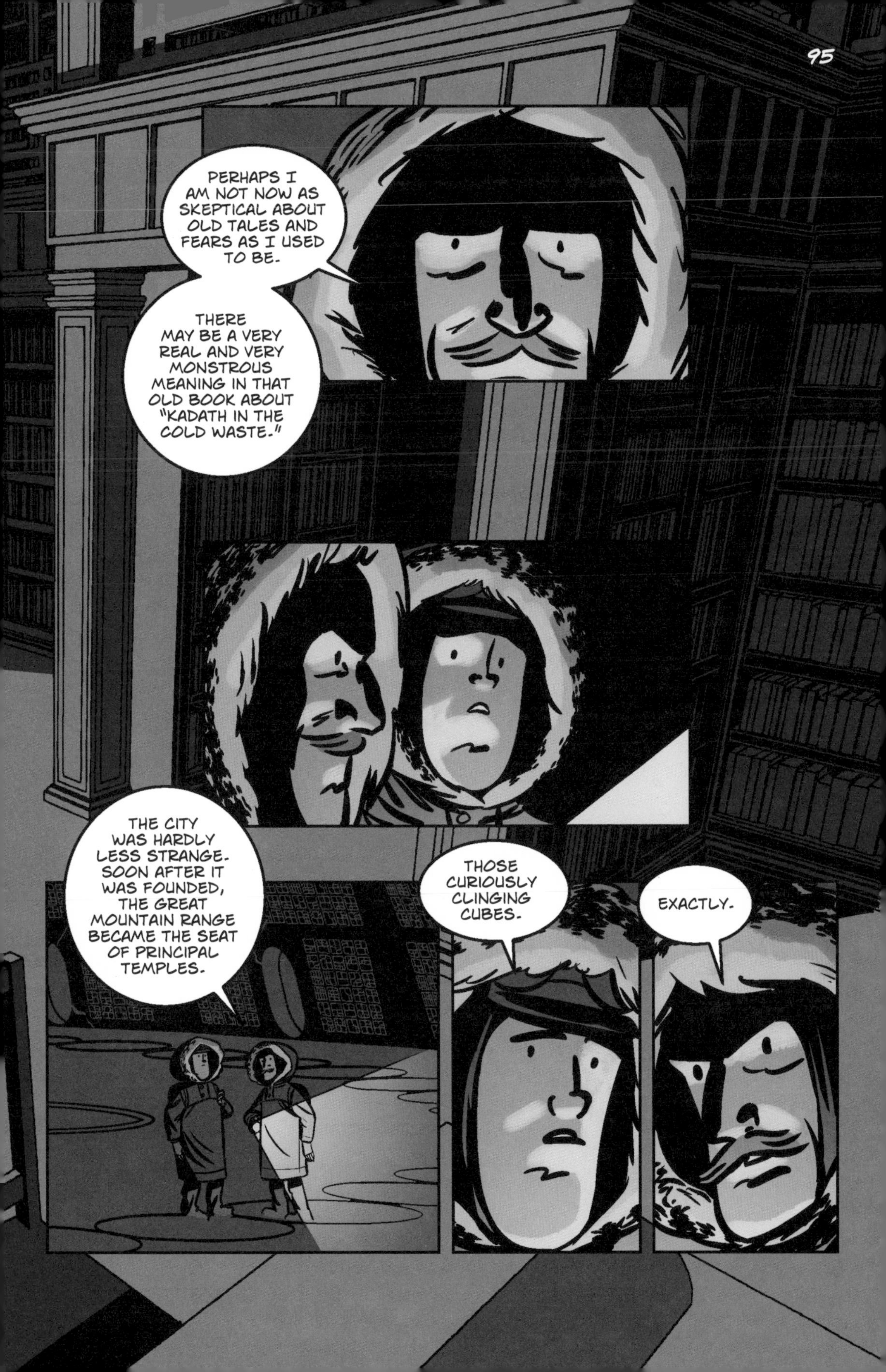
PERHAPS I AM NOT NOW AS SKEPTICAL ABOUT OLD TALES AND FEARS AS I USED TO BE.
THERE MAY BE A VERY REAL AND VERY MONSTROUS MEANING IN THAT OLD BOOK ABOUT "KADATH IN THE COLD WASTE."
THE CITY WAS HARDLY LESS STRANGE. SOON AFTER IT WAS FOUNDED, THE GREAT MOUNTAIN RANGE BECAME THE SEAT OF PRINCIPAL TEMPLES.
THOSE CURIOUSLY CLINGING CUBES.
EXACTLY.

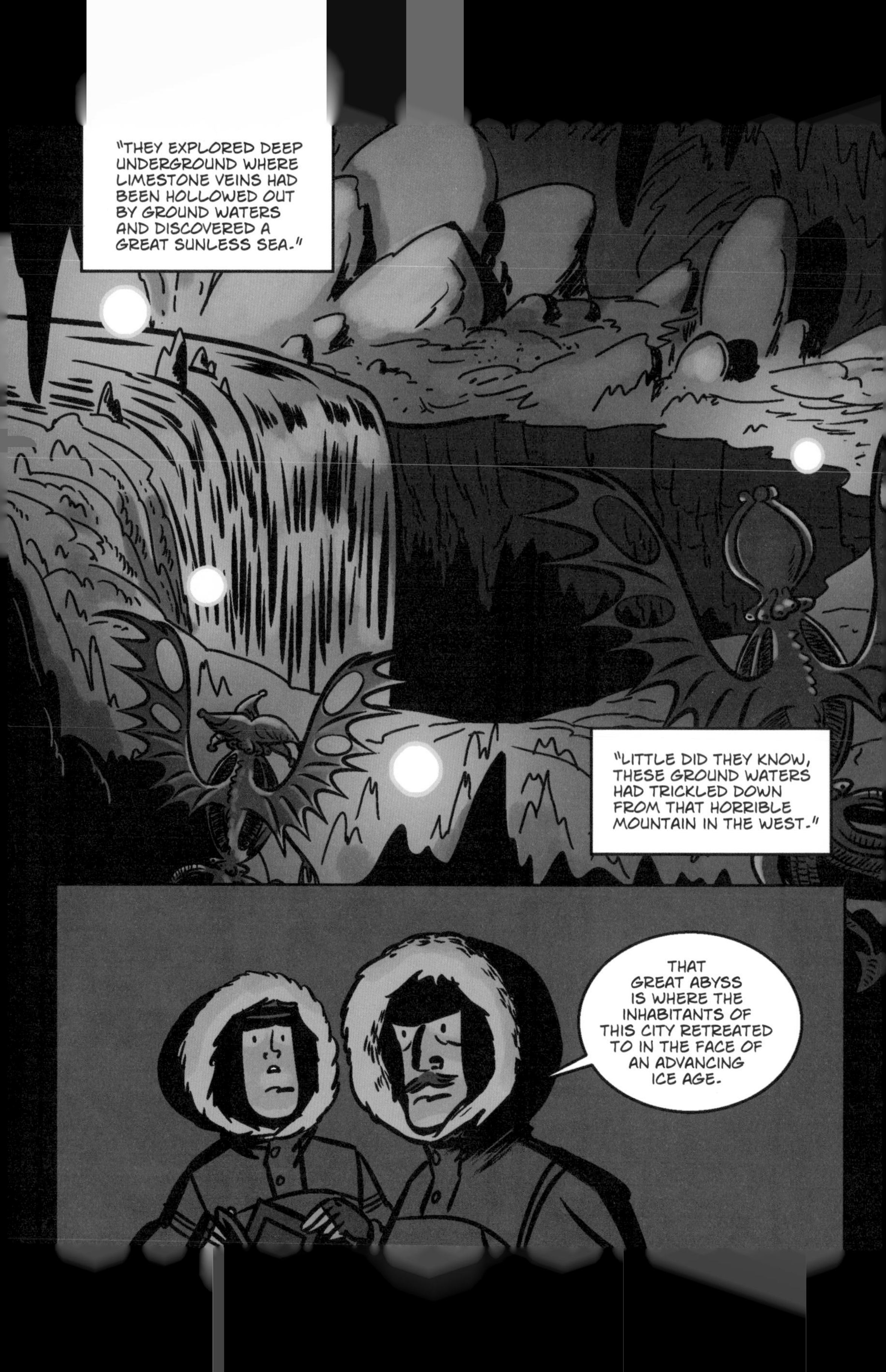
"THEY EXPLORED DEEP UNDERGROUND WHERE LIMESTONE VEINS HAD BEEN HOLLOWED OUT BY GROUND WATERS AND DISCOVERED A GREAT SUNLESS SEA."
"LITTLE DID THEY KNOW, THESE GROUND WATERS HAD TRICKLED DOWN FROM THAT HORRIBLE MOUNTAIN IN THE WEST."
THAT GREAT ABYSS IS WHERE THE INHABITANTS OF THIS CITY RETREATED TO IN THE FACE OF AN ADVANCING ICE AGE.

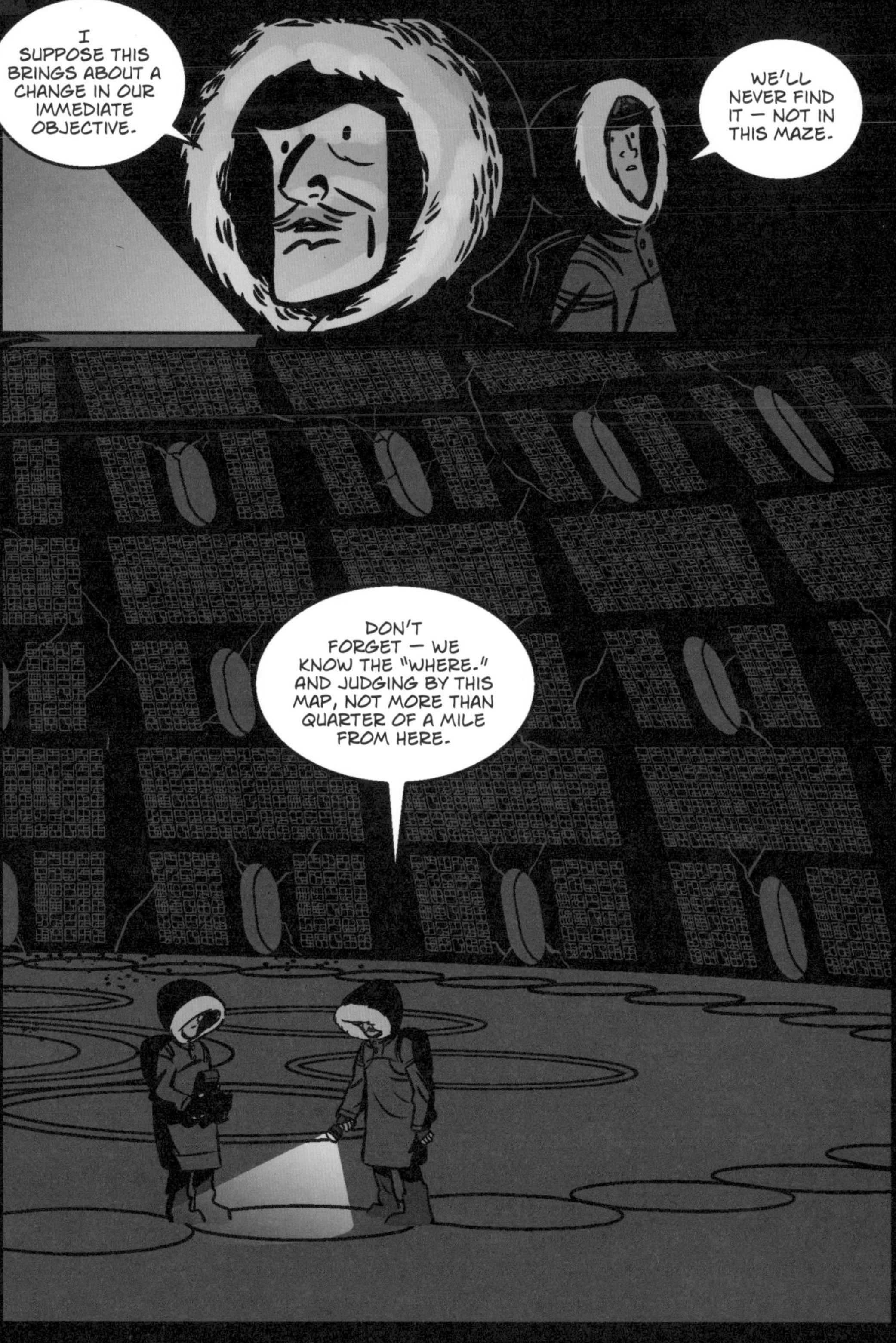
I SUPPOSE THIS BRINGS ABOUT A CHANGE IN OUR IMMEDIATE OBJECTIVE.
WE'LL NEVER FIND IT — NOT IN THIS MAZE.
DON'T FORGET — WE KNOW THE "WHERE." AND JUDGING BY THIS MAP, NOT MORE THAN QUARTER OF A MILE FROM HERE.

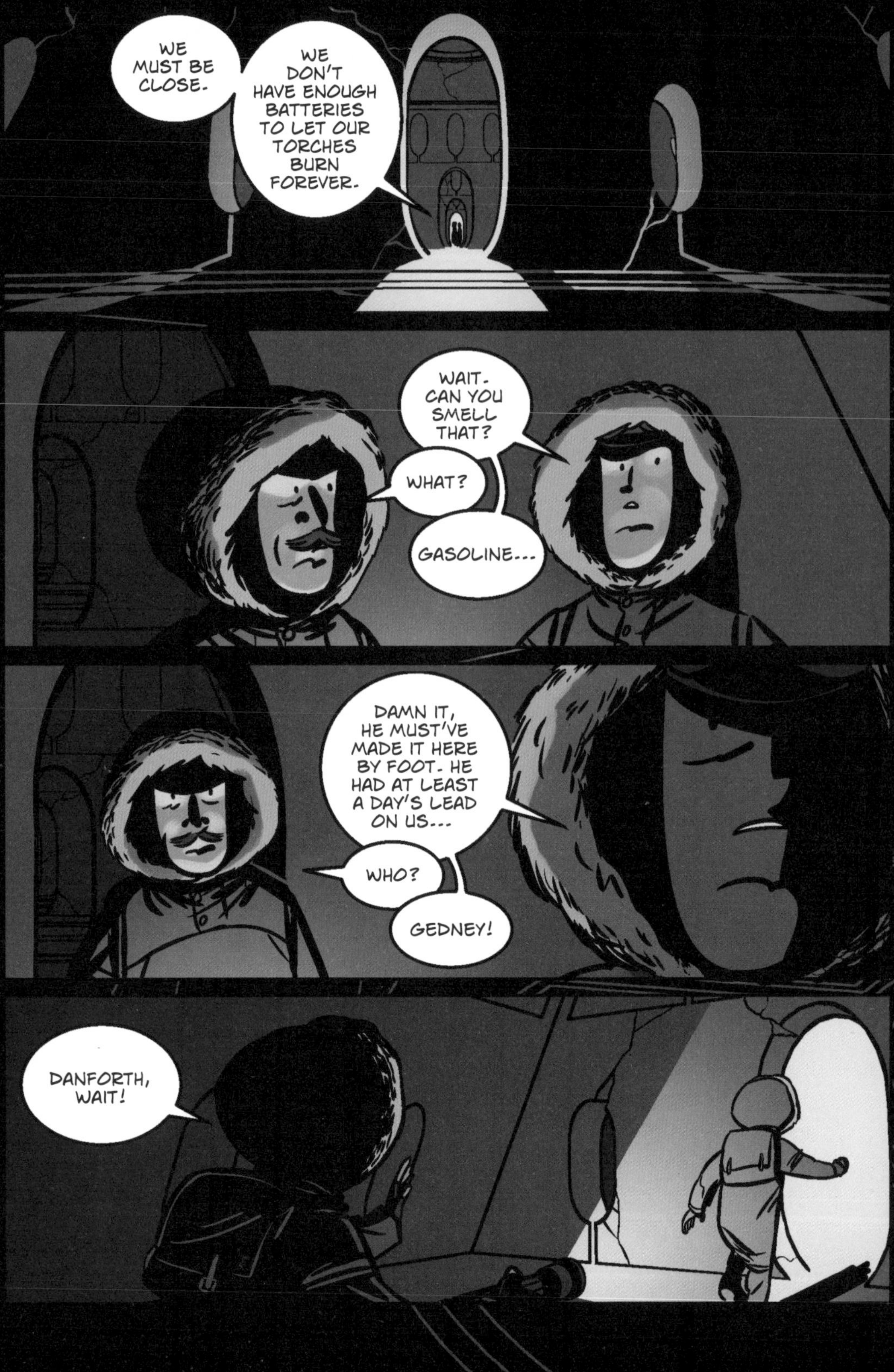
WE MUST BE CLOSE.
WE DON'T HAVE ENOUGH BATTERIES TO LET OUR TORCHES BURN FOREVER.
WAIT. CAN YOU SMELL THAT?
WHAT?
GASOLINE...
DAMN IT, HE MUST'VE MADE IT HERE BY FOOT. HE HAD AT LEAST A DAY'S LEAD ON US...
WHO?
GEDNEY!
DANFORTH, WAIT!

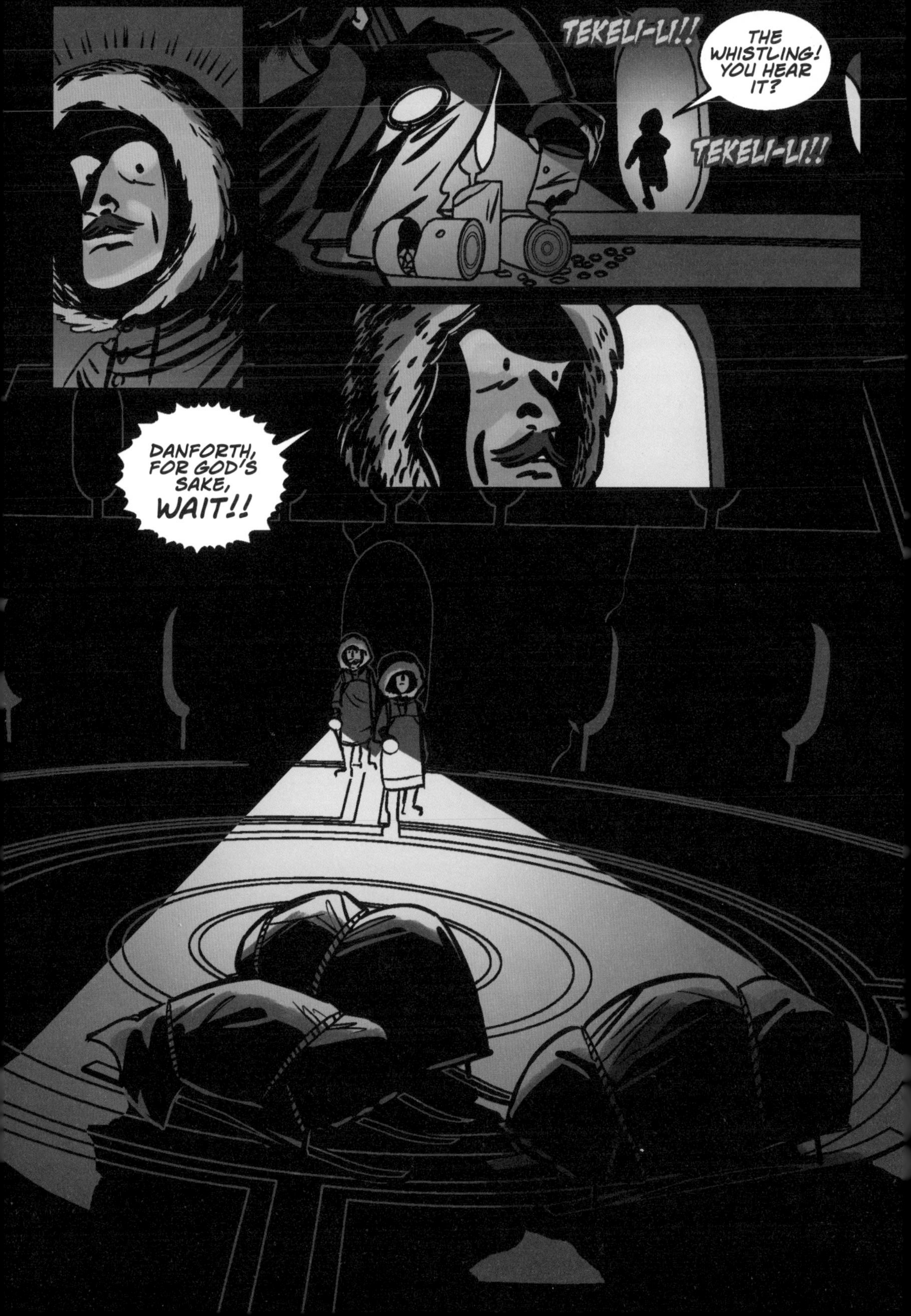
TEKELI-LI!!
THE WHISTLING! YOU HEAR IT?
TEKELI-LI!!
DANFORTH, FOR GOD'S SAKE, WAIT!!

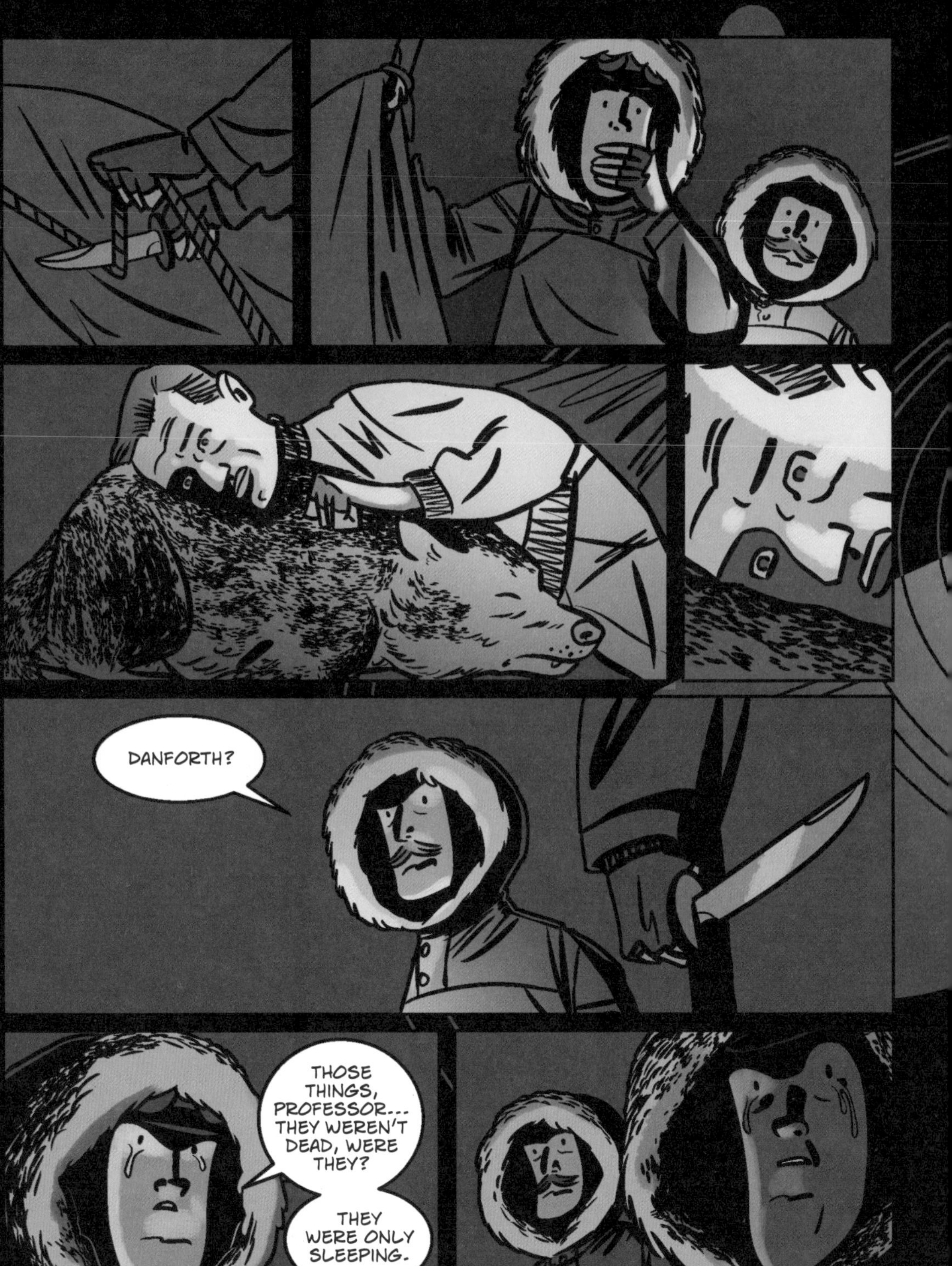
DANFORTH?
THOSE THINGS, PROFESSOR... THEY WEREN'T DEAD, WERE THEY?
THEY WERE ONLY SLEEPING.
WUK WUK WUK

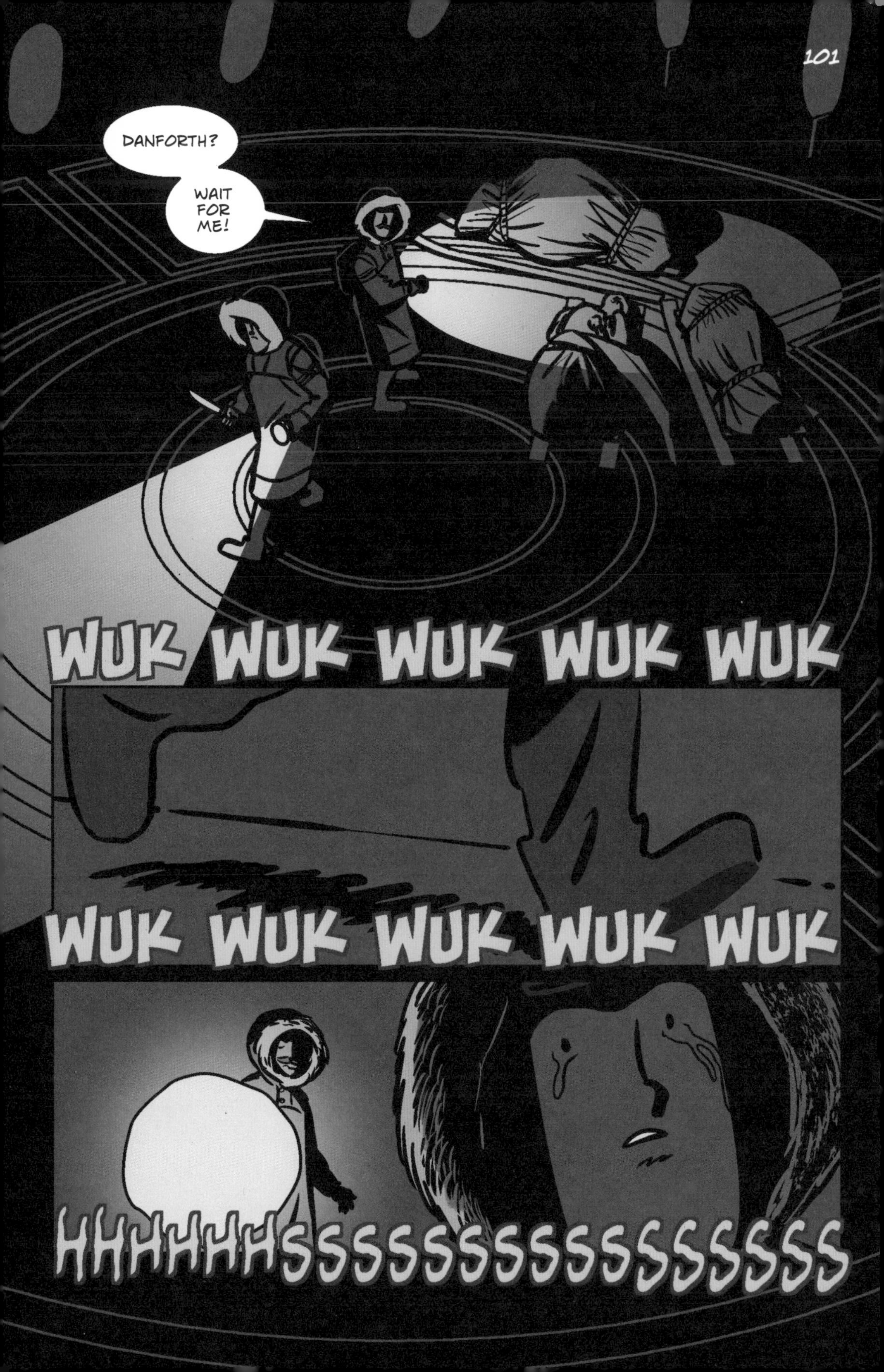
DANFORTH?
WAIT FOR ME!
WUK WUK WUK WUK WUK
WUK WUK WUK WUK WUK
HHHHHHSSSSSSSSSSSSSSSSSS

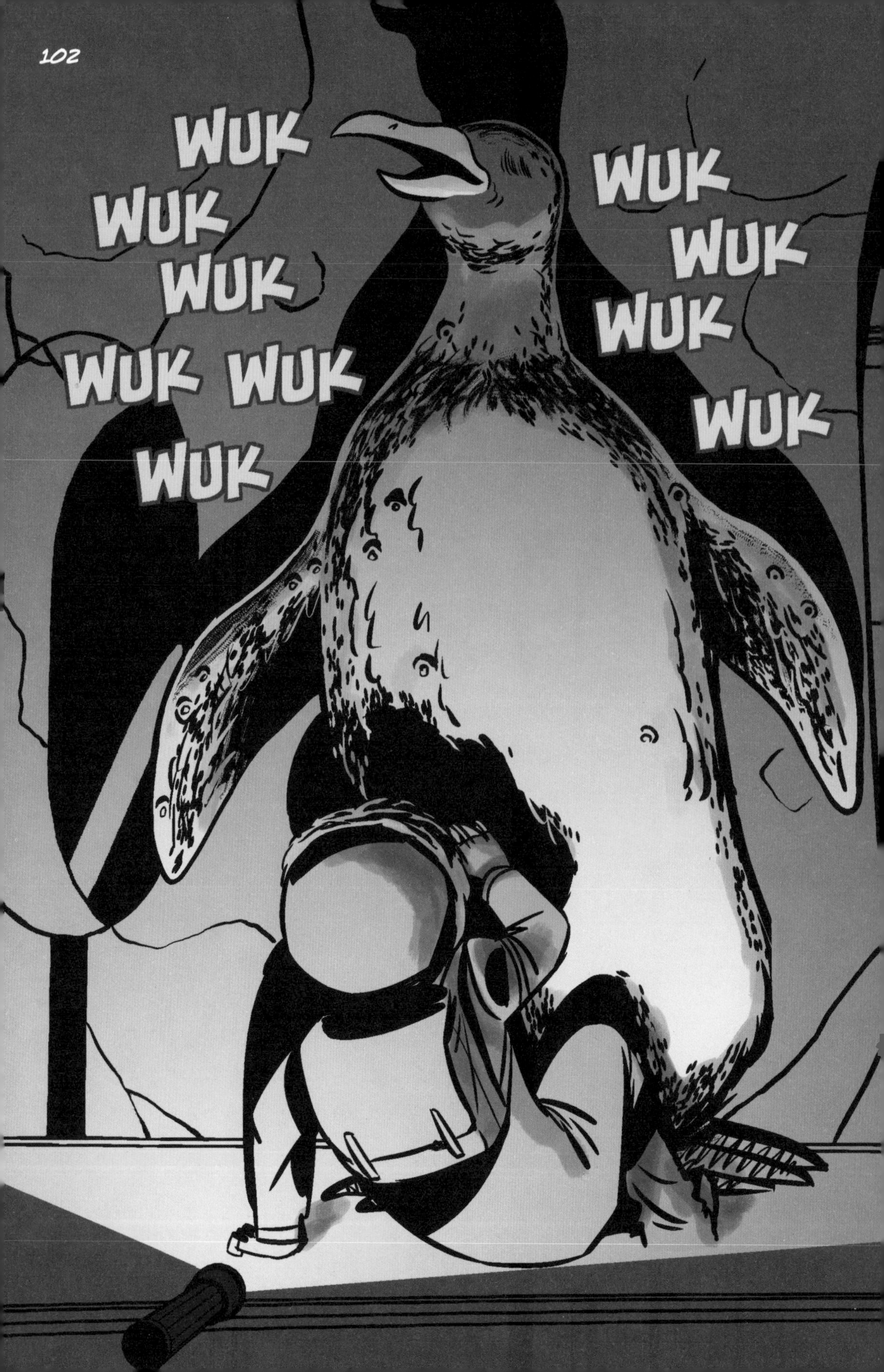
WUK
WUK
WUK
WUK WUK
WUK
WUK
WUK
WUK
WUK

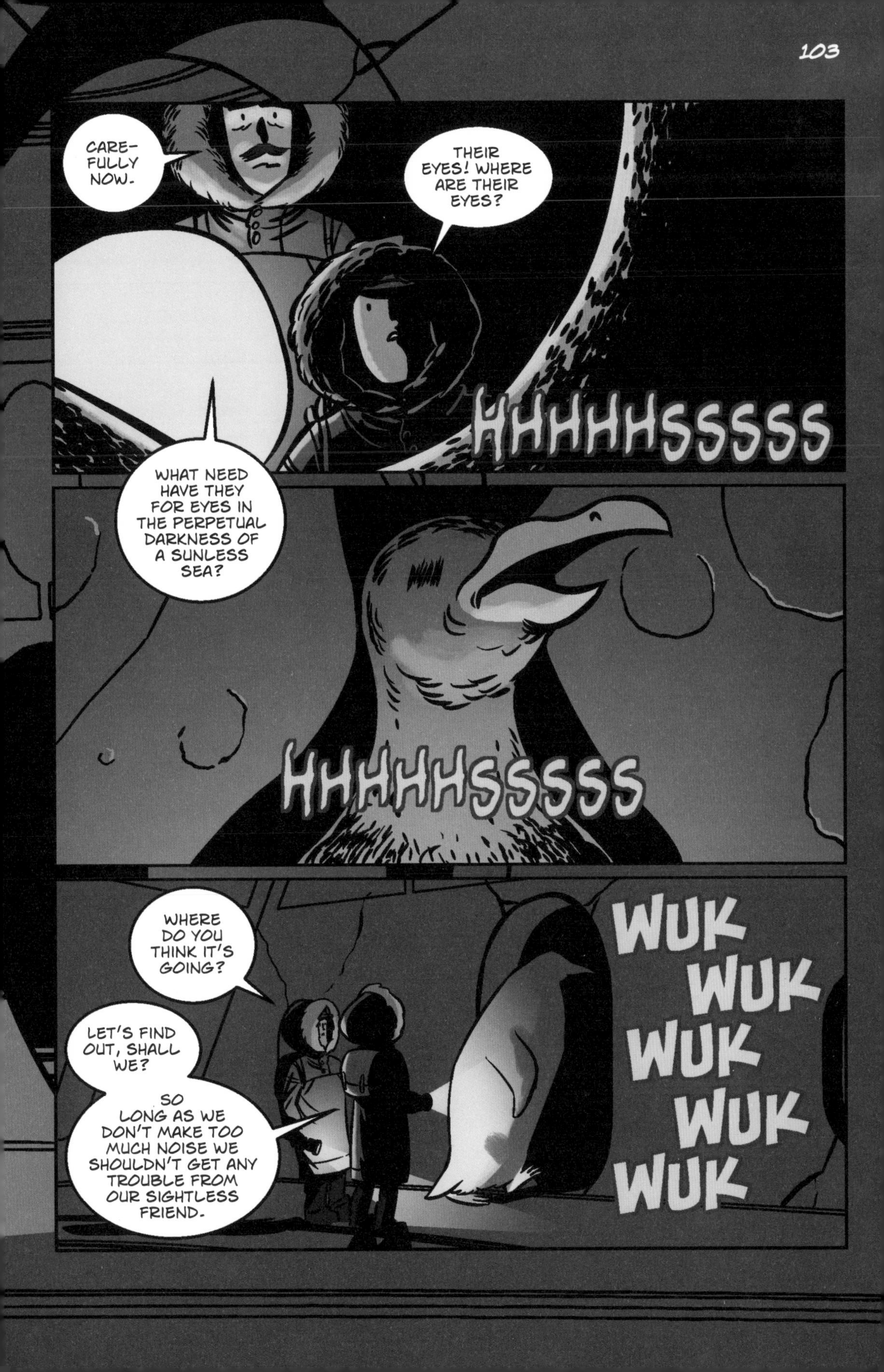
CARE-FULLY NOW.
THEIR EYES! WHERE ARE THEIR EYES?
HHHHHSSSSS
WHAT NEED HAVE THEY FOR EYES IN THE PERPETUAL DARKNESS OF A SUNLESS SEA?
HHHHHSSSSS
WHERE DO YOU THINK IT'S GOING?
LET'S FIND OUT, SHALL WE?
SO LONG AS WE DON'T MAKE TOO MUCH NOISE WE SHOULDN'T GET ANY TROUBLE FROM OUR SIGHTLESS FRIEND.
WUK WUK WUK WUK WUK

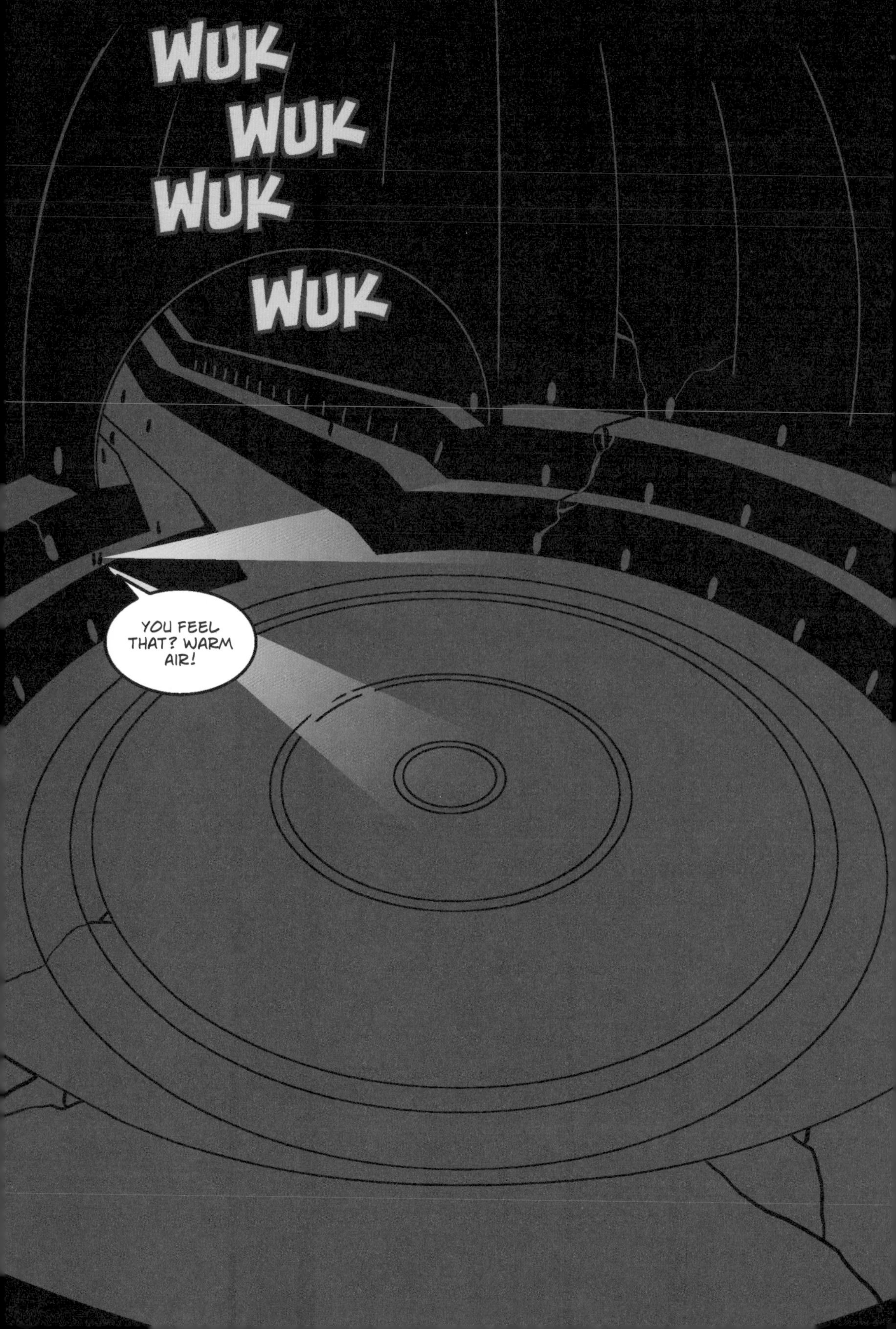
WUK
WUK
WUK
WUK
YOU FEEL THAT? WARM AIR!

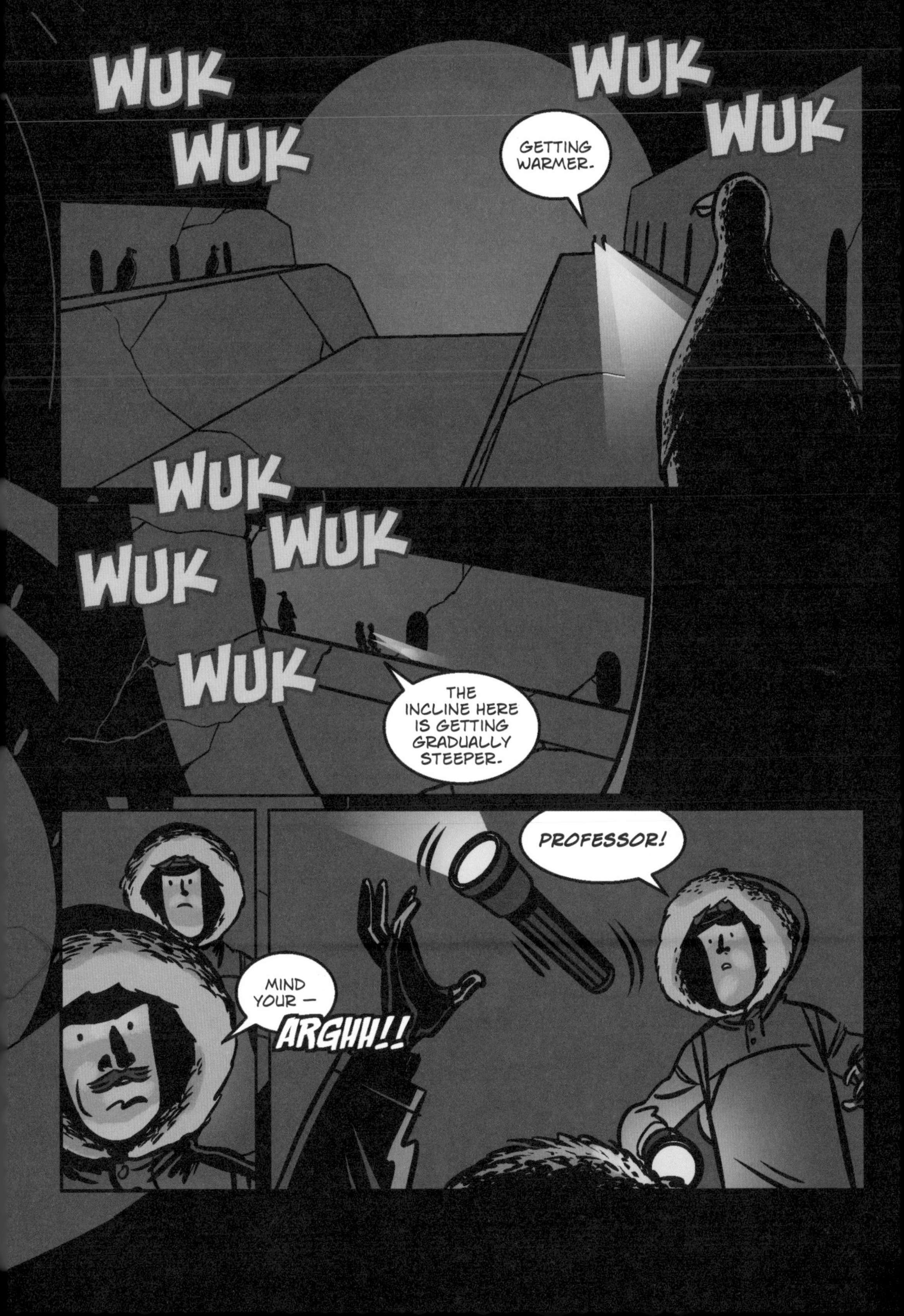
WUK
WUK
WUK
WUK
GETTING WARMER.
WUK
WUK
WUK
WUK
THE INCLINE HERE IS GETTING GRADUALLY STEEPER.
MIND YOUR —
ARGHH!!
PROFESSOR!

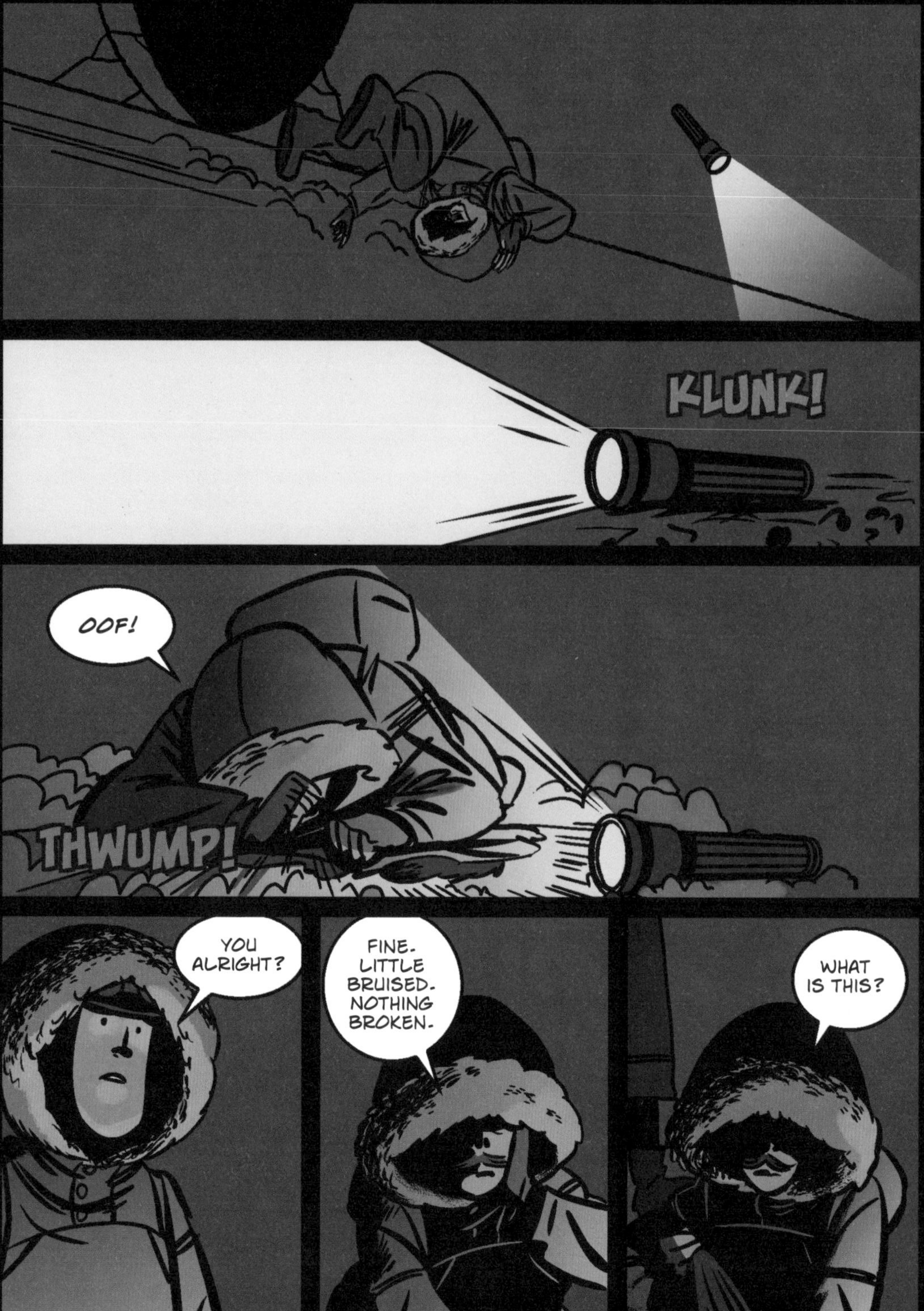
KLUNK!
OOF!
THWUMP!
YOU ALRIGHT?
FINE. LITTLE BRUISED. NOTHING BROKEN.
WHAT IS THIS?

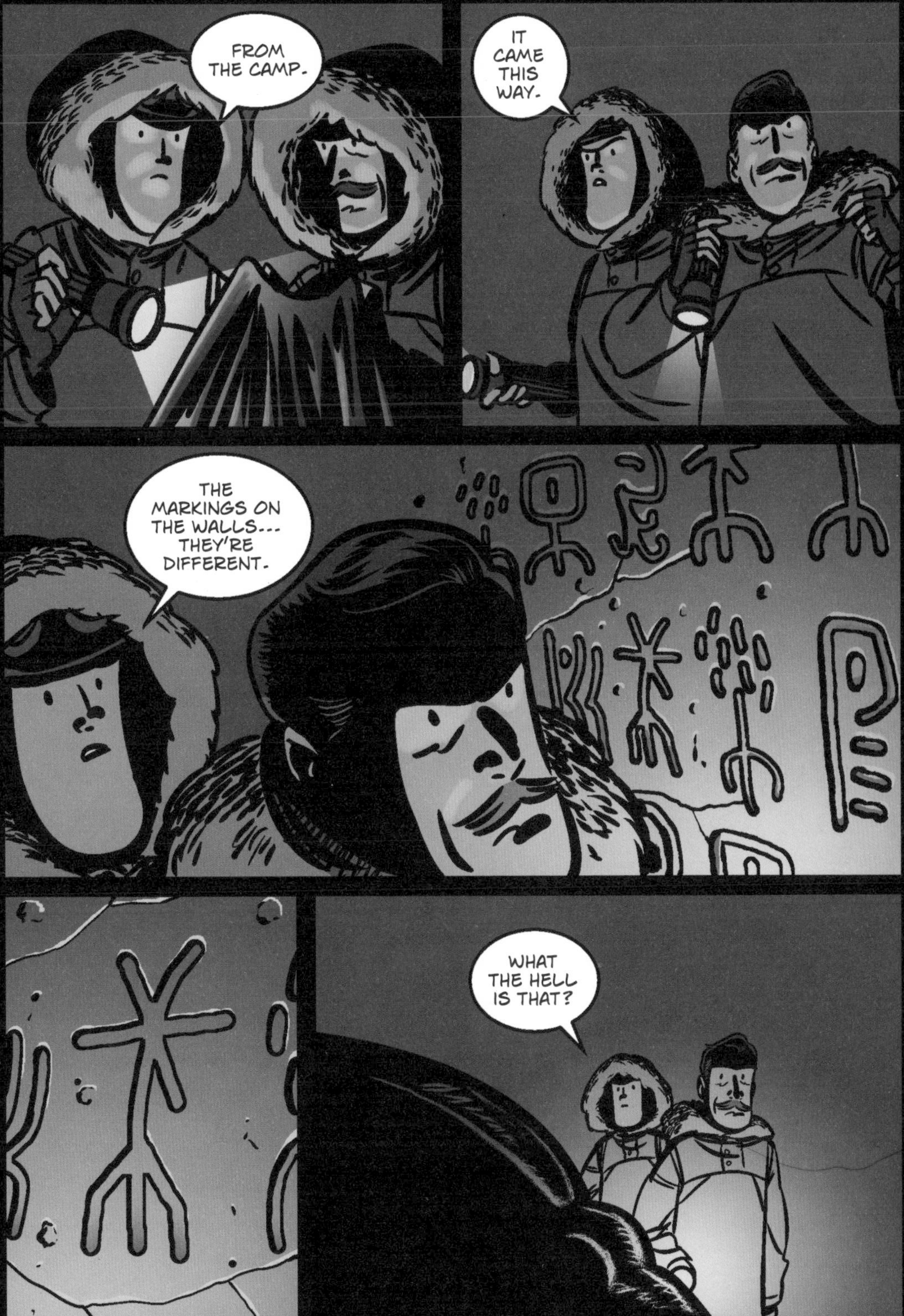
FROM THE CAMP.
IT CAME THIS WAY.
THE MARKINGS ON THE WALLS... THEY'RE DIFFERENT.
WHAT THE HELL IS THAT?

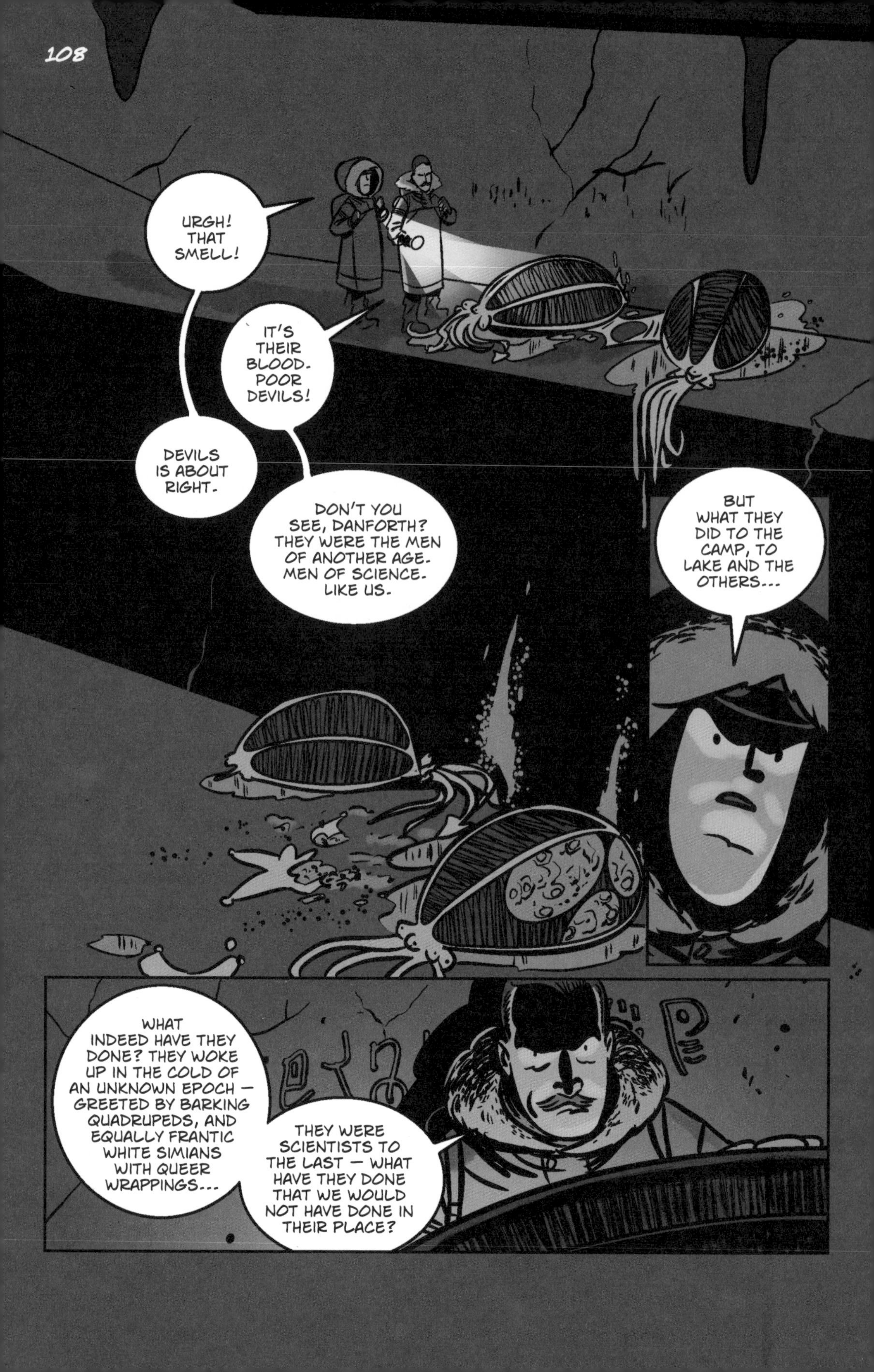
URGH! THAT SMELL!
IT'S THEIR BLOOD. POOR DEVILS!
DEVILS IS ABOUT RIGHT.
DON'T YOU SEE, DANFORTH? THEY WERE THE MEN OF ANOTHER AGE. MEN OF SCIENCE. LIKE US.
BUT WHAT THEY DID TO THE CAMP, TO LAKE AND THE OTHERS...
WHAT INDEED HAVE THEY DONE? THEY WOKE UP IN THE COLD OF AN UNKNOWN EPOCH — GREETED BY BARKING QUADRUPEDS, AND EQUALLY FRANTIC WHITE SIMIANS WITH QUEER WRAPPINGS...
THEY WERE SCIENTISTS TO THE LAST — WHAT HAVE THEY DONE THAT WE WOULD NOT HAVE DONE IN THEIR PLACE?

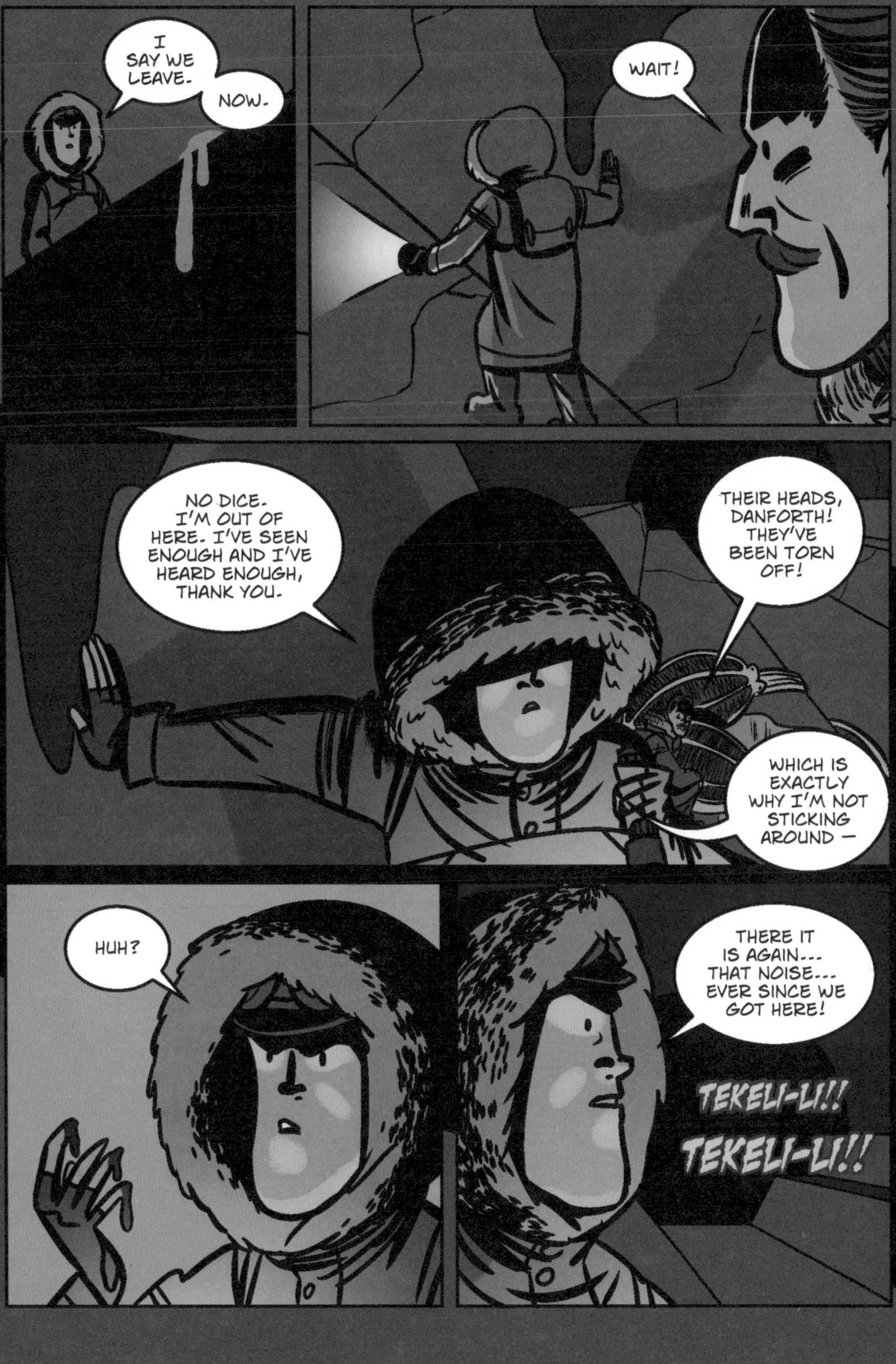
I SAY WE LEAVE.
NOW.
WAIT!
NO DICE. I'M OUT OF HERE. I'VE SEEN ENOUGH AND I'VE HEARD ENOUGH, THANK YOU.
THEIR HEADS, DANFORTH! THEY'VE BEEN TORN OFF!
WHICH IS EXACTLY WHY I'M NOT STICKING AROUND —
HUH?
THERE IT IS AGAIN... THAT NOISE... EVER SINCE WE GOT HERE!
TEKELI-LI!!
TEKELI-LI!!

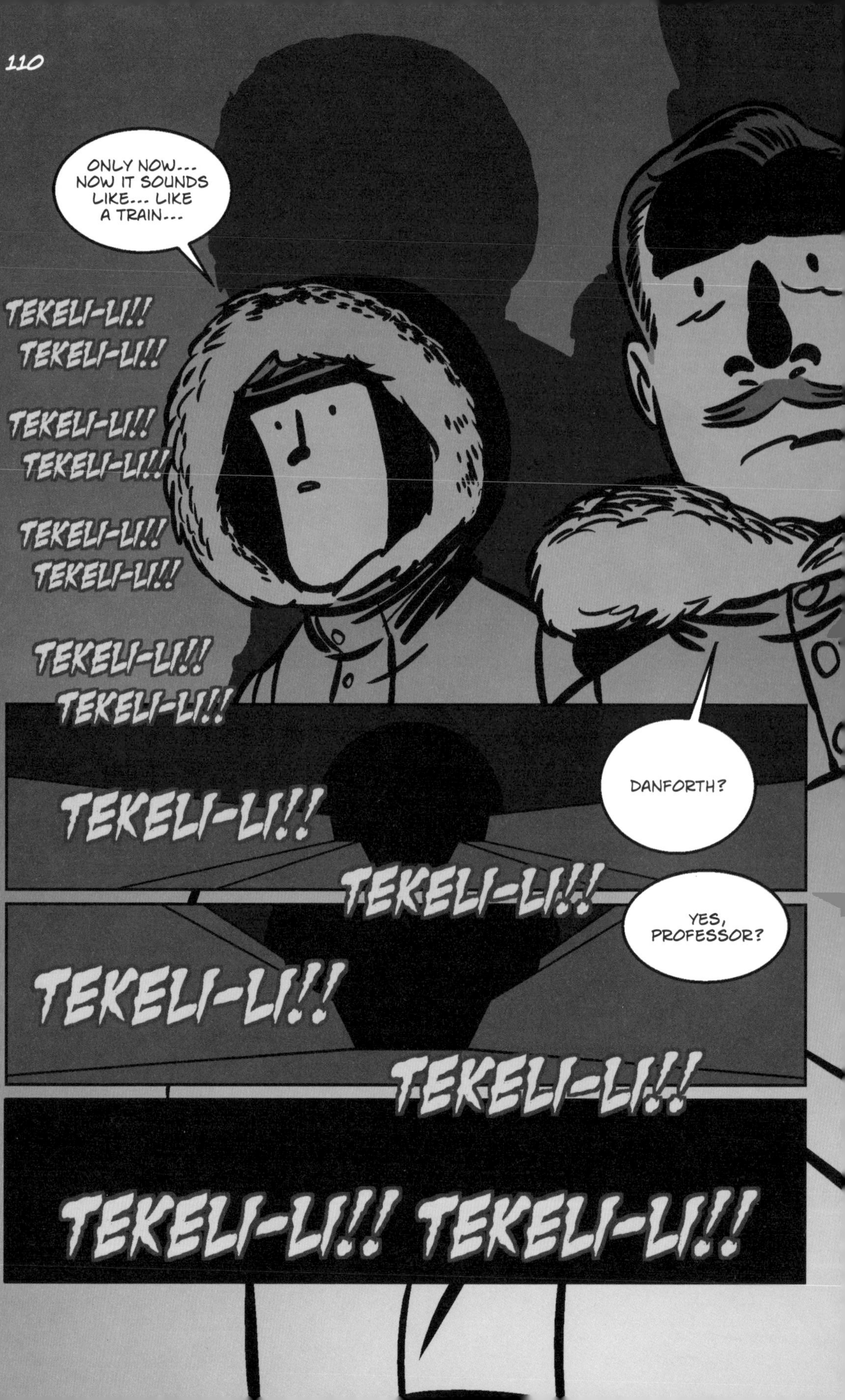
ONLY NOW... NOW IT SOUNDS LIKE... LIKE A TRAIN...
TEKELI-LI!! TEKELI-LI!!
TEKELI-LI!! TEKELI-LI!!
TEKELI-LI!! TEKELI-LI!!
TEKELI-LI!! TEKELI-LI!!
TEKELI-LI!!
DANFORTH?
TEKELI-LI!!
YES, PROFESSOR?
TEKELI-LI!!
TEKELI-LI!!
TEKELI-LI!! TEKELI-LI!!

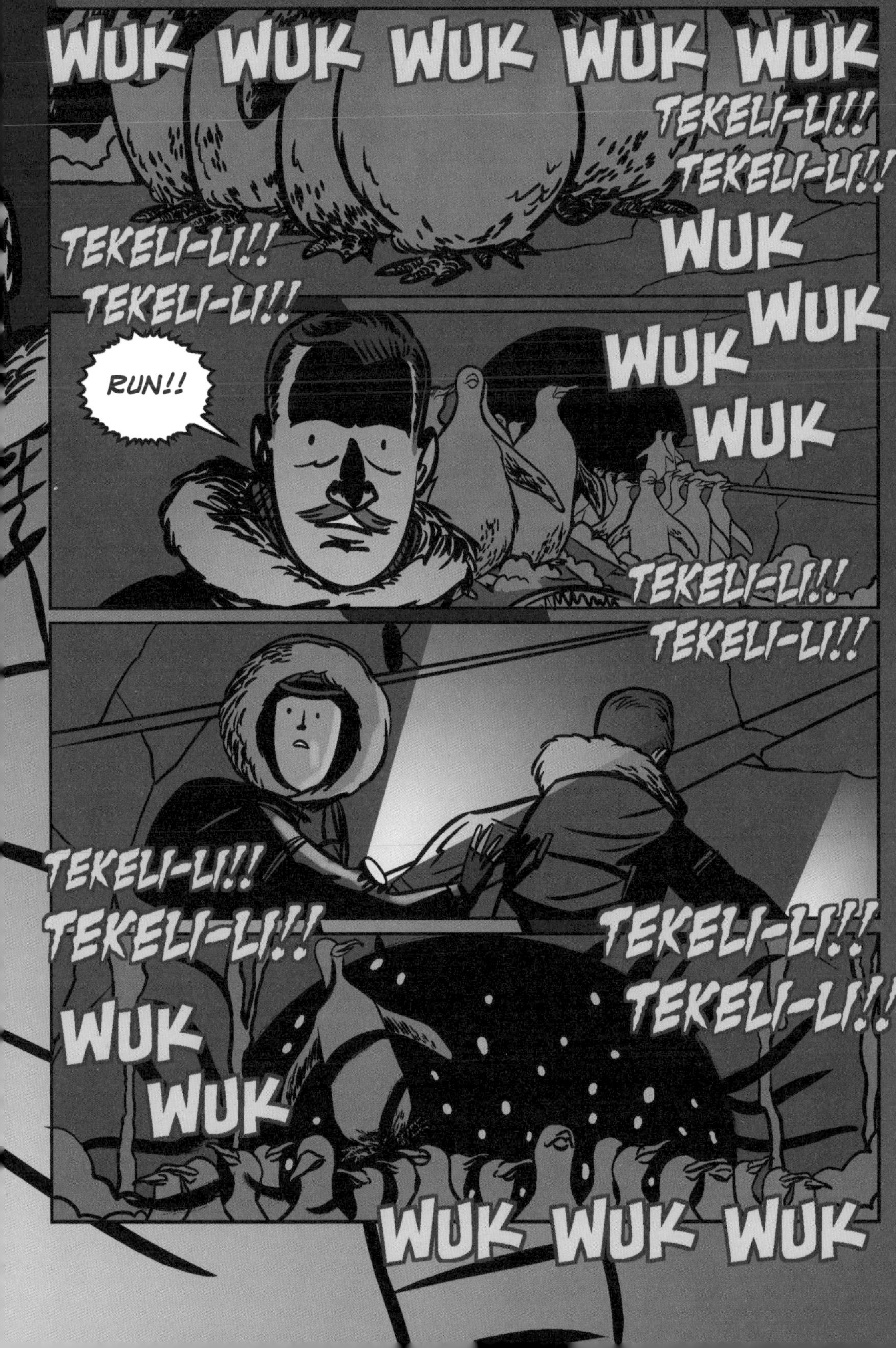
WUK WUK WUK WUK WUK
TEKELI-LI!!
TEKELI-LI!!
WUK
TEKELI-LI!!
TEKELI-LI!!
WUK
WUK
WUK
RUN!!
TEKELI-LI!!
TEKELI-LI!!
TEKELI-LI!!
TEKELI-LI!!
TEKELI-LI!!
TEKELI-LI!!
WUK
WUK
WUK WUK WUK

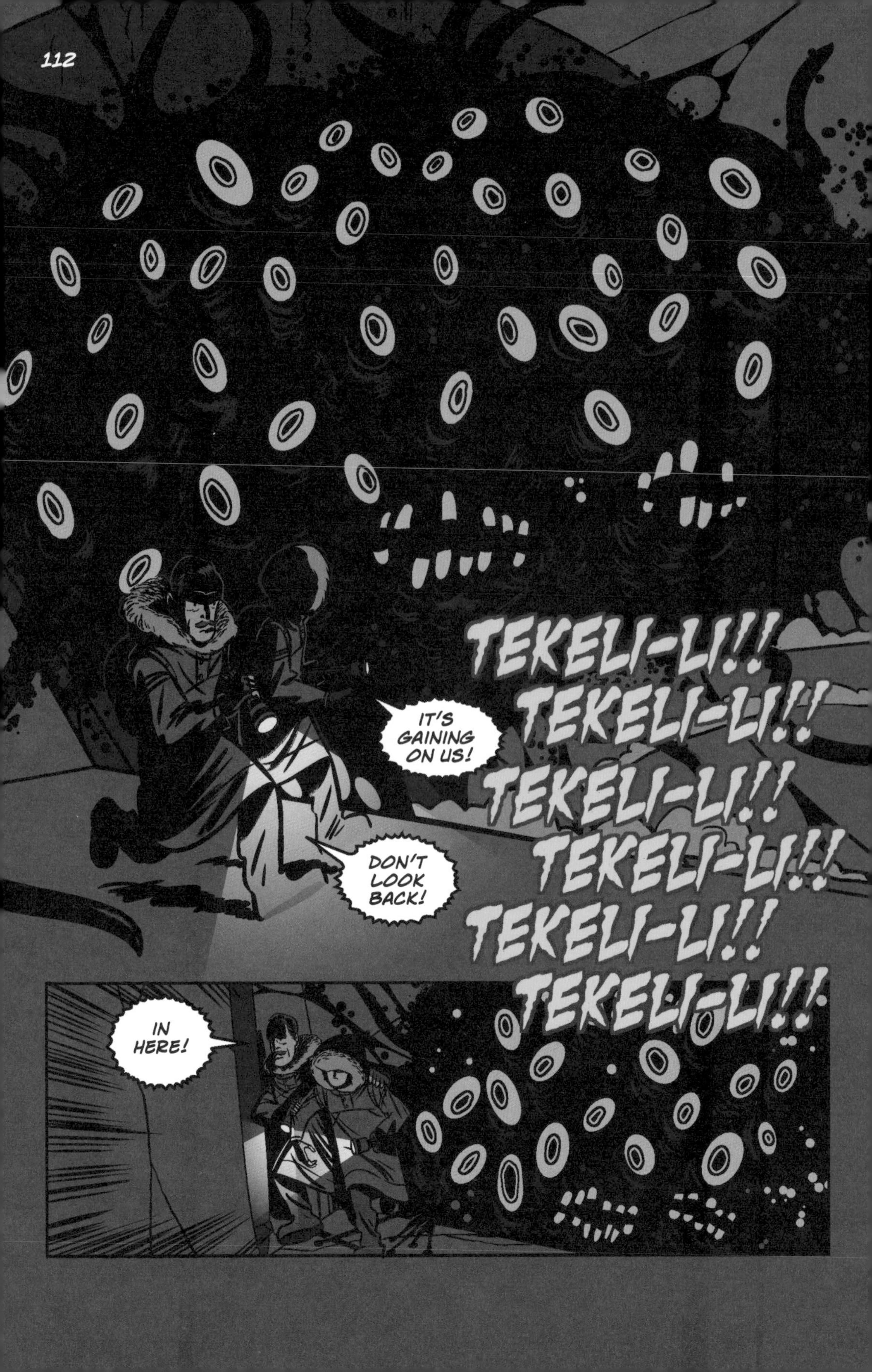
IT'S GAINING ON US!
DON'T LOOK BACK!
TEKELI-LI!! TEKELI-LI!! TEKELI-LI!! TEKELI-LI!! TEKELI-LI!! TEKELI-LI!!
IN HERE!

SOUTH STATION UNDER...
TEKELI-LI!! TEKELI-LI!!
WASHINGTON UNDER... PARK STREET UNDER KENDALL...
TEKELI-LI!! TEKELI-LI!!
CENTRAL... HARVARD...
DEAR GOD!
TEKELI-LI!! TEKELI-LI!!

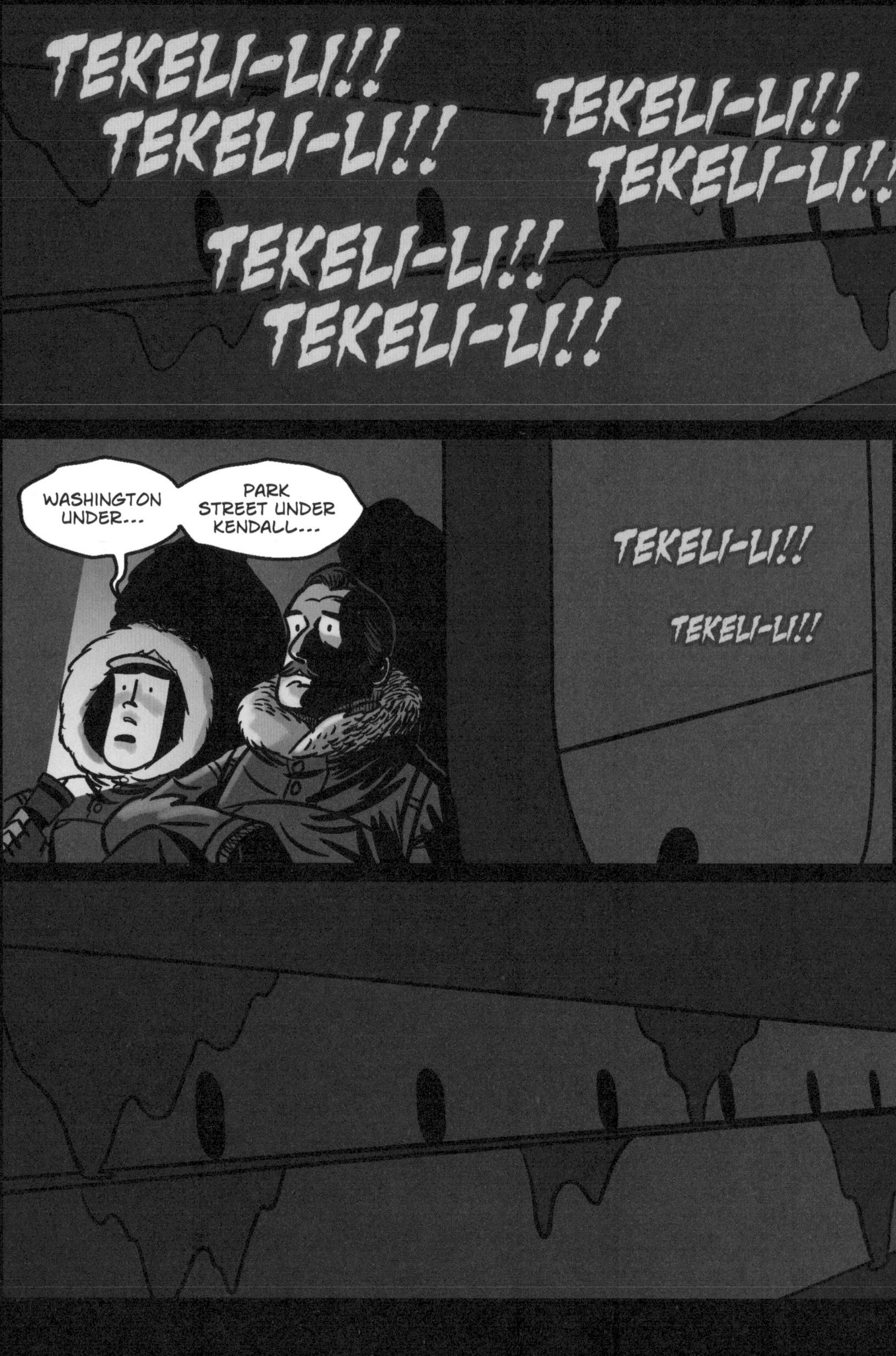
TEKELI-LI!!
TEKELI-LI!!
TEKELI-LI!!
TEKELI-LI!!
TEKELI-LI!!
TEKELI-LI!!
WASHINGTON UNDER...
PARK STREET UNDER KENDALL...
TEKELI-LI!!
TEKELI-LI!!

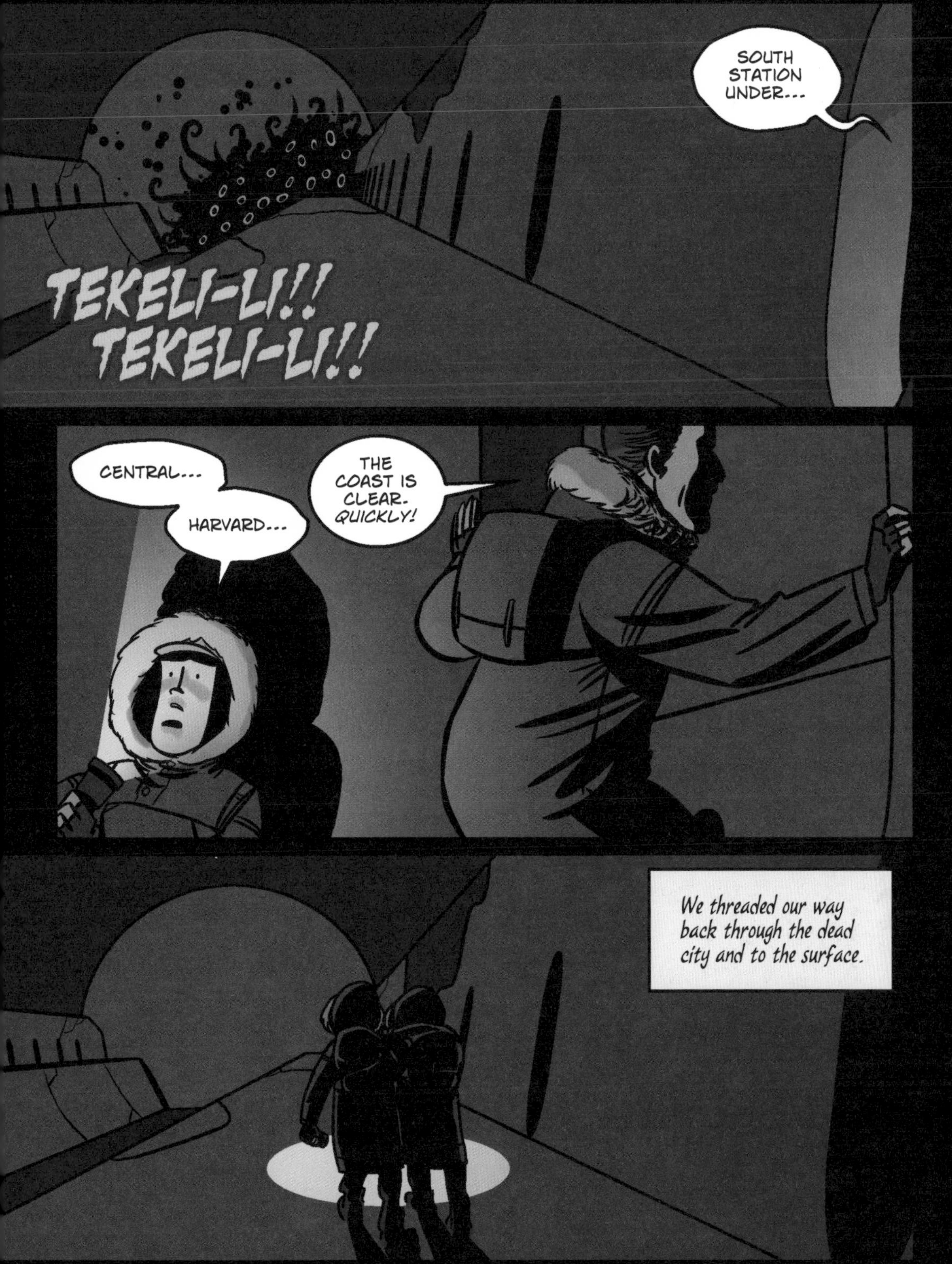
SOUTH STATION UNDER...
TEKELI-LI!! TEKELI-LI!!
CENTRAL...
HARVARD...
THE COAST IS CLEAR. QUICKLY!
We threaded our way back through the dead city and to the surface.

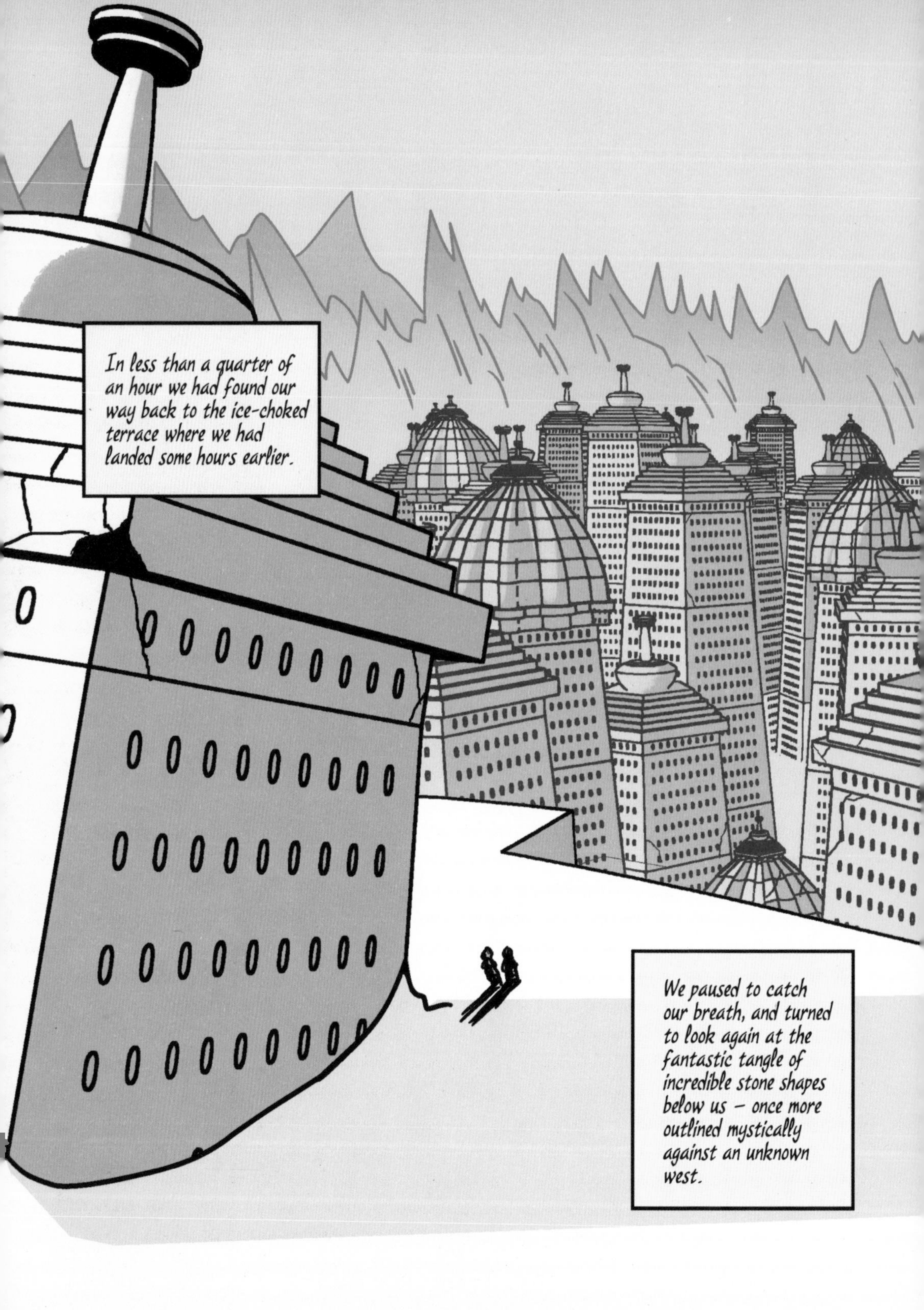
In less than a quarter of an hour we had found our way back to the ice-choked terrace where we had landed some hours earlier.
We paused to catch our breath, and turned to look again at the fantastic tangle of incredible stone shapes below us – once more outlined mystically against an unknown west.

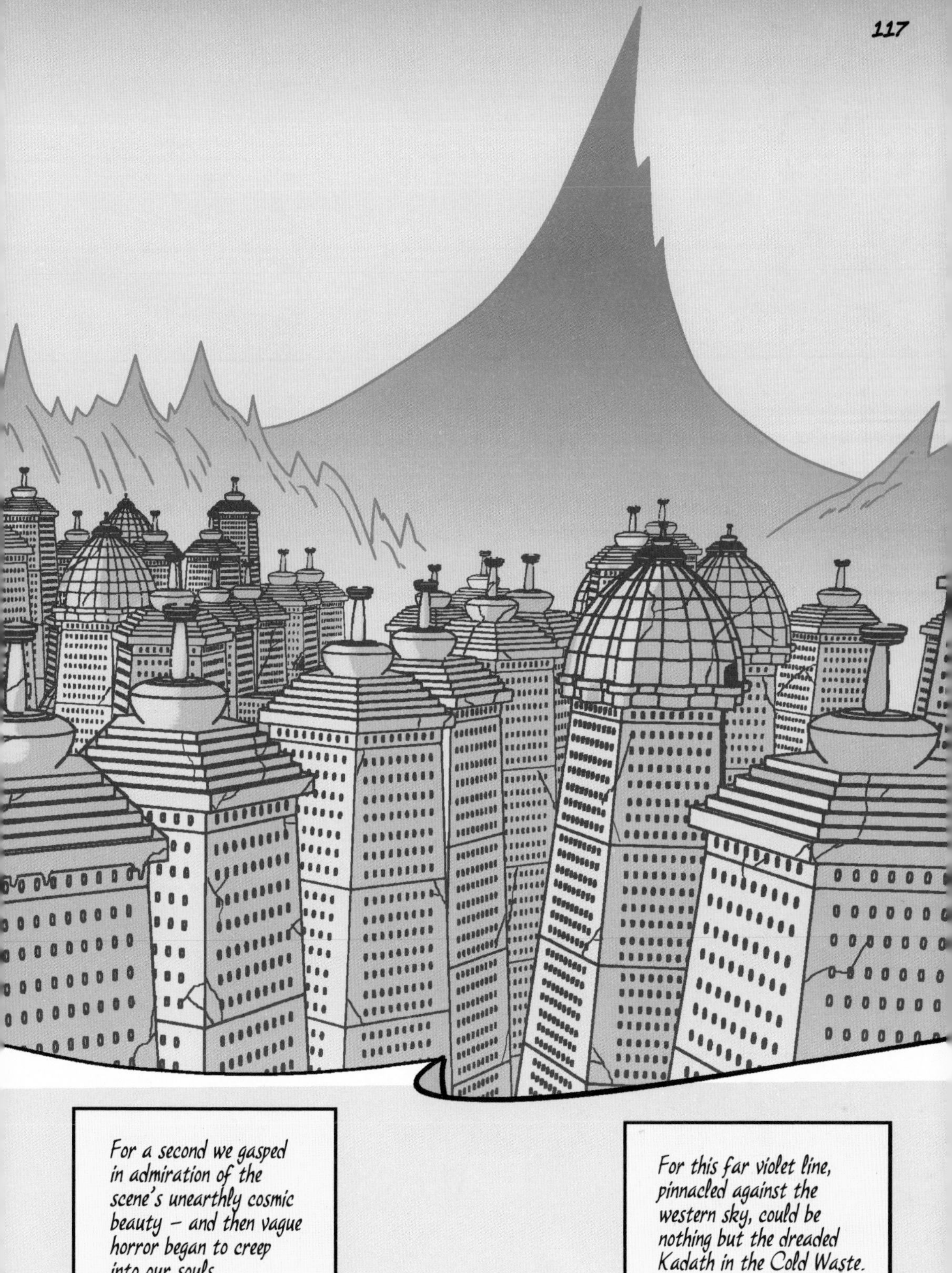
For a second we gasped in admiration of the scene's unearthly cosmic beauty – and then vague horror began to creep into our souls...
For this far violet line, pinnacled against the western sky, could be nothing but the dreaded Kadath in the Cold Waste.

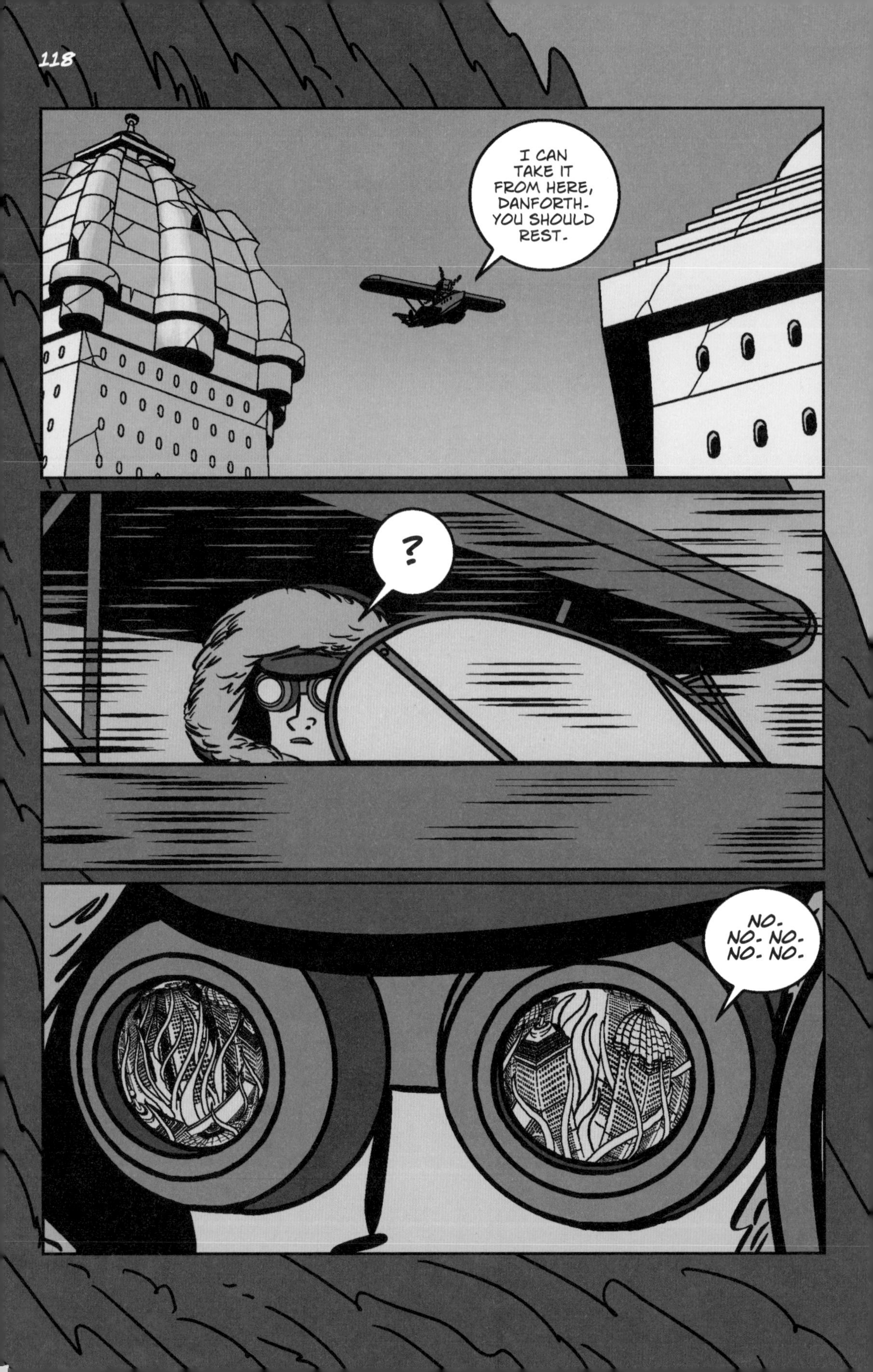
I CAN TAKE IT FROM HERE, DANFORTH. YOU SHOULD REST.
?
NO. NO. NO. NO. NO.

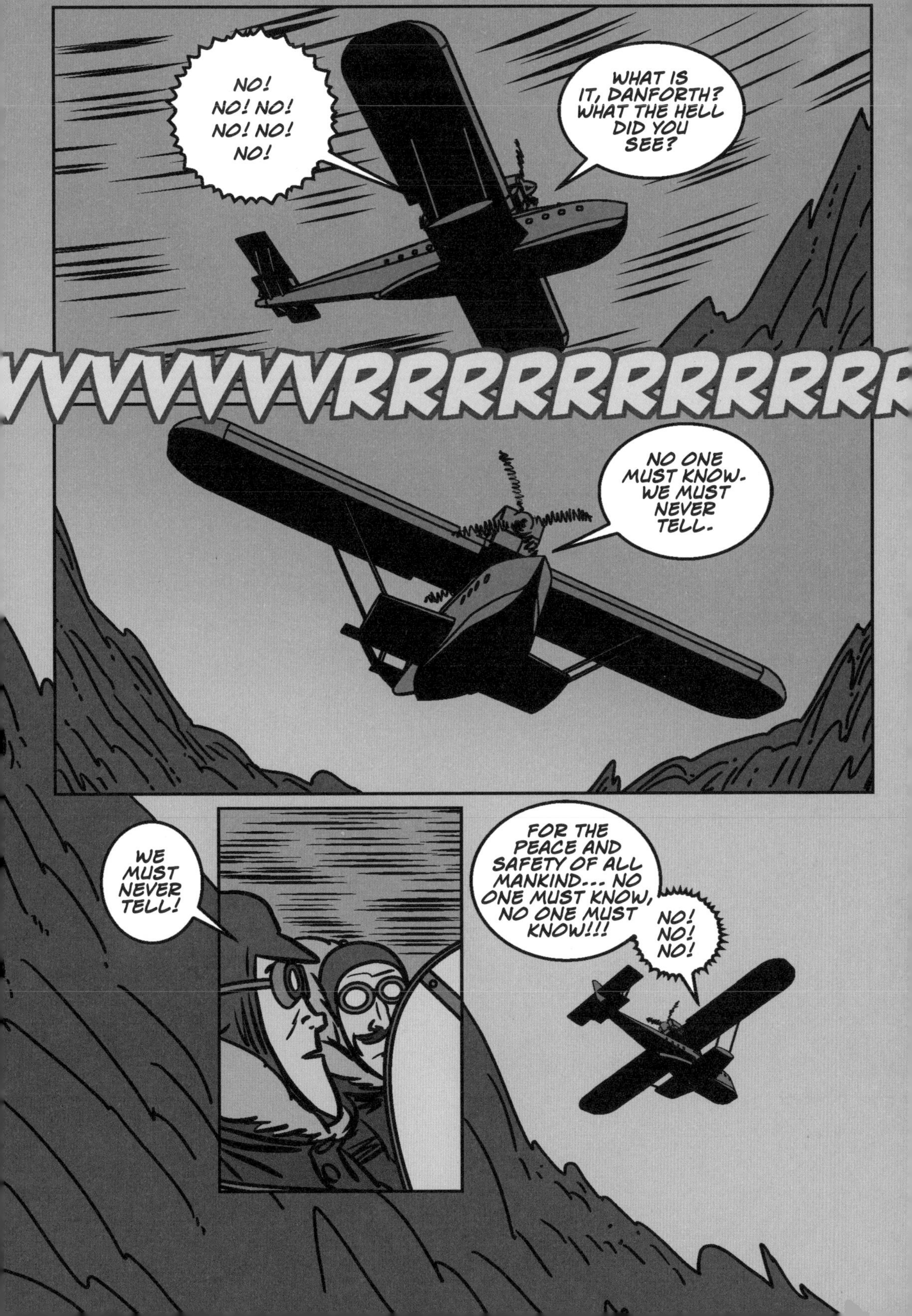
NO! NO! NO! NO! NO! NO!
WHAT IS IT, DANFORTH? WHAT THE HELL DID YOU SEE?
VVVVVVVVRRRRRRRRRRRR
NO ONE MUST KNOW. WE MUST NEVER TELL.
WE MUST NEVER TELL!
FOR THE PEACE AND SAFETY OF ALL MANKIND... NO ONE MUST KNOW, NO ONE MUST KNOW!!!
NO! NO! NO!

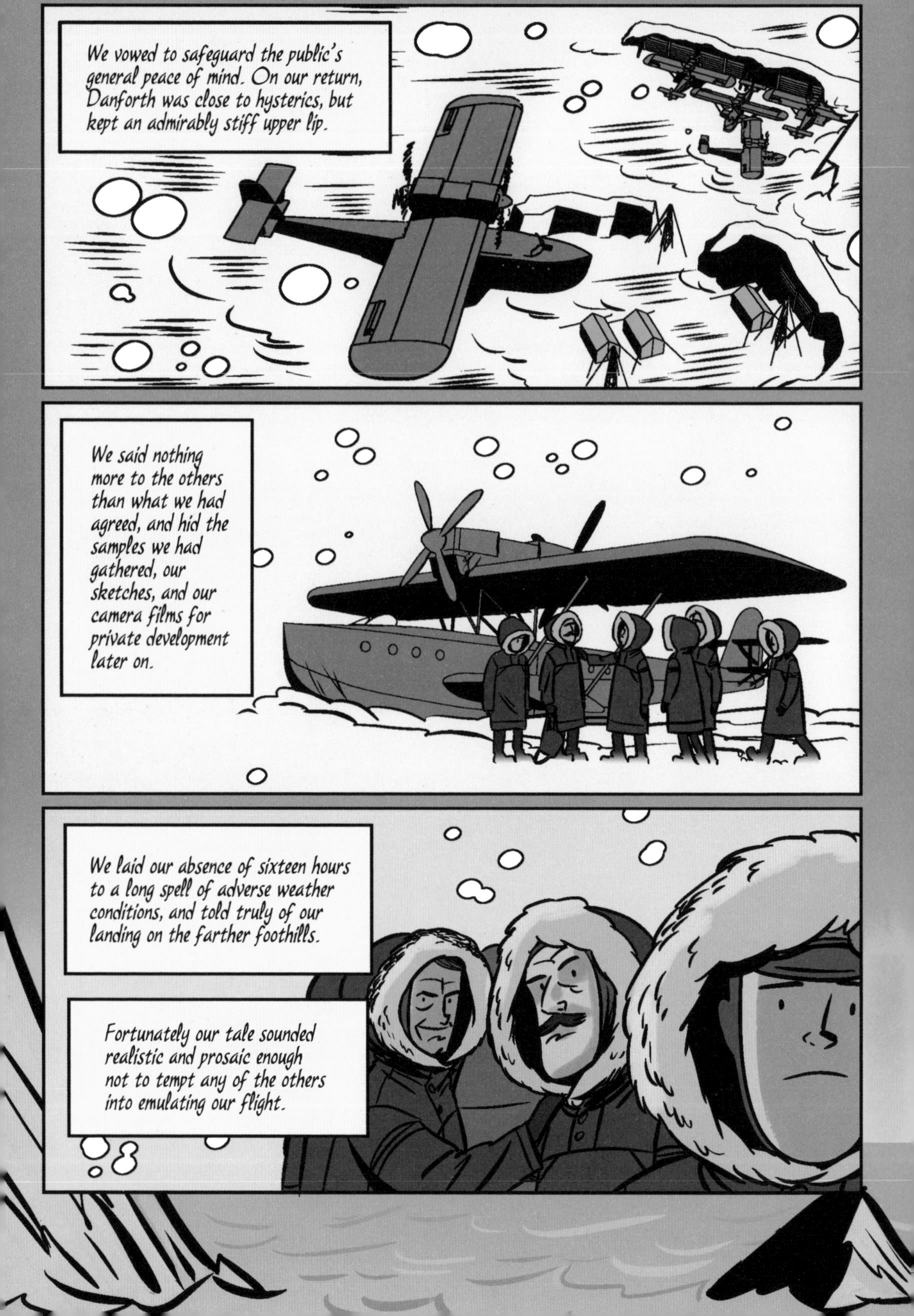
We vowed to safeguard the public's general peace of mind. On our return, Danforth was close to hysterics, but kept an admirably stiff upper lip.
We said nothing more to the others than what we had agreed, and hid the samples we had gathered, our sketches, and our camera films for private development later on.
We laid our absence of sixteen hours to a long spell of adverse weather conditions, and told truly of our landing on the farther foothills.
Fortunately our tale sounded realistic and prosaic enough not to tempt any of the others into emulating our flight.

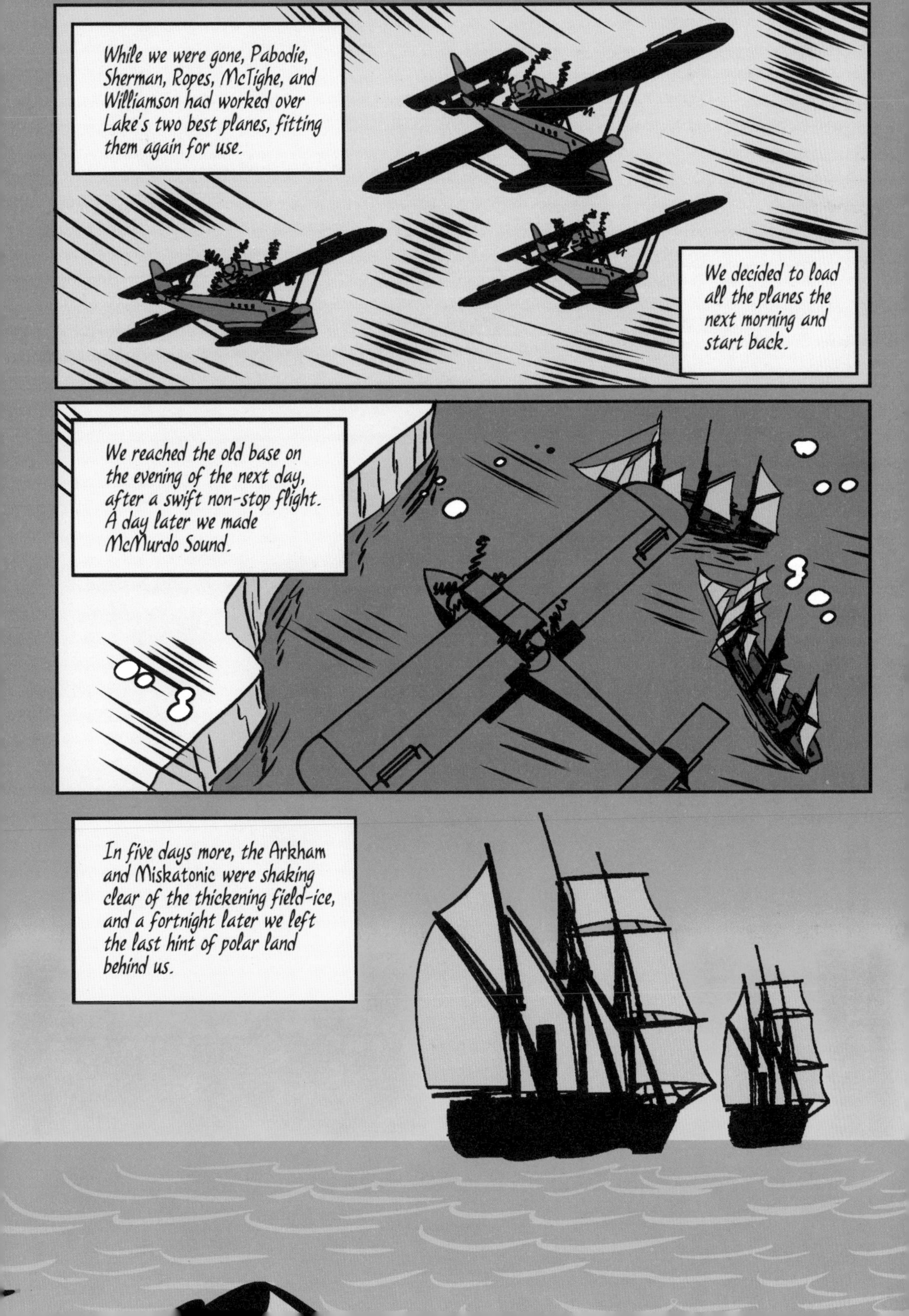
While we were gone, Pabodie, Sherman, Ropes, McTighe, and Williamson had worked over Lake's two best planes, fitting them again for use.
We decided to load all the planes the next morning and start back.
We reached the old base on the evening of the next day, after a swift non-stop flight. A day later we made McMurdo Sound.
In five days more, the Arkham and Miskatonic were shaking clear of the thickening field-ice, and a fortnight later we left the last hint of polar land behind us.

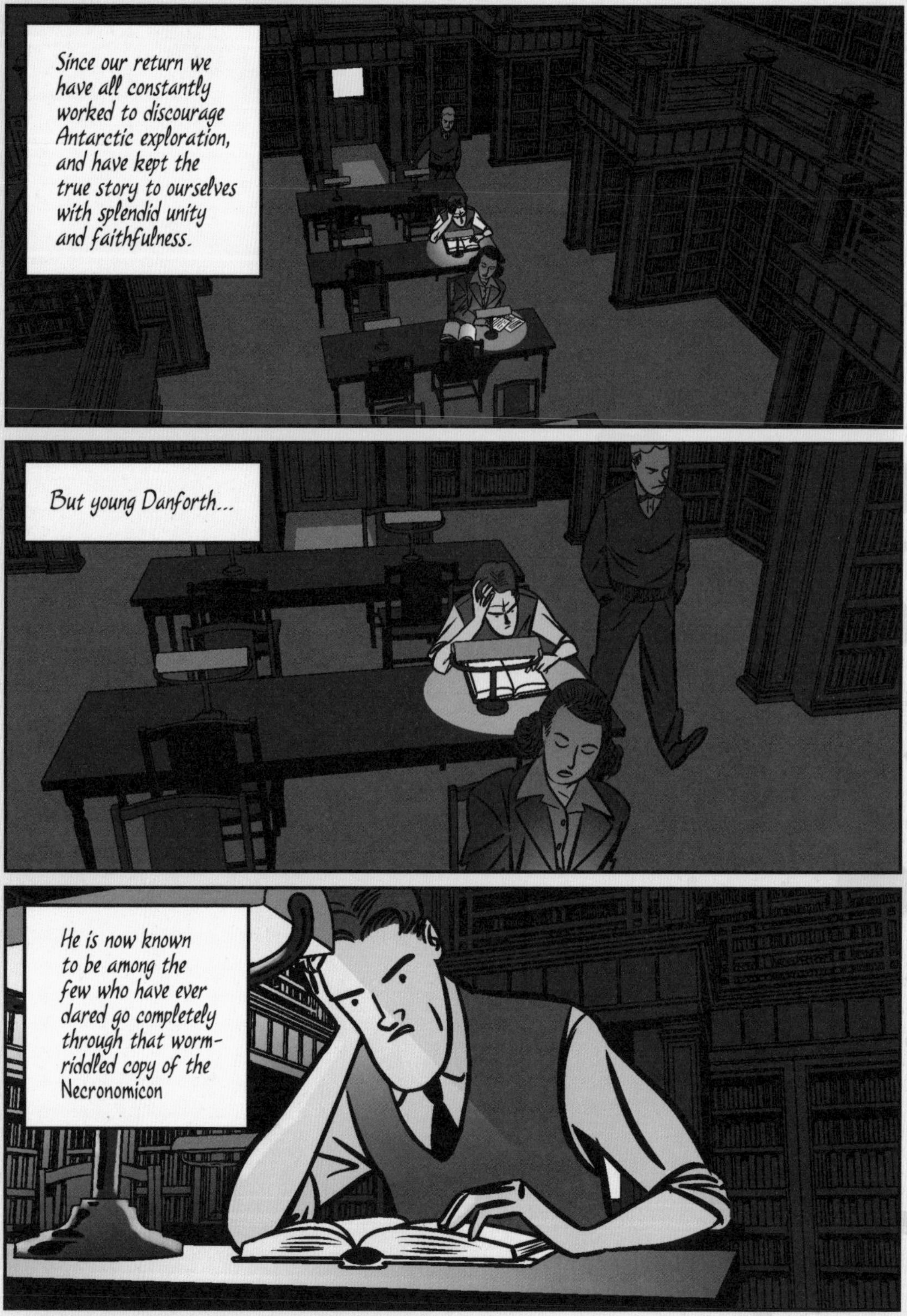
Since our return we have all constantly worked to discourage Antarctic exploration, and have kept the true story to ourselves with splendid unity and faithfulness.
But young Danforth...
He is now known to be among the few who have ever dared go completely through that worm-riddled copy of the Necronomicon

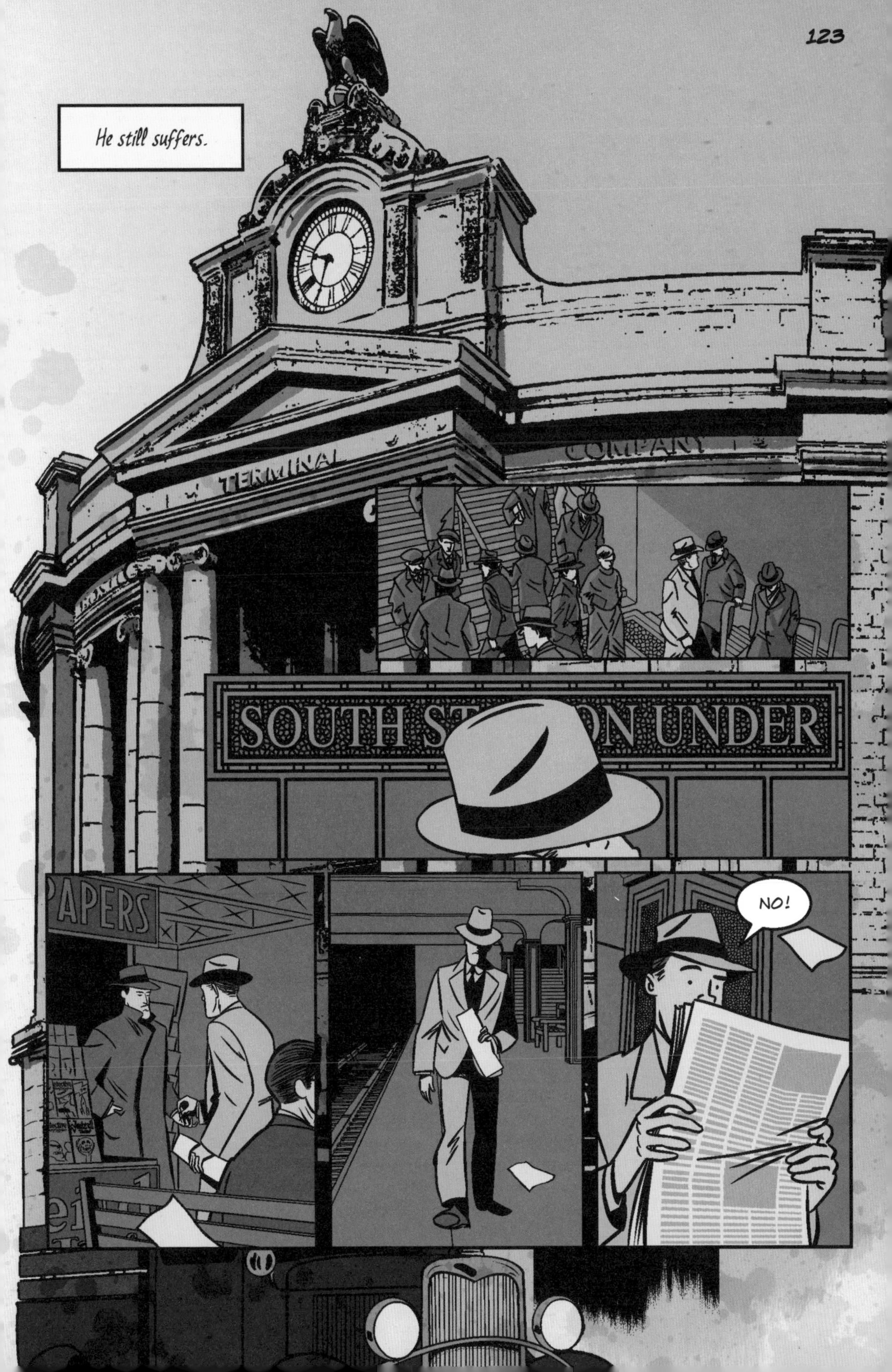
He still suffers.
TERMINAL
COMPANY
SOUTH ST ON UNDER
PAPERS
NO!

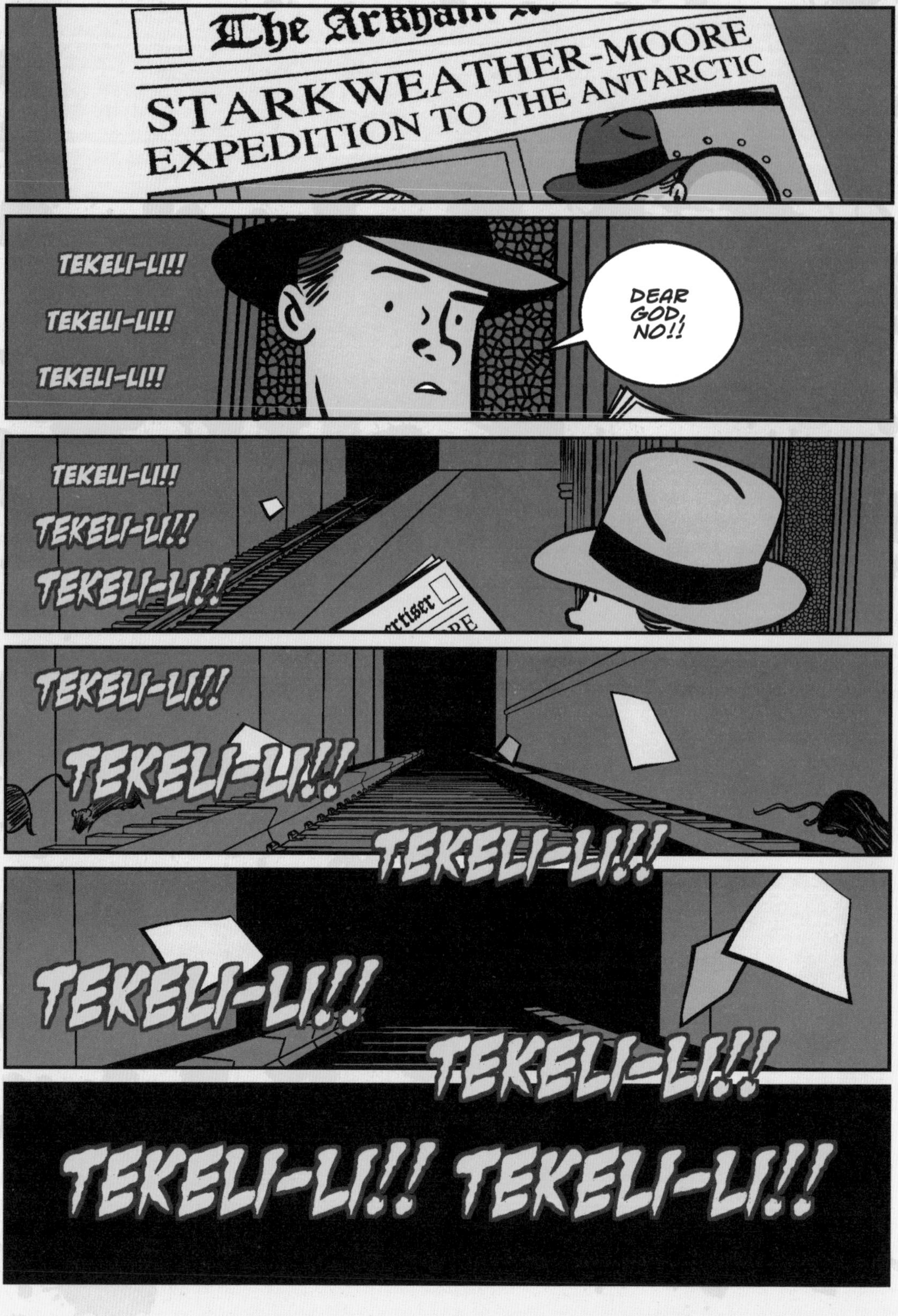
The Arkham
STARKWEATHER-MOORE
EXPEDITION TO THE ANTARCTIC
TEKELI-LI!!
TEKELI-LI!!
TEKELI-LI!!
DEAR GOD, NO!!
TEKELI-LI!!
TEKELI-LI!!
TEKELI-LI!!
TEKELI-LI!!
TEKELI-LI!!
TEKELI-LI!!
TEKELI-LI!!
TEKELI-LI!!
TEKELI-LI!! TEKELI-LI!!